NORTHWEST
Reprints

Northwest Reprints
Series Editor: Robert J. Frank

Other titles in the series:

Beyond the Garden Gate (by Sophus K. Winther, introduction by Barbara Meldrum)

Botanical Exploration of the Trans-Mississippi West (by Susan Delano McKelvey, introduction by Stephen Dow Beckham)

Down in My Heart (by William Stafford, introduction by Kim Stafford)

Driftwood Valley: A Woman Naturalist in the Northern Wilderness (by Theodora C. Stanwell-Fletcher, introduction by Wendell Berry, afterword by Rhoda M. Love)

Frontier Doctor (by Urling C. Coe, introduction by Robert Bunting)

Happy Valley (by Anne Shannon Monroe, introduction by Karen Blair)

A Homesteader's Portfolio (by Alice Day Pratt, introduction by Molly Gloss)

The Land Is Bright (by Archie Binns, introduction by Ann Ronald)

Narrative of a Journey across the Rocky Mountains to the Columbia River (by John Kirk Townsend, introduction by George A. Jobanek)

Nehalem Tillamook Tales (told by Clara Pearson, collected by Elizabeth Jacobs, introduction by Jarold Ramsey)

On the Highest Hill (by Roderick Haig-Brown, introduction by Laurie Ricou)

Oregon Detour (by Nard Jones, introduction by George Venn)

Requiem for a People: The Rogue Indians and the Frontiersmen (by Stephen Dow Beckham, with a new introduction by the author)

Tall Tales from Rogue River: The Yarns of Hathaway Jones (introduction by Stephen Dow Beckham)

Timber (by Roderick Haig-Brown, introduction by Glen A. Love)

The Viewless Winds (by Murray Morgan, introduction by Harold Simonson)

The Wallowas: Coming of Age in the Wilderness (by William Ashworth, with a new afterword by the author)

Wildmen, Wobblies, and Whistle Punks: Stewart Holbrook's Lowbrow Northwest (introduction by Brian Booth)

Yamsi: A Year in the Life of a Wilderness Ranch (by Dayton O. Hyde, introduction by William Kittredge

Preface

but there were things
That covered what a man was, and set him apart
From others, things by which others knew him. The place
Where he lived, the horse he rode, his relatives, his wife,
His voice, complexion, beard, politics, religion or lack of
it,
And so on. With time, these things fall away
Or dwindle into shadows: river sand blowing away
From some long-buried old structure of bleached boards
That appears a vague shadow through the sand-haze,
and then stands clear,
Naked, angular, itself.
　　　　　from "Trial and Error," H.L. Davis

People new to a region are especially interested in what
things might set them apart from others. In works by
Northwest writers, we get to know about the place where we
live, about each other, about our history and culture, and
about our flora and fauna. And with time, some things about
ourselves start to come into focus out of the shadows of our
history.

To give readers an opportunity to look into the place
where Northwesterners live, the Oregon State University
Press is making available again many books that are out of
print. The Northwest Reprints Series will reissue a range of
books, both fiction and nonfiction. Books will be selected for
different reasons: some for their literary merit, some for their
historical significance, some for provocative concerns, and
some for these and other reasons together. Foremost,
however, will be the book's potential to interest a range of
readers who are curious about the region's voice and
complexion. The Northwest Reprints Series makes works of
well-known and lesser-known writers available for all.

RJF

Adventures of the First Settlers

on the

Oregon or Columbia River

1810-1813

by
Alexander Ross

Introduction by
William G. Robbins

Oregon State University Press
Corvallis

The paper in this book meets the guidelines for permanence and durability of the Committee on Production Guidelines for Book Longevity of the Council on Library Resources and the minimum requirements of the American National Standard for Permanence of Paper for Printed Library Materials Z39.48-1984.

Library of Congress Cataloging-in-Publication Data
Ross, Alexander, 1783-1856
    Adventures of the first settlers on the Oregon or Columbia River : 1810-1813 / by Alexander Ross ; introduction by William G. Robbins.
        p. cm. — (Northwest reprints)
    ISBN 0-87071-528-3 (alk. paper)
    1. Northwest, Pacific—History—19th century. 2. Frontier and pioneer life—Northwest, Pacific. 3. Fur trade—Northwest, Pacific—History—19th century. 4. Columbia River Valley—History—19th century. 5. Oregon—History—To 1859. 6. Ross, Alexander, 1783-1856. 7. Fur traders—Northwest, Pacific—Biography. 8. Indians of North America—Northwest, Pacific—History—19th century. 9. Astoria (Or.)—History—19th century. I. Title. II. Series.

F880 .R812 2000
979.5'02—dc21

                                00-026825

This edition reproduces the 1904 edition by Reuben Gold Thwaites, published by the Arthur H. Clark Company as Volume VII of Early Western Travels, 1748-1846, later reprinted by the University of Nebraska Press as a Bison Book. This edition, like the Bison Book edition, omits an appendix containing a Chinook vocabulary and a table of weather conditions at Astoria in 1811.

Oregon State University Press
101 Waldo Hall
Corvallis OR 97331-6407
541-737-3166 • fax 541-737-3170
http://.osu.orst.edu/dept/press

Contents

Series Preface
iii

Introduction by William G. Robbins
ix

Adventures of the First Settlers
on the
Oregon or Columbia River, 1810-1813
by Alexander Ross
19

Scene on the Columbia River by John Mix Stanley, ca. 1852.
Oil on canvas. $17^{1}/8$ x $21^{1}/8$ inches. Courtesy Amon Carter
Museum, Fort Worth, Texas, accession number 1972.45.
Cover shows detail.

Introduction
by William G. Robbins

When British and American sea captains George Vancouver and Robert Gray sailed along the North Pacific Coast in 1792, they initiated a series of reports and journal entries that sang the praises of nature's abundance and its *potential* for improvement, the degree to which the natural bounty of the Northwest could be enhanced by an industrious people. But for all the fame and fortune of those early captains, the land-based explorers and fur traders who followed left the most durable and lasting narratives about the region. The host of partners, clerks, and engagés associated with the great continental fur companies provided the first ethnographic commentaries on aboriginal people and the first broadly communicated geographic knowledge about the country, and suggested the promise of vast material rewards to those who would capitalize on the natural wealth of the Columbia River country. The most celebrated among those accounts, of course, were the voluminous journal observations of the American explorers, Meriwether Lewis and William Clark. And the Corps of Discovery, it is widely known, stimulated American interest in the far western reaches on the continent.

Among those excited by the published reports about the Lewis and Clark expedition was the German-born, New York-based businessman, John Jacob Astor, a man whose entrepreneurial ambitions envisioned a fur-trading network that spanned the continent from the Missouri to the Columbia. He planned a two-pronged effort to reach the Columbia, one by sea and a second overland expedition. With close ties to important officials in the United States government, including presidents and cabinet officers, Astor's Pacific Fur Company promised both profits and patriotism. According to historian James Ronda: "Fur and flag would join forces to plant American sovereignty along the Great River of the West."[1] Astor shrewdly selected experienced Canadian traders and *voyageurs* to head the effort, many of them from the small Quebec settlement of Lachine outside Montreal. Lachine had long served as a human and material supply point for the great western fur trade, and when word spread of Astor's grand scheme to establish a trading venture in the Columbia River country, Alexander Ross, one of the principal figures in the enterprise, noted that *voyageurs* from near and far "flocked thither to enroll themselves under the banner of this grand undertaking."

Alexander Ross, an immigrant from Scotland, was one of the first to sign on as a clerk. with the enterprise. "A down-on-his-luck schoolmaster who needed a job and a fresh start,"[2] Ross and two other clerks, Canadians Ross Cox and adventure-seeking Gabriel Franchère, produced the three most notable recollections of Astor's grandiose plans for a trading empire on the North Pacific.[3] Of those accounts, *Adventures of the First Settlers on the Oregon or Columbia River,*[4] first published in 1849, provides the most detailed, informed, and candid voice about that very early commercial endeavor on the North Pacific. During his fifteen years west of the Continental Divide, Ross worked for three different masters: Astor's Pacific Fur Company, the Montreal-based North West Company, and finally the Hudson's Bay Company. He proved to be a survivor in this contest for commercial supremacy and empire, shifting his allegiance from one company to the next as opportunity presented itself. Like the great French foreign minister Talleyrand, who survived a variety of regimes through and beyond the French Revolution, Ross made the easy transition from one fur-trading company to the next.

Alexander Ross was literally aboard the Astor enterprise from its inception. Assigned (or condemned!) to ocean passage to Pacific waters, Ross boarded the Tonquin in New York harbor on September 6, 1810, one of thirty-three passengers bound for the Columbia River. After an adventure-filled sail around Cape Horn with the tyrannical Captain Jonathan Thorn, a man of "jealous and peevish temper," at the helm, the ship stood off the stormy surf at the mouth of the Columbia River the following March. Tragic comedy followed in the next few days when the impatient captain, in front of an incredulous crew and fur company personnel, ordered the first mate and four others overboard to examine the bar in the tumultuous waters; their boat quickly disappeared in the towering waves. Finally, a few days later, wind and tide and good fortune combined to hurtle *Tonquin* safely across the bar on March 26, 1811. But that effort brought further loss of life when still another boat was swamped attempting to find safe passage for the ship. *Adventures* makes it strikingly clear that the lower Columbia was a setting where the power of nature overwhelmed and dominated all human activity. "Every succeeding day," Ross reported, "was marked by some new and alarming disaster." The Astorians' struggles with the elements, however, were only beginning.

The small Pacific Fur Company party immediately set about the arduous task of clearing land on the south side of the river, the site selected for "the new establishment." Because the immense trees grew so thick—and despite strenuous work—the men made little progress clearing space for the site of the Astor enterprise. On some occasions, several of the huge trees would hang in the tops of others, thus keeping the group in "awful suspense" and making it doubly difficult "to extricate one from the other." And then it took several days to remove the enormous stump. During two months of hard work, Ross reported that three men were killed by natives, two were hurt by falling trees, and another lost his hands when they were blown off by gunpowder. He concluded that the selection of the site "for the emporium of the west, might challenge the whole continent to produce a spot of equal extent presenting more difficulties to the settler."

But the Astorians were persistent and aggressive in expanding their presence in the region. As some party members planted a small garden and laid the foundations for the first buildings, others, including Alexander Ross, were moving upriver, establishing contact with the Indians who inhabited its shores and reporting about the surrounding countryside. As he did with his ethnographic reporting, Ross drew vivid word pictures of a rich and abundant physical landscape, and like many of his contemporaries, he singled out the Willamette Valley for special praise. The "Wallamitte," he said, was a most favorable place for agriculture, "salubrious and dry" and with sufficient heat "to ripen every kind of grain in a short time." To another Astorian, Robert Stuart, the country above Willamette Falls was "delightful beyond expression," with bottomlands "composed of an excellent soil" and thinly covered with a scattering of trees "to give variety to the most beautiful Landscapes in nature." Stuart also noted the existence of a "first rate salmon fishery" on the Columbia.[5] Like his colleague, Alexander Ross also reported bountiful salmon runs, indeed, "as fine as any in the world." Because the fish were caught in great numbers during the summer season, Ross reasoned that salmon offered great potential "were a foreign market to present itself."

The Astorians were not the only distant and aggressive interlopers with designs on the riches of the Columbia River watershed. In mid-July of that first year on the River of the West, Ross reported that David Thompson, "northwest-like, came dashing down the Columbia in a light canoe, manned with eight Iroquois and an interpreter." One of the partners in the expanding North West Company, Thompson "saw and examined everything" and did all he could to discourage the Astorians, a strategy his company used, according to Ross, "to extend their own trade at the expense of ours." With a good bit of pride, he noted that Thompson failed to deter the Pacific Fur Company operatives, having forgotten that "he was speaking to north-westers—men as experienced and as cunning as himself." And so the stage was set for increased competition in the contest for trade advantage (and imperial supremacy) on the Columbia, a rivalry that the Astorians apparently welcomed. Once again, Canadians, including those who kept journal accounts of their experiences (Ross, Gabriel Franchère, and Ross Cox), were at the center of those efforts. In retrospect, we can say that Alexander Ross and his associates represented the leading edge of market-rooted initiatives that were in the process of dramatically altering the native subsistence economy and replacing it with rudimentary market-exchange mechanisms. The presence of Ross and the Astorians on the Columbia River indicates the far-reaching implications of market capitalism; it also illustrates the influence of metropolitan centers on distant places rich in raw materials valuable to the great urban centers around the globe. In that sense, Ross and the Astorians and their North West and Hudson's Bay Company successors ultimately took their orders from primary sources of capital and decision making in New York, Montreal, and London. The cutting edge for the changes that were taking place on the North Pacific slope, therefore, had its origins in the Atlantic-centered world and its great metropolitan houses of capital. While the Pacific Fur Company, the North West Company, and the Hudson's Bay Company contended for imperial ascendancy in the region, they were changing forever the lives of native people (and introducing devastating exogenous diseases as well).

Like other texts of its kind, *Adventures of the First Settlers* treats the Columbia River country as a vast commons, a spacious arena free and open to newcomers, irrespective of the presence and cultural worlds of native people. Indians who were unwilling to provide the necessary labor to assist fur traders in portaging around the rapids and falls on the Columbia were "troublesome," "importunate," and "forward." Natives on the lower river were "hostile and annoying to the whites at Astoria," prone to thievery, and on occasion behaved like "sordid and treacherous rogues." In his choice of descriptive words, Ross shared broadly held stereotypes about native people. But there is more to *Adventures* than mere caricaturing of Columbia River Indians; Ross was an astute observer of their language patterns, their dietary habits, and their complex social and cultural worlds. During an extended stay at Fort Okanogan, most of it in the service of the North West Company, the enterprising Ross took copious notes about the local Sinkaietks band, recording information about their everyday activities, their stories about creation, and virtually everything else associated with Sinkaietk life. In four informative chapters, he provides remarkable detail about Sinkaietk social customs, marriage practices, edible roots and berries, diseases, medicinal practices, and descriptions of their winter and summer seasonal "habitations." His marriage in 1813 to the prominent daughter of a Sinkaietk headman unquestionably aided his effort.

Adventures exhibits a remarkable grasp of the complexities of Indian diplomacy and politics. In one of his most trenchant commentaries concerning the Indians who fished along the stretch of the mid-Columbia River, Ross estimated that during the salmon season as many as three thousand natives gathered along the section of the river known as the Long Narrows. During the remaining months of the year, he speculated that the permanent residents "do not exceed 100 persons." Native people came to this stretch of the river, according to Ross, "for gambling and speculation; for trade and traffic, not in fish, but in other articles." The Long Narrows, he reported in an oft-quoted statement, "is the great emporium or mart of the Columbia." Ross also sketched a vivid description of Celilo Falls at the head of the Narrows, the most spectacular fishing spot on the river, a place where the entire volume of the Columbia River passed through a narrow opening during the low-water months: "Through this gap it rushes with great impetuosity; the foaming surges dash through the rocks with terrific violence." Although others among his peers rank ahead of him as a naturalist, Ross did notice—as he passed upriver—the remarkable transition in ecozones from the tree-shrouded Columbia Gorge with its marine climate to the open and barren landscape of the arid interior. "The contrast," he wrote, "is sudden, striking, and remarkable."

John Jacob Astor's Pacific Fur Company's main post inside the bar of the Columbia River was ultimately a short-lived enterprise, reverting to the Montreal-controlled North West Company in the midst of the War of 1812. And when the Northwesters and the Hudson's Bay Company engaged in open conflict for control of the rich fur-producing region stretching from Manitoba west to the Pacific, the British government ended what it deemed destructive competition and forced the smaller firm to merge with the more powerful Hudson's Bay Company. Alexander Ross moved easily with those shifting tides. As if he were preparing the reader for his decision to join the North West Company, the author of *Adventures* becomes increasingly critical of Astor and the support he provided to his Pacific operations. Astor is described as penurious, guilty of "reckless indifference for the lives of his people," and "like the wind," his orders were ever-changing. Ross singled out for special criticism the arbitrary powers that Astor left to his sea captains and cited the words of one of the Pacific Fur Company partners that Astor's underhanded policies and "the conduct of his captains had ruined the undertaking."

Adventures, of course, must be read as hindsight; the book represents more than mere journal entries quickly prepared for publication. Despite the author's disclaimer that allowance be made "for any changes that may have taken place since this account was written—thirty years ago," *Adventures* is a work of reflection, unquestionably crafted from detailed notes but written from the perspective of two decades of time. Ross, who retired with his native wife to the Red River settlement in 1826, eventually fancied himself as a writer, publishing *Adventures* in 1849 and *The Fur Hunters of the Far West*, published in London in two volumes, in 1855. The latter is the only first-hand account of North West Company activities between 1813 and its merger with the Hudson's Bay Company. Roaa also authored *The Red River Settlement: Its Rise, Progress, and Present State* (1856), according to Canadian historian Gordon Friesen,[6] the classic narrative of the origins of modern Winnipeg.

In this, as in the Pacific Fur Company book, Ross was a shrewd observer with an uninhibited willingness to pass judgment on his contemporaries. But while he is a bit of a grumbler, his writing gives a living presence to landscapes and events of nearly two centuries past. More important, *Adventures of the First Settlers* is one of the charter literary documents for the Pacific Northwest. In this account, Alexander Ross proves himself to be a true adventurer with a splendid literary gift for bringing those experiences to the public..

Notes

1 James P. Ronda, *Astoria and Empire* (Lincoln: University of Nebraska Press, 1990), 2.
2 ibid., 91.
3 Ross Cox, *The Columbia River*, Edgar I. Stewart and Jane R. Stewart, editors (1831; Norman: University of Oklahoma Press, 1957); and Gabriel Franchère, *Journal of a Voyage on the North West Coast of North America during the Years 1811, 1812, 1813, and 1814*, W. Kaye Lamb, ed. (1854; Toronto: Champlain Society, 1969).
4 Alexander Ross, *Adventures of the First Settlers on the Oregon or Columbia River* (1849; Lincoln: University of Nebraska Press, 1986).
5 Phillip Aston Rollins, ed., *The Discovery of the Oregon Trail: Robert Stuart's Narrative* (New York: Charles Scribner's Sons, 1935), 32.
6 Gordon Friesen, *The Canadian Prairies: A History* (Toronto: University of Toronto Press, 1984), 506.

Long. West.

Quadra & Vancouvers I.ᵈ

50

Nootka S.
Breakers p.
Ayoquat
Nittinat S.
C. Flattery
Mᵗ Olympus

Destruction I.
Bullfinch H.

C. Disappointment
COLUMBIA RIVER
Point Adams

C. Lookout

45

C. Foulweather

C. Perpetua

Fᵗ Umpqua

C. Orford
or Blanco

Fᵗ Langley
Mᵗ ...
Fᵗ Oaka...

Pᵗ Discovery
Hoods ...

Nesqally Puget S.ᵗ

Cowlitz R.
Fᵗ Astoria

Fᵗ Vancouver
Falls   Falls

Walamette R.

Umpqua R.

Far   West   Mount...
Mᵗ ...

MAP OF
THE COLUMBIA
to illustrate
ROSS'S ADVENTURES

George & Cⁿ. Lithography, 54 Hatton Garden.

48

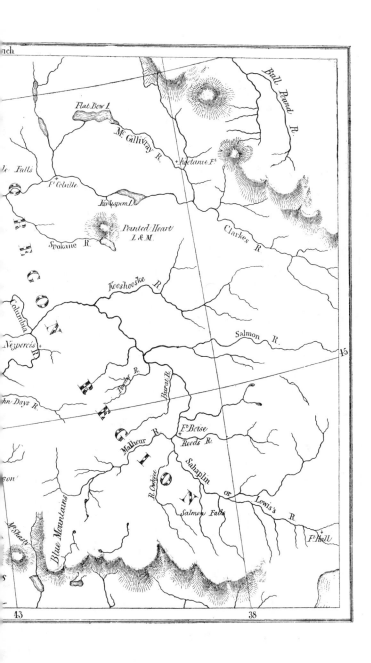

PREFACE

HAVING been one of the first commercial adventurers to the Columbia River, and having spent fifteen years of my life travelling among the savage tribes west of the Rocky Mountains, I was induced, from time to time, to note down such incidents and opinions, illustrative of savage life and manners, as appeared to me either new or interesting.

To the characteristic details of Indian life, I have added that of personal adventure, the trials and misfortunes which the first adventurers had to undergo among the Indians in that quarter; connecting therewith an account of the trade and commerce of the country during the early days of that bold spirit which animated the first explorers of the Columbia.

These different subjects have been arranged and [iv] linked together in their natural order, so as to form one complete narrative, embodying the history of "the Pacific Fur Company."

It is not an arm-chair narrative, derived from hearsay tales, but the result of practical experience on the spot. From beginning to end, I had personally to act my part in the scenes described; they passed under my own eyes; and the account altogether may derive more value from being authentic than from any adventitious embellishment bestowed on it.

While on this part of our subject, it may be observed that there is an error which most travellers, especially those pioneers who first penetrate into dark and remote regions, fall into: they generally run into the extreme, and spoil a simple story by colouring. Not content to leave nature in its simple garb, they must brighten or darken, magnify or diminish, everything they describe, until at last the real likeness of the thing is entirely effaced, and truth itself, by over-refinement, is thrown into the shade.

What belongs to oneself is generally viewed with a partial eye; and perhaps that partiality influences [v] my own opinion as to the interest of the subject before us. In reference to this subject, however, others have written on it as well as myself. Let our readers, therefore, judge for themselves.

In presenting the present work to the public, I have no very sanguine expectations. All I aim at is to lay before my readers a faithful and impartial statement of what took place, during my own times, in a quarter hitherto but little known.

Freedom from imperfection is not to be expected; yet, on the whole, I hope that this volume will prove to the calm inquirer, in all matters connected with the subject generally, a sure and satisfactory guide: allowance being made for any changes that may have taken place since this account was written—thirty years ago.

Red River Settlement, Rupert's Land.
  Aug. 1, 1846.

CONTENTS

CHAPTER I

Introductory remarks—John Jacob Astor—Grasping views —Early traders of Canada—The Hudson's Bay Company— American fur companies—Astor's policy—Russian settlements—Coasting vessels—The Pacific Fur Company— Flattering results—Oregon territory—New association— Mr. Hunt—Golden prospects—Proposals accepted—List of adventurers—Land party—Sea party—The ship *Tonquin*—Remarks—Opinion against opinion—Observations —Land expedition departs—Sea party set off for New York —Bark canoe—Spectators—Canadian voyageurs . . 33

CHAPTER II

The *Tonquin* sails—Quarrels on board—The captain's character—Accommodations—A sudden squall—Flying fish— The captain's harshness—Cape de Verd Islands—Alarm of fire—A suspicious sail—Crossing the line—Springing a leak—Short allowance of water—Immense wave—The Falkland Islands—Rocky passage—Wild fowl—Port Egmont Bay—The party on shore—Mr. Farnham's gray goose—Old graves renewed—Epitaphs—Party left behind —New dangers—Mr. Robert Stuart's determined conduct —Feuds on board—Cape Horn doubled—The weather— Pilot fish—Trade winds—Rogues' mess—Little pilot— Mouna Roa—A man overboard—The mate in irons . 43

[viii] CHAPTER III

Karakakooa Bay—The sailors desert—The captain's conduct— Productions of Owhyhee—Tocaigh Bay—Governor Young —Royal proclamation—Woahoo—Ourourah, the residence of Tammeatameah—Harbour fees—Excursion on shore—The Queen's umbrella—The King's appearance—

Royal palace and guards—Arsenal, or royal workshop—
Royal dinner—His Majesty's fleet—Morais, or places of
public worship—Sacred or puranee ground tabooed—
Storm—A sailor left to his fate among the natives—Parting visit from his Majesty—His meanness—Diving of the
natives—Native proas: how made—Clothing—Customs
and peculiarities—Character of the women—White men
at the Sandwich Islands—The King's disposition towards
foreigners—Captain Cook—Pahooas, or war spears—A
sham fight—Religion—Tammeatameah conqueror and
king—Apparent happiness of the natives—Prophetic hint
—Distressed situation of a boat 57

CHAPTER IV

Departure from the Sandwich Islands—Bad weather—Live
stock destroyed—Columbia River—A boat and crew lost—
Captain's conduct towards Mr. Fox—Mouth of the river—
Bar and breakers—Cape Disappointment—Point Adams
—Narrow escape of the long boat—Sounding the bar—A
boat and crew left to perish—The ship in the breakers—
Critical situation—Melancholy narrative of Steven Weeks
—Search made for the lost boat, and narrow escape—Long
boat swamped—Fidelity of the natives—Preparations for
leaving the ship—Captain Thorn—The voyage concluded 74

CHAPTER V

Preparations for landing—Site of the new emporium of the west
—Astor's representative—Hard work—Huge trees—Natives—Comecomly—Mode of felling the trees—Danger—
Trying scenes—Three [ix] men killed—Three wounded—
Party reduced by sickness—Disaffection—Conduct of the
deputy—Desertion—Mr. Astor's policy—Climate—Indian rumours—Comecomly's intrigues and policy—Trip
to the cascades—Mr. M'Kay and north-west notions—
Anecdote—Exploring party to the north—Several persons killed—Hostile threats of the Indians—Potatoes and
other seeds planted—New building—Astoria—Departure
of the ship—Dangerous situation of the whites—Great

assemblage of Indians — People under arms — Blunderbuss
accident — Alarming moment — Two strangers arrive — Mr.
Thompson at Astoria — M' Dougall's policy — The two
great functionaries 88

CHAPTER VI

The ten tribes — Number of warriors — Their laws — Chief's
arbitrary power — Dress, games, and arms of the men —
Dress of the women, slaves, and basket-making — Lewdness
of the women — Food, ornaments — The salmon — Superstitious customs — Sturgeon — Fathomfish — Roots and
berries — Circulating medium — Econé, or Good Spirit —
Ecutoch, or Bad Spirit — Etaminua, or priests — Keelalles,
or doctors — War canoes — Diseases — Winter houses—
Temporary, or Summer houses — Fleas — Practice of flattening the head — Colonization — Wallamitte — Cowlitz,
or Puget's Sound — Conclusion . . . 102

CHAPTER VII

First expedition into the interior — Number of the party —
Tongue Point — Canoe swamped — Sailing difficulties —
Indian villages — Cedars — First night's encampment —
Mount Coffin — Cowlitz — Wallamitte — Columbia Valley
— Point Vancouver — Difficulties — The Cascades — Con-
course of Indians — General appearance of the country —
The portage — Description of the cascades — The roll of
tobacco — Pilfering — Mr. Thompson — Exchange of men
— The Long Narrows — Warlike appearance of the Indian
cavalry — Button contract — Critical situation of the party
— Camp of gamblers — The Narrows [x] — Hard work at
the carrying place — A day's work — Description of the
portage — Number of Indians — Aspect of the country —
The plains begin — End of the woods — Want of sleep —
Demeanour of the Indians 115

CHAPTER VIII

Columbia Falls — A canoe swamped — Suspicious behaviour of
the Indians — Stratagem — Umatallow — Walla-Walla —
Great body of Indians — Harangues — Indian ceremonies

—The great forks—Difference in the waters—Length of
the forks—The British flag—Mr. Thompson's design—
Indian ideas—Salmon—European articles—Tummatapam
—Departure from the Forks—Indian honesty—Eyakema
—Marl-hills—Dead children—Superstitions—Priest's
Rapid—Rattle-snakes—Appearance of the country—
Kewaugh-chen—Perilous situation of a canoe—The two
sisters—The old Indian—Hunting party—Horses—The
priest—Piss-cows—Sopa—Great assemblage of Indians
—The comet—Oakinacken—Distance from Astoria—
Indian-council—Resolve to winter—Some account of the
place—The stolen watch—The priest dismissed—Voyage
concluded—The two strangers—First building—Division
of the party—Lonely winter—The lost party—Indian
trade—Mr. Stuart's adventures   131

CHAPTER IX

Anxieties at Astoria—Indians depart—A schooner built—The
Dolly's first trip—Criminal curiosity—The powder keg—
The schooner condemned—Mr. Astor's cargoes—His
policy—Remarks on the North-West coast—Unwelcome
rumours—Calpo's statement—Rumours renewed—Hard
cases—Joe Lapierre—Kasiascall's account of the *Tonquin*
—Strange Indian—Kasiascall's conduct—His character—
His design on Astoria—Remarks   .   .   . 159

[xi] CHAPTER X

Land expedition—Hunt and M'Kenzie—Montreal recruits—
La Chine—Devout farewell—Mackina in 1810—Fur
traders of the South—Frolic parties—Comparison between
the South and North—Arrival at St. Louis—Recruiting
service—Yankees—Canoe-men—Delays at St. Louis—
Difficulties—Mr. Miller—The Missouri—Canadian
voyageurs—Winter quarters—Mr. Hunt revisits St. Louis
—M'Kenzie—Mr. Astor's policy—The Yankees desert—
Winter quarters broken up—Rocky Mountains—Pilot
knobs—New scenes—Columbia River—The horses abandoned—Take to canoes—The canoes abandoned—Trap-

pers—Mr. Miller—Party on foot—Hardships—Starvation—Conflicting councils—Gloomy prospects—Property *en cache*—The party divided—Three men perish—M'Kenzie's speech—He arrives at Astoria—Mr. Crooks and òthers left behind—Mr. Hunt's arrival at Astoria—Voyage concluded   173

CHAPTER XI

Doings at Astoria—Three parties on foot—Their object—M' Lellan's resolution—Hostile attack at the Long Narrows —Mr. Reed—Two Indians shot—Heroic conduct of M' Lellan—Difficulties adjusted—Advance of the party—Remarks—Arrival at Oakinacken—Departure again for Astoria—Scene at Umatallow—Mr. Crook's adventures and suffering—Yeck-a-tap-am—Umatallow left—Merit rewarded—Arrival of the party at Astoria—The ship *Beaver* there also   186

CHAPTER XII

General meeting of the partners—Resolutions passed—Departure of the parties for the interior—Mr. Clarke—The cascades—Wyampam, or the Long Narrows—Situation of the party—Loss of time—Mr. M'Kenzie—A stroll through the Indian camp—Mr. Clarke's alarms—Command transferred—Reed's rifle recovered—A robber in irons—The five shots—Yeck-a-tap-am rewarded—Mr. Stuart's departure [xii] for St. Louis—Second division—Summer trip to She Whaps—Boullard and his squaw—Mr. Stuart's arrival at Oakinacken—Departure for She Whaps—Winter operations at Oakinacken—Visits—Travelling scenes—A night in the snow—Jacque and his powder-horn—Mr. Stuart's account of his journey—Arrival at Walla Walla ⟍ . 194

CHAPTER XIII

Mr. Clarke—Stragglers—Hard Travelling—Cox's pilgrimage—Visit to Spokane—Trade—Mr. Pillet—Mr. Farnham—Cootanais and Flatheads—M'Lennan—Plunge in the lake —Adventures—Outposts—Catatouch chief—Curiosity—

Fracas — Introduction of civilization — Commotion — M'Kenzie — Great Snake River — Caches robbed — Canadian wanderers — Character of the Shahaptains — Visit to Spokane — M'Tavish — Account of the war — Winter travels — M'Kenzie at Astoria — New resolves — M'Kenzie's return to his post — Indian chiefs — Bold enterprize — Property recovered — Chiefs and their horses — Strategems — Indians outwitted — Plotting — Friendly Island — Conference — Marauding propensities — Treaty of peace — System changed — Plentiful market — The island abandoned — Arrival at Walla Walla — Commotions among the savages — Tummeatapam — Arrival at Astoria . . . 207

CHAPTER XIV

Mr. Stuart — Snake River — Trappers — Joyous meeting — Trapper's resolution — Crow Indians' troubles — Horses change masters — Mr. Stuart on foot — M'Lellan left alone — Hardships of the party — Famine — Le Clerc's horrid proposition — The old bull — The old horse — Pilot-knobs — Winter quarters — Unwelcome visitors — Change of quarters — Spring — Travelling at random — An Otto-Indian — River Platte — Two traders — News of the war — The Missouri — The old horse given for an old canoe — St. Louis — Mr. Astor — Wallamitte — Falls — Scenery — Habits of the Collap-poh-yea-ass tribes — Concourse of savages — M'Dougall's letter — [xiii] M'Kenzie's stratagem — Indian disappointment — The ship *Beaver* — Coasting voyage — Mr. Astor's policy — Captains — Their instructions — Mr. Hunt baulked in his plans — The Boston merchants — Mr. Astor's conduct — Difficulties of Mr. Hunt's situation — The ship *Albatross* — All the parties at head-quarters   222

CHAPTER XV

Meeting of the partners — Warm discussion — M'Kenzie — Eloquence of the times — Reasons for dissolving the company — Dissenting partners converted — Final resolve — The deputy's powers — Departure of the brigade — A canoe lost — A man's leg in jeopardy — Rumours at the narrows —

Snake party — Rumours renewed — Tummeatapam's coun-
sel — Hostile appearance at the forks — Number of Indians
— Nez Percés' fleet — Fears of the whites — Indian visit —
Strong guard — Mr. Clarke — Relic of the silver goblet —
Mr. Hunt at Astoria — Face of affairs changed — Mr.
Hunt departs from Astoria — North-West squadron — A great
Eri duped — Bill of sale — Petty manœuvring — Rumours
of ships — The Astorians at their post — Bill signed — As-
toria delivered up — North-West Company   .   . 236

CHAPTER XVI

Mr. Franchere — Comecomly's anxiety — His report of a sail —
His attachment to the Americans — Laframboise, the inter-
preter — Mr. M' Dougall's visit — The *Racoon* sloop-of-war
— Comecomly grows partial to the British flag — North-
West partners — British officers — Astoria changed to Fort
George — Captain Black's character — Mr. Hunt's voyage
— Commodore Porter — Mr. Hunt leaves the Marquesas
— Arrival at the Sandwich Islands — Rumours — The ship
Lark — Eight persons perish — Columbian affairs — The
property delivered — No ice — The people assembled — Voy-
age — The Cascade banditti — Two North-West canoes —
North-West affray at the cascades — Mr. Stuart wounded —
Mr. Keith's conduct — Preparations for war — The great
expedition — Conduct of the Cath-le-yach-é-yach Indians —
Expedition fails — The effect — Remarks   .   . 246

[xiv] CHAPTER XVII

Party to the Wallamitte — Hunt's voyage concluded — The brig
Pedlar — M' Dougall suspected — His character vindicated
— Mr. Hunt's remarks on the late concern — His liberality
— His farewell address to the clerks — Final departure from
Columbia — The party for Canada — Efforts and disappoint-
ments — Snake expedition — The melancholy story of Pierre
Dorion's wife — Massacre of the Snake party — Remarks —
A winter in the Blue Mountains — List of casualties — Astor's
hopes disappointed — Comment on the late concern   . 261

CHAPTER XVIII

Origin of the Oakinackens — Religion — Good Spirit — Evil
Spirit — Ideas of a future state — Ceremonies — End of this
world — Extent of country — Names and number of tribes —
Warriors — Population — Royal family — The great chief,
or Red Fox — Wild hemp — Long journeys — Barter —
Emblem of royalty — Government — Indian ideas — Council
of chiefs — Manners — Employments — Plurality of wives —
Brawls — Dress and clothing — Stratagems — A savage in
wolf's clothing — Painted faces and sleek hair   .   . 272

CHAPTER XIX

Marriage contracts — National custom — Exchange of presents
— Nocturnal visits — The object — Purchasing the bride —
Customs on the occasion — Feuds and quarrels — Tla-quill-
augh, or Indian doctor — His office — Precarious life —
Mode of paying him — Manner of treating the sick — Customs and ceremonies on the occasion — Hard duty — Superstitions — Knowledge of roots and herbs — Curing wounds
— Diseases, or general complaints — Gambling — Tsill-all-
a-come, or the national game — Manner of playing it — Bets
— Gambling propensities — Hot baths — Manner of using
them — On what occasions — Indian qualifications — Gymnastic exercise — Comparison — General remarks   . 283

[xv] CHAPTER XX

Social habits — Winter habitations — Economy of the winter —
Summer employments — Collecting of food — Fish barriers
— Salmon — Division of labour — Roots and berries —
Scenes at the fish camp — Mode of catching the deer —
Preparation of food — Furnaces or ovens — Implements of
warfare — Spampt, how made — Pine moss — Bread, how
prepared — Great war-dance — Manner of fighting — Treat-
ies of peace — Scalps — Slaves — Funeral ceremonies —
Mode of interment — Graves — Superstitions — Emblems —
Customs — Mourning — Punishments — Sedate habits and
docile dispositions   295

CHAPTER XXI

Calculation of time—Singular manner of naming children—
Peculiar modes of address—Anecdote of an Indian chief—
Indian forbearance—Conduct of the whites in Indian coun-
tries—Comparison of crime between Indians and whites—
Manner of swaddling infants—Hardships during infancy—
Savage customs—Indian constitution—Chief cause of
scanty [population—A day's journey—Calculation of
distance—Rough roads—Indian ideas—Social habits—
Some remarks on the system adopted for converting
Indians to the Christian faith   304

APPENDIX

Chinook Vocabulary   321
Table of the Weather at the Mouth of the Columbia   .   . 330

ADVENTURES OF THE FIRST SETTLERS ON THE COLUMBIA RIVER

CHAPTER I

Introductory remarks — John Jacob Astor — Grasping views — Early traders of Canada — The Hudson's Bay Company — American fur companies — Astor's policy — Russian settlements — Coasting vessels — The Pacific Fur Company — Flattering results — Oregon territory — New association — Mr. Hunt — Golden prospects — Proposals accepted — List of adventurers — Land party — Sea party — The ship *Tonquin* — Remarks — Opinion against opinion — Observations — Land expedition departs — Sea party set off for New York — Bark canoe — Spectators — Canadian voyageurs.

WHEN I first conceived the idea of writing the following narrative, my design was to begin with a brief outline of the discoveries already made on the coast of the Pacific, from Drake in 1579 to Vancouver in 1792;[1] or, rather, down to the present time; but, on second thoughts, I felt convinced that enough had been done already in that branch of [2] inquiry; or, at least, that the further prosecution of it might be better left to those who aspire to literary fame. Mine is an humbler ambition — not to figure as an author, but to record faithfully, as a trader, the events in which I bore a part; and, in so doing, to gratify a desire kindled by an acquaintance with strange scenes

---

[1] For a brief account of the discoveries of the Northwest Coast, see Thwaites, *Rocky Mountain Exploration* (New York, 1904), chap. i. For notes on Vancouver and Drake, see Franchère's *Narrative*, volume vi of our series, notes 2, 66. Further references to this *Narrative*, in the following notes, will be to that reprint.— ED.

and new fields of action, in a remote country which is still
but little known.

The progress of discovery contributes not a little to the
enlightenment of mankind; for mercantile interest
stimulates curiosity and adventure, and combines with
them to enlarge the circle of knowledge. To the spirit of
enterprise developed in the service of commercial speculation, civilized nations owe not only wealth and territorial
acquisitions, but also their acquaintance with the earth
and its productions. The illustration of these remarks
will be found in the following pages.

———

Mr. Astor of New York, a German by birth, but a
citizen of the United States, raised himself, by his adventurous and enterprising spirit, from small beginnings
to be one of the wealthiest and most eminent merchants in
America. Soon after his arrival in the United States,
about the year 1784, he commenced his commercial
career in the traffic of furs: at first on a very narrow scale,
but gradually expanding as his means increased. In this
way he made visits to Canada, purchasing furs in that
country, and shipping them from thence to the London
market: [3] and it is supposed that at this period his
buoyant and aspiring mind conceived the vast project of
grasping in his own hands, at some future day, the whole
fur trade of North America. [2]

The valuable furs and peltries scattered in former days
over the extensive forests, lakes, and rivers of the Canadas,
like the rich mines of Potosi and Mexico, invited many
adventurers. The French, for some time after settling
there, carried on an irregular but lucrative traffic in furs

———

[2] For brief sketch of John Jacob Astor, see Franchère's *Narrative*, volume
vi. of our series, note 8.— ED.

and peltries, with very little opposition, until the year 1670, when the Hudson's Bay Company, established by royal charter, took possession of the territory now called "Rupert's Land," or Hudson's Bay. The Canada, or as it was more generally called, the North-West Company, was formed in 1787; and these soon became the two great rival companies of the north, as we shall have occasion to notice more fully hereafter. Next on the theatre of action appeared the Mackina Company, which swept the warm regions of the south, as the two others did those of the wintry north, until the American Fur Company, established by Mr. Astor in 1809, commenced operations; but he, finding the Mackina fur traders somewhat in his way, bought out that Company, and added its territorial resources in 1811 to those of the American Fur Company. This body corporate was entitled the South-West, in contradistinction to the North-West Company. [2]

Mr. Astor now saw himself at the head of all the [4] fur trade of the south, and his intention was to penetrate through the barriers of the Northern Company, so as eventually to come into possession of all the fur trade east of the Rocky Mountains. With this plan still before him, he now turned his views to the trade on the coast of the Pacific, or that new field lying west of the Rocky

---

[2] For the history of the great fur-trade companies, see Turner, "Character and Influence of the Fur Trade in Wisconsin," Wisconsin Historical Society *Proceedings*, 1889; Chittenden, *History of American Fur Trade in Far West* (New York, 1902); J. Long's *Voyages*, volume ii of our series, preface. The Mackinac Company, composed of British subjects, was formed before the surrender of the Upper Lakes posts to the Americans (1796). It operated chiefly in the West and Southwest; and in 1807, Americans on Lake Ontario fired upon its brigade. See Michigan *Pioneer and Historical Collections*, xxv, pp. 250–257. This company was a source of dispute between Canada and the United States until Astor purchased its stock. At the time of sale, the North West Company's partners held a controlling interest.— ED.

Mountains, and which forms the subject of our present narrative. In this quarter the Russians alone had regular trading ports, opposite to Kamtschatka, where they still carry on a considerable trade in furs and seal skins, sending them across the Pacific direct to China. Their capital is limited, and their hunting grounds almost entirely confined to the sea-coast and islands around their establishments. The American coasting vessels also frequent this quarter, collecting vast quantities of valuable furs, which they convey to the Chinese market. This casual traffic by coasters, yielded to their owners in former days, by means of the returning cargo, an average clear gain of a thousand per cent. every second year; but these vessels are not so numerous of late, nor are the profits thus made so great as formerly.

The comprehensive mind of Mr. Astor could not but see these things in their true light, and perceive that if such limited and desultory traffic produced such immense profits, what might not be expected from a well-regulated trade, supported by capital and prosecuted with system: at all events, the Russian trader would then be confined within [5] his own limits, and the coasting vessels must soon disappear altogether.

Towards the accomplishment of the great plan which he had in view, Mr. Astor now set about opening a new branch of the fur trade on the Pacific, under the appellation of the "Pacific Fur Company," the grand central depôt of which was to be at the mouth of the Columbia River, the "Oregon of the Spaniards." [4] By this means he contemplated carrying off the furs of all the countries

[4] The word "Oregon" was not an appellation of the Spaniards, but appears to have first been employed in 1778 by the English traveller, Captain Jonathan Carver (concerning whom see J. Long's *Voyages*, volume ii of our series, note 5). On the meaning thereof, see Oregon Historical Society *Quarterly*, June, 1900; also H. H. Bancroft, *History of Oregon* (San Francisco, 1886), i, pp. 17–25.— ED.

west of the Rocky Mountains; at the same time forming a chain of trading posts across the Continent, from the Atlantic to the Pacific, along the waters of the great Missouri: connecting by this chain the operations of the South-West Company on the east, with that of the Pacific Fur Company on the west side of the dividing ridge.

This grand commercial scheme, appearing now plain and practicable, at least to men of sanguine disposition, gave much satisfaction to the American public, who, from the results contemplated, became deeply interested in its success; for all the rich cargoes of furs and peltries thus to be collected annually over the vast expanse were to be shipped in American vessels for the great China mart, there to be sold, and the proceeds invested in a return cargo of teas, silks, beads, and nankeens, and other articles of high demand in the United States; which would not only prevent to some extent the American specie from going out of the Union for such articles, but also turn the barren wilds of the north and far [6] west into a source of national wealth. Some, however, of the more sagacious and influential among the Americans themselves observed to Mr. Astor at the time, that his plan would be likely to give umbrage to the British, and arouse them to assert more speedily their claims of prior discovery to the Oregon quarter, and that such a step would operate against him. To these suggestions Mr. Astor simply observed, ''that he had thought of that, but intended chiefly to employ in his undertaking British subjects, and that he should on that account give less offence; besides,'' added, he, ''the claims of prior discovery and territorial right are claims to be settled by Government only, and not by an individual.''

Mr. Astor's plans, hitherto known only to a few, now began to develope themselves more publicly. On the first intimation of the scheme, the North-Westerns took the alarm; for having already, in the prosecution of their trade, penetrated to the west side of the Rocky Mountains, in the direction of New Caledonia and the north branch of the Columbia, where they expected to reap a rich harvest, they viewed Astor's expedition to that quarter with a jealous eye, according to the old adage that "two of a trade seldom agree;" but others again extolled the brilliant project, as the brightest gem in the American Union, and particularly many of the retired partners of the North-West Company, who, not being provided for in some late arrangements, had left that concern in disgust, and therefore were the most likely [7] to oppose with effect the ambitious views of their former coadjutors. These were just the men Mr. Astor had in his eye; men of influence and experience among savages, and who from their earlier days had been brought up in, and habituated to, the hardships of the Indian trade. To several of these persons Mr. Astor disclosed his plans and made proposals, whereupon Messrs. M'Kay, M'Kenzie, M'Dougall, and Stuart, entered into his views, and became partners in the new concern. [5] The former of these gentlemen had accompanied Sir Alexander M'Kenzie in his voyages of discovery to the North Polar Sea in 1789, and to the Pacific in 1793, the narratives of which are before the public; and most of the others had equal experience, and were all of them in some way or other related to the great men at the head of the North-West Company.[6]

Articles of association and co-partnership were therefore entered into and concluded at New York, in the spring

---

[5] For brief biography of these partners of the Pacific Fur Company, see Bradbury's *Travels*, volume v of our series, note 4; Franchère's *Narrative*, notes 9, 10.— ED.

[6] Concerning Mackenzie's discoveries, see Franchère, note 4. McKay accompanied Mackenzie upon his second voyage to the Pacific, not upon his first expedition to the Arctic.— ED.

of 1810, between those gentlemen and Mr. Astor, establishing the firm of the Pacific Fur Company, as already noticed; to which firm five other partners, namely, Messrs. Hunt, Crooks, Miller, M'Lellan, and Clarke, were soon afterwards added.[7] The association was not a joint-stock concern; Mr. Astor alone furnished the capital, amounting to 200,000 dollars, divided into 100 shares of 2000 dollars each, with power to increase the capital to 500,000 dollars.

The association was formed for a period of twenty [8] years, but with this proviso, that it was to be dissolved if it proved either unprofitable or impracticable, after a trial of five years; during which trial, however, Mr. Astor, as stock-holder, was alone to bear all expenses and losses, the other partners giving only their time and labour. Of the above shares, Mr. Astor held fifty in his own hands; Mr. Hunt, as his representative and chief manager of the business, five; while the other partners, who were to carry on the trade with the Indians, were to have four each, in the event of the business succeeding. The remaining shares were reserved for the clerks, who joined the concern as adventurers, without any other remuneration than their chances of success at the end of the five years' trial. The only exceptions were Mr. Robert Stuart and myself, who were to have our promotion at the end of the third year. From the proportion of interest, or number of shares in the hands of the stockholder and his representative, it will appear evident that the other partners, however unanimous they might be, could never have gained a majority of votes in any case over those which might have been by proxy appointed to represent Astor.

At the head depôt, or general rendezvous, was to be

---

[7] Relative to Hunt, Crooks, McClellan, and Miller, see Bradbury's *Travels*, volume v of our series, notes 2, 3, 72; for Clarke, see Franchère, note 81.— ED.

stationed Mr. Astor's representative. The person appointed to this important trust was Wilson Price Hunt, a gentleman from New Jersey, who alone, of the whole party, had never been engaged in the Indian trade; yet his active habits, perseverance, and enterprise, soon made good his want of experience, [9] and enabled him to discharge the duties of his station. In him was also vested the chief authority, or, in his absence, in M'Dougall. It was therefore to either or to both of these gentlemen that all Mr. Astor's measures were made known, and all his cargoes consigned.

At the time when these novel schemes were first agitated, I was in Upper Canada; and the first intimation I had of them was in a letter from Mr. M'Kay, the senior partner, requesting an interview with me at Montreal. To Montreal I accordingly went in the month of May; and there, for the first time, I saw the gilded prospectus of the new Company, and, accepting the proposals made to me by Mr. Astor, was the first to join the expedition; — and who at the time would not have joined it, for, although the North-Westerns tried to throw all the cold water of the St. Lawrence on the project, yet they could not extinguish the flame it had spread abroad. The flattering hopes and golden prospects held out to adventurers, so influenced the public mind, that the wonder-stricken believers flocked in from all quarters to share in the wonderful riches of the far west.

It need not be wondered at, if, under the influence of such extravagant expectations, many applicants appeared; but in accordance with Astor's plan, that the business should be carried on only by persons of well-tested merit and experience, for on their habits of perserverance and enterprise alone rested all hopes [10] of ultimate success, his assistants were selected with more than ordinary care, every poor fellow that engaged being led to believe that his fortune was already made. Here Messrs. Franchere, Pillet, M'Gillis, Farnham, and M'Lennan, besides Mr. Stuart and myself, joined the adventurers;[8] besides five tradesmen or mechanics, and twenty-four canoe men, the best that could be found of their classes.

Operations were now deemed requisite for the accomplishment of the Company's views; therefore, while one party, headed by Mr. Hunt, was ordered to make its way across the Continent by land, another party, headed by Mr. M'Kay, was to proceed by sea in the *Tonquin*, a ship of 300 tons, and mounting twelve guns. The *Tonquin's* course was round Cape Horn, for the north-west coast. The Columbia River was to be the common destination of both parties. The land party at its outset consisted of only seventeen persons, but Mr. Hunt's object was to augment that number to about eighty as he passed along, by means of American trappers and hunters from the south. Here M'Kenzie strongly recommended Mr. Hunt to take all his men from Canada, as too much time might probably be lost in collecting them from the south; and besides, Canadians, as he thought, would answer much better; but Mr. Hunt adhered to his first plan.

The arrangement of these two expeditions, in which M'Kay, whose life had been spent in voyaging through the Indian countries, and who was nowise [11] qualified as a merchant, had resigned the inland voyage to a gentleman, bred to mercantile pursuits, but unacquainted with this

---

[8] For what is known of these clerks, see Franchère, notes 76, 84. For Robert Stuart, see Bradbury's *Travels*, in our volume v, note 117.— ED.

new mode of travelling, exhibited such an egregious inversion of the ordinary rules of prudence, as gave rise to much comment.

Matters being so far settled, Mr. Hunt, who was now seconded by Mr. M'Kenzie, left La Chine, nine miles south of Montreal, with the land expedition, in the beginning of July; and, on the 20th of the same month, the ship party, consisting of three partners, five clerks, Mr. Stuart, and myself, five mechanics, and fourteen canoe men, left Montreal for New York, where we were to embark. Of this number, however, M'Kay and eight of the most expert voyageurs proceeded in a bark-canoe through the States: on all such occasions there is a kind of mutual understanding between both parties, that is, between the canoe men and the canoe, the former undertaking to carry the latter over the land part of the journey, while the latter is bound to carry the others safe over water. The appearance of this unusual kind of craft on the American waters, with the cheerful chantings of its crew, their feathered caps and sylvan appearance, as they approached the gay city of New York, attracted such a crowd of spectators of all classes around them, as left but little space to land; but what was the astonishment, when, in the twinkling of an eye, two of the crew were seen to shoulder their craft, capable of containing [12] two tons weight, and to convey it to a place of safety on terra firma. Mr. Astor, who happened to be present, was so delighted with the vivacity and dexterity of the two men, that he gave them an eagle to drink his health; then turning round, observed to some gentlemen who were standing by, that "six Americans could not do what these two brawny fellows had done," which observation gave rise to some further remarks, when

Mr. M'Kay, with an air of confidence, challenged the swiftest New York boat for a three mile race, offering to bet ten to one on his canoe men, but, after what had been witnessed, no one appeared disposed to risk his money. It is scarcely necessary in this place to observe, that the Canadian voyageurs are among the most expert and venturesome canoe men in the world.

[13] CHAPTER II [9]

The *Tonquin* sails — Quarrels on board — The captain's character — Accommodations — A sudden squall — Flying fish — The captain's harshness — Cape de Verd Islands — Alarm of fire — A suspicious sail — Crossing the line — Springing a leak — Short allowance of water — Immense wave — The Falkland Islands — Rocky passage — Wild fowl — Port Egmont Bay — The party on shore — Mr. Farnham's gray goose — Old graves renewed — Epitaphs — Party left behind — New dangers — Mr. Robert Stuart's determined conduct — Feuds on board — Cape Horn doubled — The weather — Pilot fish — Trade winds — Rogues' mess — Little pilot — Mouna Roa — A man overboard — The mate in irons.

ON the 6th of September, 1810, all hands — twenty-two belonging to the ship, and thirty-three passengers — being on board, the *Tonquin* set sail, and a fresh breeze springing up, soon wafted her to a distance from the busy shores of New York. We had not proceeded far when we were joined by the American frigate *Constitution*, which was to escort us clear of the coast. On the 7th, in the afternoon, we passed Sandy Hook lighthouse, and the next day the *Constitution* returned, we dismissed our pilot, and were soon out of sight of land, steering a S.E. course. [14] So

[9] Compare the following description of the voyage of the "Tonquin" with that of Franchère; on the "Constitution," Captain Thorn, and the Hawaiian Islands, see *ibid.*, notes 18, 19, 21.— ED.

far all was bustle and confusion upon deck, and every place in the ship was in such topsy-turvy state, with what sailors call live and dead lumber, that scarcely any one knew how or where he was to be stowed; and it was in settling this knotty point that the crusty supremacy of the high-minded captain was first touched. Captain Jonathan Thorn had been brought up in the American navy, had signalized himself, and upon the present occasion he stood upon his own quarter-deck. Matters went on well enough till we came to the mechanics: these young men had been selected from the most respectable of their class, had been promised by their employers situations as clerks in the trade whenever vacancies should occur, and in consequence, serving in the twofold capacity of clerks and tradesmen, they were entitled, by their engagements, whilst on board ship to the same treatment as the other clerks; but behold when the captain came to assign them their place, it was not in either the second or the third cabin, no, nor in the steerage, but before the mast among the common sailors. In vain did they remonstrate, and equally vain was it for them to produce copies of their engagements; right or wrong, forward they must go; but that was not all; to the grievance of bad accommodations was added that of an insult to their feelings, by being compelled, as a further punishment for their obstinacy, to perform the duties of common seamen both by day and night. After this bit of a row with the captain, they applied for [15] redress to the partners on board, the very persons with whom they had executed their agreements. The partners interposed, and in their turn remonstrated with the captain, but without effect; he remained inexorable. Both parties then getting into a violent passion, Mr. M'Kay said, ''That his people would defend themselves rather than suffer such treatment." On hearing this, the captain, suddenly turning round on his heel, defied Mr. M'Kay and his people, adding, "that he would blow out the brains of the first man who dared to disobey his orders on board his own ship." In the midst of this scene, Mr. David Stuart, a good old soul, stept up, and by his gentle and timely interference put an end to the threatening altercation.

This was the first specimen we had of the captain's disposition, and it laid the foundation of a rankling hatred between the partners and himself, which ended only with the voyage, and not only that, but it soon spread like a contagion amongst all classes, so that party spirit ran high: the captain and his people viewing the passengers as the passengers did them, with no very cordial feelings. Whilst these feuds agitated the great folks at the head of affairs, we amused ousrelves with conjectures as to the issue of the contest. A new leaf was to be turned over, the captain forbade the partners the starboard side of the quarter-deck; the clerks, the quarter-deck altogether; and as for the poor mechanics and Canadians, they were ruled ever after with a rod of iron. All this [16] time the *Tonquin* was speeding her way proudly over the wide bosom of the Atlantic, until the 18th, in the morning, when she was struck with a sudden squall, which backed all the sails and placed her in a critical position for about two minutes; her stern going down foremost was almost under water, when all at once she recovered and relieved our anxiety. The next day two sail were descried a head, all hands were mustered on deck, and each had his station assigned to him in case of coming to close quarters. For some days past the flying fish appeared in immense numbers, passing frequently through the ship's rigging, and now and then falling on the deck. We measured one of them and found its length to be 5½ inches, circumference of the body 2 inches; the wings, situate near the gills, resemble in texture the wings of the bat, and measure, when stretched, 5 inches between the tips. In their flight they generally rise to 15 or 20 feet above the surface of the water, and fly about 150 yards at a time. As soon as their wings get dry they fall again into the water, and only fly to avoid their pursuers. They are the prey of the dolphin and other large fishes.

On the 6th of October we made one of the Cape de Verd Islands, on the coast of Africa. It proved to be Bonavista, in lat. 16° N. and long. 22° 47′ W. The land, covered with a blue haze, appeared broken, barren, and rocky. The weather was overcast, and we had heavy rain and thunder at the time. Near this place immense shoals of porpoises kept skipping [17] on the surface of the water going southwards. They were said to prognosticate the near approach of bad weather. We found the changes of the weather here very remarkable, from calm to rough, from foul to fair; clear, cloudy, wet, dry, hazy, and squally alternately, with the usual finale of mist and rain, and not unfrequently all these changes within the twenty-four hours.

After leaving the land, some of the gentlemen amused themselves one fine evening with shooting at a mark suspended from the ship's stern, under which a boat lay secured; soon afterwards, in the dusk of the evening, smoke was seen to issue from that quarter; the alarm of fire was given, and in an instant all the people assembled on deck in a state of wild confusion, some calling out to broach the water casks, others running to and fro in search of water, some with mugs, others with decanters, while the *mâitre de cuisine* was robbed of his broth and dish water—no one, in the hurry and bustle of the moment, ever thought of dipping the buckets alongside. At length to the inexpressible joy of all, it was discovered that the smoke was occasioned only by the wadding of the guns setting fire to some old junk which was lying in the boat astern. This gentle warning, however, put an end to such sport in future. Some angry words took place between the captain and Mr. Fox, the first mate, on which the latter was suspended from duty, and ordered below: no other reason could be assigned for this act but [18] the friendly and sociable terms existing between the mate and the partners; for by this time such was the ill-feeling between the captain and the passengers generally, that scarcely a word passed between them. After three days' confinement Mr. Fox was reinstated.

Just as we entered the trade winds, a sail appeared about two leagues to leeward; she gained fast upon us, and dogged us all day, and the next morning was close under our stern. She appeared to be an armed brig, and pierced for twenty guns, and looked very suspicious; very few hands, however, were to be seen on her deck, which might haye been a manœuvre to decoy us alongside. We were prepared for combat, at least as far as a good display of numbers on deck: for to our numbers, and not to either our skill or discipline, did we chiefly trust, and it is probable this show had the desired effect, for she soon bore away and we saw her no more.

On the 25th, in long. 26° 24' W. we crossed the equinoctial line, and here the usual ceremony of ducking was performed on such of the sailors as had never before entered the southern hemisphere. The heat was intense, the weather a dead calm, and the ocean smooth as a sheet of glass. The thermometer stood at 92° in the shade.

In lat. 3° 17' S. and long. 26° 40' W. we spoke a brig from Liverpool bound to Pernambuco. On nearing this old and ghastly-looking hulk, which apparently had but few hands on board, we thought [19] ourselves exceedingly strong compared to her, and I suppose from the bold front we presented, put her in as much bodily fear as the armed brig some days before did us.

On the 10th of November a violent gale came on, which lasted for fifty hours without intermission, and did us considerable damage, our jib and jib-boom being both carried off, and a leak of considerable extent sprung; but as it was easy of access, we soon got it stopped again. In the night of the 14th, an alarm of fire was again given; but after much confusion it ended without serious consequences. Of all calamities that of fire on board ship seems to be the most terrific, and every precaution was taken to prevent any accident of the kind, for at nine o'clock every night all the lights were, by the captain's orders, put out, and this rule was strictly observed during the voyage. In these latitudes we saw many turtle, and caught some of them sleeping on the water, one of which weighed forty-five pounds; we also frequently met with what the sailors call a Portuguese man-of-war, or seabladder, floating on the surface of the waters.

In lat. 35° S. and 42° 17' W. we experienced another tempestuous gale, which lasted upwards of forty hours. During this violent storm the ship laboured hard, and sustained damage. Two new leaks were observed, and many of the sails blown to rags. Although the top and top-gallant masts had been lowered, six of the guns got dismounted, and [20] kept for some time rolling like thunder on the deck, and the ship in a constant heavy sea. For seventeen hours she scudded before the wind, and went in that time two hundred and twenty miles; nothing alarming, however, took place until eight o'clock in the morning of the second day, when a very heavy sea broke over the stern, and filled us all with consternation. This wave, like a rolling mountain, passed over her deck ten feet high, and broke with a tremendous crash about the mainmast; yet, fortunately, no lives were lost, for on its near approach we all clung to the rigging, and by that means saved ourselves. On the weather moderating the carpenter was soon at work, and succeeded effectually in stopping the leaks. On the 20th our allowance of water, already short by one-half, was lessened to a pint and a half per man, and on the 2nd of December to a pint each man per day—then a gallon of brandy was offered for a pint of fresh water! but on the 5th, when the joyful sight of land was announced, a hogshead of water was offered in return for a pint of brandy. In the afternoon of this day, we made the N. W. point of one of the Falkland Islands, the rugged and solitary features of which presented a truly romantic appearance. Near this spot are three remarkable peaked rocks, or insular bluffs, of considerable height, and nearly equal distance from each other. We soon afterwards came close in with the shore, and beheld a rocky surface, with an aspect of hopeless sterility. [21] Here we came to an anchor; but the captain not liking the place changed his resolution of taking in water there.

During the few hours, however, which we spent on shore, while the ship lay at anchor, one of the sailors, named Johnston, strolled out of the way. The captain, nevertheless, gave orders to weigh anchor, declaring that he would leave the fellow to his fate; but after much entreaty he consented to wait an hour, adding, that if the man did not return in that time he should never more set foot on board his ship. A party immediately volunteered to go in search of the lost tar. This party after beating about in vain for some time, at last though of setting fire to the few tufts of grass which here and there alone decked the surface. This expedient succeeded, and the man was found, having fallen asleep near the water's edge. But the hour had unfortunately elapsed, and the loss of a few minutes more so enraged the captain, that he not only threatened the man's life, but maltreated all those who had been instrumental in finding him. We then set sail, and had much difficulty in effecting a passage through a narrow strait which lay before us, interrupted in many places by ledges of rocks, which were literally covered with seals, penguins, white and grey geese, ducks, shags, albatrosses, eagles, hawks, and vultures. After making our way through this intricate pass, we again came to anchor.

[22] On the 7th of December we anchored in Port Egmont Bay, for the purpose of taking in a supply of water. The bay or inlet of Port Egmont is about a mile long, and half a mile broad, and sheltered from almost every wind that blows. All hands now were set to work; two of the mates and two-thirds of the crew, together with the mechanics and Canadians, commenced replenishing the water-casks, whilst the other two mates with the remainder of the people were employed on board repairing the rigging, and putting everything in a fit condition for a new start. During these operations the partners and clerks, and frequently the captain also, went sporting on shore, where wild fowl of all kinds stunned our ears with

their noises, and darkened the air with their numbers, and were generally so very tame, or rather stupid, that we often killed them with sticks and stones, and the sailors in their boats often knocked down the ducks and penguins with their oars in passing the rocks. The only quadruped we saw on land was a wolverine of ordinary size, which one of our party shot.

Our tent was pitched on shore, not above four hundred yards from the ship; this was our sporting rendezvous. On the 10th all the water-casks were ready, and the captain on going on board that evening said to Mr. M'Dougall, that the ship would probably sail the next day. Soon after, however, Messrs. M'Kay and M'Dougall also went on board, where they passed the night; but coming ashore [23] the next morning, they told us that the ship would not sail till the 12th, and that all hands were ordered on board on that night.

In the mean time Mr. Farnham, one of the clerks, had caught a grey goose, which he tied to a stone between our hut and the landing-place, in order to have some sport with it. Soon afterwards the captain, happening to come on shore, and seeing the goose, he up with his gun to shoot at it. Thinking, however, that he had missed it, he instantly reloaded and fired again, and seeing the goose flutter he ran up to catch it, when he discovered his mistake, on which we all burst out a laughing. Nettled at this, he immediately turned round and went on board again. Meantime, Messrs. M'Dougall and Stuart started across the point after game; whilst Mr. M'Kay, myself, and some others, went up the bay a little to repair two old graves which we had discovered in a dilapidated state the day before. On one of these graves was the following rudely-cut inscription on a board:—"William Stevens, aged twenty-two years, killed by a fall from a rock, on the 21st of September, 1794;" on the other, "Benjamin Peak died of the smallpox on the 5th of January, 1803, ship *Eleonora*, Captain Edmund Cole, Providence, Rhode Island."

While we were thus eagerly employed, little did we suspect what was going on in another quarter; for, about two o'clock in the afternoon, one of our party called out, "The ship's off!"—when all of us, [24] running to the top of a little eminence, beheld, to our infinite surprise and dismay, the *Tonquin*, under full sail, steering out of the bay. We knew too well the callous and headstrong passions of the wayward captain to hesitate a moment in determining what to do; with hearts, therefore, beating between anxious hope and despair, some made for the boat, whilst others kept running and firing over hill and dale to warn Messers. M'Dougal and Stuart, who had not yet returned. In half an hour we were all at the water's edge; the ship by this time was three miles out at sea. We were now nine persons on shore, and we had to stow, squat, and squeeze ourselves into a trumpery little boat, scarcely capable of holding half our number. In this dreadful dilemma, we launched on a rough and tempestuous sea, and, against wind and tide, followed the ship. The wind blowing still fresher and fresher, every succeeding wave threatened our immediate destruction. Our boat already half full of water, and ourselves, as may be supposed, drenched with the surges passing over her, we gave up all hope of succeeding in the unequal struggle, and a momentary pause ensued, when we deliberated whether we should proceed in the perilous attempt or return to land. The ship was now at least two leagues ahead of us, and just at this time the man who was bailing out the water in the boat unfortunately let go and lost the pail, and one of our oars being broken in the struggle to recover it, our destiny seemed sealed beyond a doubt. A second deliberation [25] ended in the resolve to reach the ship or perish in the attempt. The weather now grew more violent; the wind increased; and, what was worst of all, the sun had just sunk under the horizon, and the fearful night began to spread its darkness over the turbulent deep. Every ray of hope now vanished: but so short-sighted is man, that the moment when he least expects it, relief often comes from an unseen hand; and such was our case; for in an instant our hopeless anxiety was turned into joy by the ship suddenly making down to our assistance: but here again we had a new danger to contend with; for, on coming alongside, we were several times like to be engulfed or dashed to pieces by the heavy seas and rolling of the ship. The night was dark; the weather stormy; and death in a thousand forms stared us in the face. At length, after many ineffectual attempts and much manœuvring, we succeeded in getting on board; having been in the boat upwards of six hours. That the captain's determination was to leave us all to our fate, there is not the least doubt; for he declared so afterwards, in a letter written to Mr. Astor from the Sandwich Islands, and he was only prevented from carrying his purposes into effect by the determined conduct of Mr. Robert Stuart, who, seizing a brace of pistols, peremptorily told the captain to order about ship and save the boat; or, he added, "You are a dead man this instant."

During the night the gale increased almost to a hurricane, so that two of our sails were torn to pieces, [26] and the side-rails broke by the labouring of the ship; so we had to lie-to under a storm-staysail for six hours. The reader is here left to picture to himself how matters went on after the scene just described. All the former feuds and squabbles between the captain and passengers sink into insignificance compared to the recent one. Sullen and silent, both parties passed and repassed each other in their promenades on deck without uttering a word; but their looks bespoke the hatred that burnt within. The partners on the quarter-deck made it now a point to speak nothing but the Scotch dialect; while the Canadians on the forecastle spoke French — neither of which did the captain understand; and as both groups frequently passed hours together, cracking their jokes and chanting their outlandish songs, the commander seemed much annoyed on these occasions, pacing the deck in great agitation. Yet all this time the ship good was hastening on her way.

On the 15th we saw Staten Land, whose forked peaks and rugged surface exhibited much snow. Soon afterwards, Terra del Fuego came in sight; and on the 19th, at 9 o'clock in the morning, we had a full view of Cape Horn. But adverse winds meeting us here, we were unable to double it before Christmas morning, and were carried, in the mean time, as far south as lat. 58° 16'. While in these latitudes, notwithstanding the foggy state of the weather, we could read common print at all hours of the night on deck without the aid of artificial light. The sky was [27] generally overcast, and the weather raw and cold, with frequent showers of hail and snow, but we saw no ice. Here the snow birds and Cape pigeon frequently flew in great numbers about the ship. After doubling the Cape, a speckled red and white fish, about the size of a salmon, was observed before the ship's bow, as if leading the way. The sailors gave it the name of the pilot-fish.

With gladdened hearts, we now bent our course northward on the wide Pacific. On the 19th of January, 1811, all hands passed the ordeal of inspection, or as the sailors more appropriately called it, the ''general turn-out;'' and as none could guess what this new manœuvre portended, we all judged it to be a relic of man-of-war discipline, which the captain introduced merely to refresh his memory; but the proceeding must be described:—After breakfast, all hands were summoned on deck, and there ordered to remain, while the officers of the ship got up the trunks, chests, hammocks, dirty shirts, and old shoes belonging to each individual, on deck. They were then ordered to empty out the contents of the boxes, examine, and expose the whole to view, each man's paraphernalia separately. While this was going on, the bystanders were ordered to claim any article belonging to them in the possession of another. This declaration cleared up the matter, and set our judgment right as to the captain's motives; but to the credit of all, very little stolen property was found—being only three articles, namely, a pamphlet, a clasp-knife, [28] and a spoon, and even as to them the theft was not very well proved; but the three individuals implicated were nevertheless condemned, and placed on what is called the ''rogue's mess'' for a month.

On the 24th we again crossed the Equator, and entered the northern hemisphere, and here the pilot-fish that joined us at Cape Horn disappeared. During a run of upwards of 5,000 miles, our little piscatory pilot was never once known, by day or night, to intermit preceding the ship's bow. On the 10th of February, the cloud-capped summit of the towering Mouna Roa—a pyramidal mountain in Owhyhee, and the loftiest in the Sandwich Islands—was visible at the distance of 50 miles.

As we drew near to the land, going at the rate of eight

knots an hour, a Canadian lad named Joseph LaPierre
fell overboard. This was an awkward accident, as all
eyes were at the time gazing with admiration on the
scenery of the land. In an instant, however, the sails
were backed, boats lowered, and everything at hand
thrown overboard to save the drowning man; but before
he could be picked up the ship had distanced him more
than a mile, and when the boatswain reached the ship with
the body, the captain, in his usual sympathizing mood,
peremptorily ordered him about to pick up all the
trumpery which had been thrown into the water. This
took a considerable time. The apparently lifeless body
was then hoisted on board, and every means tried to
restore animation, and at last, by rolling the body in warm
[29] blankets, and rubbing it with salt, the lad recovered,
after being thirty-eight minutes in the water, and though
unable to swim.

Mr. Fox, who had again fallen under the captain's
displeasure, and who had been, in consequence, off duty
for a week past, was reinstated this morning. This was no
sooner done, however, than the fourth mate, the captain's
own brother, was put into irons. The young Thorn was
as factious and morose a subject as his brother; with this
only difference, that he had less power to do mischief. He
had maltreated one of the passengers; and the captain,
in order to show impartiality, awarded him the above
punishment.

[30] CHAPTER III [10]

Karakakooa Bay—The sailors desert—The captain's conduct—Productions of Owhyhee—Tocaigh Bay—Governor Young—Royal proclamation—Woahoo—Ourourah, the residence of Tammeatameah—Harbour fees—Excursion on shore—The Queen's umbrella—The King's appearance—Royal palace and guards—Arsenal, or royal workshop—Royal dinner—His Majesty's fleet—Morais, or places of public worship—Sacred or puranee ground tabooed—Storm—A sailor left to his fate among the natives—Parting visit from his Majesty—His meanness—Diving of the natives—Native proas: how made—Clothing—Customs and peculiarities—Character of the women—White men at the Sandwich Islands—The King's disposition towards foreigners—Captain Cook—Pahooas, or war spears—A sham fight—Religion—Tammeatmeah conquerer and king—Apparent happiness of the natives—Prophetic hint—Distressed situation of a boat.

ON the 13th of February the ship anchored in Karakakooa Bay, in the island of Owhyhee, and within a mile of the place where the unfortunate Captain Cook fell in 1779. The Sandwich Islands are eleven in number, and lie between the 19th and 22nd parallels of N. latitude, and the meridians of 151° and 160° W. longitude. The climate is warm but healthy, and more temperate and uniform than [31] is usual in tropical countries; nor is it subject to hurricanes and earthquakes. In their customs and manners the natives resemble the New Zealanders, and like them are a warlike people: all classes tattoo their bodies.

Karakakooa Bay is about a mile or more in extent, but

[10] Compare Ross's account of the Hawaiian Islands with that of Franchère, especially notes 22–34.— ED.

sheltered only on one side, which presents a high rugged front of coral rock, resembling a rampart or battery in the bottom of the bay, facing the ocean, with two bushy trees on it waving in the wind like flags. The shores, with the exception of the above-mentioned rock, are everywhere low, with here and there clumps of cocoa-nut and other trees, which give a pleasing variety to the scene; and the land, rising gradually as it recedes to a considerable height, looks down over intervening hill and dale upon the delightful little villages of Kakooa and Kowrowa.

We were now near land, and the captain's conduct to both passengers and crew had fostered a spirit of desertion among the sailors: Jack Tar, slipping off in the night, was seen no more. This new feature in our affairs portended no good, but brought about a sweeping change, for the captain had now no resource but to place his chief confidence in those whom he had all along maltreated and affected to despise. In this state of things, the natives were employed to bring back the deserters. One Roberts, a yankee, was confined below; Ems, a Welshman, was tied up and flogged; Johnston, an Englishman, [32] was put in irons; and Anderson, the boatswain, could not be found. Storming and stamping on deck, the captain called up all hands; he swore, he threatened, and abused the whole ship's company, making, if possible, things worse. I really pitied the poor man, although he had brought all this trouble upon himself: with all his faults he had some good qualities, and in his present trying situation we all forgot our wrongs, and cheerfully exerted ourselves to help him out of his difficulties. The clerks were appointed to assist the officers, and the Canadians to supply the place of the sailors in keeping watch and doing the other duties on shore; while the partners, forgetting former animosities, joined hand in hand with the captain in providing for the wants of the ship.

Order being now restored, the partners and some of the clerks went occasionally on shore; meantime, the natives having paid several visits on board, and sounded our bargain-making chiefs (for they are shrewd dealers), a brisk trade commenced in plantains, bananas, yams, taro, bread-fruit, sweet potatoes, sugar-canes, cocoa-nuts, and some pork, the principal productions of the place. We had not been long here, however, till we learned that the chief of the island resided at a place called Tocaigh Bay, some distance off; and as we expected a further and better supply there, we sailed for that place, where we had an interview with the governor, a white man, named John Young. He received us kindly, and with [33] every mark of attention peculiar to an Indian chief; showed us his wife, his daughter, his household, and vassals—a strange assemblage of wealth and poverty, filth and plenty.

Governor Young was a native of England, and belonged to an American ship, the *Eleanor*, of which he was boatswain. That vessel, happening to touch at the Sandwich Islands in 1790, left Young there to shift for himself; but his nautical skill and good conduct soon recommended him to the reigning prince, Tammeatameah, and he is now Viceroy or Governor of Owhyhee. He is about 60 years of age, shrewd, and healthy; but, from his long residence among the natives, he has imbibed so much of their habits and peculiarities, that he is now more Indian than white man.

We had not been long at the village of Tocaigh, when Governor Young gave us to understand that no rain had fallen in that neighbourhood during the four preceding years, and that in consequence provisions were very scarce, and good water was not to be found there at any time. These details were discouraging. The natives, however, began a brisk trade in fruits and vegetables; we, however, were desirous of purchasing hogs and goats, but were told that the sale of pork had been prohibited by royal proclamation, and that, without the permission of the king, who resided in the island of Woahoo, no subject could dispose of any. Anxious to complete our supplies, we immediately resolved on sailing to Woahoo.

[34] On the 21st of February, we cast anchor abreast of Ourourah, the metropolis of Woahoo, and royal residence of Tammeatameah. This is the richest and most delightful spot in the whole archipelago. On our approaching the land, two white officers came on board; the one a Spaniard, secretary to his majesty; the other a Welshman, the harbour master: the latter brought us safe to anchor in Whyteete Bay, for which service he demanded and was paid five Spanish dollars.

The royal village of Ourourah is situate at the foot of a hill, facing the ocean, on the west side of the island. The houses were 740 in number, and contained 2025 inhabitants. It will appear strange that so few inhabitants should require so many houses, but this will be explained hereafter. Behind the village there is an extensive field under fine cultivation—perhaps it may measure 500 acres; but its appearance was greatly injured by irregular enclosures, or rather division lines, formed of loose stones running on the surface, intersecting and crossing each other in every possible direction, for the purpose of marking the plot claimed by each individual or family: the whole is cultivated with much skill and industry, the soil teemingly rich, and the labour abundant, with here and there small water-courses and aqueducts.

Immediately after coming to anchor, Captain Thorn, accompanied by Mr. M'Kay and Mr. M'Dougall, waited on his majesty, Tammeatameah, [35] and after dining with him, returned on board. In the afternoon his majesty and three queens returned the visit in state, the royal canoe being paddled by sixteen chiefs, with the state arm-chest on board. Their majesties were received with becoming ceremony. The flag was displayed, and three guns fired. The king was conducted to the cabin followed by his valet, who held a spitting-box in his hand, but the queens preferred remaining on deck. While here, they very unceremoniously disrobed themselves, plunged overboard, and after swimming and sporting for some time in the water, came on board again and dressed themselves, after which they joined Tammeatameah in the cabin, where they did ample justice to a good collation, drank two bottles of wine, and left us apparently well pleased with their reception. The chiefs remained all the time in the royal yacht alongside.

Tammeatameah appeared to be about fifty years of age; straight and portly, but not corpulent; his countenance was pleasing, but his complexion rather dark, even for an Indian. He had on a common beaver hat, a shirt, and neckcloth, which had once been white; a long blue coat with velvet collar, a cassimere vest, corduroy trousers, and a pair of strong military shoes; he also wore a long and not inelegant sword, which he said he got from his brother, the king of England.

During these interviews and visits of ceremony, the captain had broached the subject of pork to [36] his majesty; but this was not the work of an hour nor of a day; pork was a royal monopoly, and the king well knew how to turn it to his advantage on the present occasion, for several conferences were held, and all the *pros* and *cons* of a hard bargain discussed, before the royal contract was concluded. Time however, brought it about, and the negociation was finally closed; the king furnished the requisite supplies of hogs, goats, poultry, and vegetables, for all of which a stipulated quantity of merchandise was to be given in return. Business now commenced, and good water and provisions were brought to the ship in boat-loads; and as the king further pledged himself, that if any of the sailors deserted he would answer for their safe delivery again, this assurance, although the words of kings are not always sacred, had the effect of relieving the passengers from the ship's duties; we were, therefore, enabled to go on shore.

On walking up to the royal city on our first landing, we were met by two of the queens, accompanied by a page of honour. They were all three walking abreast, the page in the middle, and holding with his two hands a splendid parasol of the richest silk, measuring six feet eight inches in diameter. From this umbrella hung twelve massy tassels, weighing at least a pound each. The ladies were very communicative, and after detaining us for nearly half an hour passed on. We were soon afterwards introduced to his majesty, who honoured us with a glass of arrack. Here [37] we had a full view of the royal palace, the royal family, and the life-guards. The palace consisted of thirteen houses, built so as to form a square. All the buildings of the country are a kind of wicker work, remarkable for their neatness and regularity; and although slender, they appear to be strong and durable; nor did there appear any difference between the royal buildings and the other houses of the place, the square and court-yard excepted. The king occupied three of these houses;

one for eating, another for sleeping, and the third for business, which may be called the audience chamber. Each of the queens occupied three also; a dressing house, a sleeping house, and an eating house. His majesty never enters any of the queens' houses, nor do they ever enter any of his: in this respect, they are always tabooed. There is a house set apart exclusively for their interviews. The established custom of the land is that each family, however poor, invariably occupies three houses; and this will explain why so many houses are required for so few inhabitants.

We also saw two of the king's sons; one of them was in disgrace and tabooed; that is, interdicted from speaking with anybody. We were next shown the life-guards, consisting of forty men, accoutred in something of the English style, with muskets, belts, and bayonets; but their uniform was rather old and shabby. The parade-ground, or place where the guards were on duty, lay just behind the royal buildings, on a level square green spot made up for the [38] purpose, and on which were placed eighteen four or six pounders, all mounted, and apparently in good order.

From this we proceeded to a long narrow range of buildings, where a number of artisans were at work, making ship, sloop, and boat tackling, ropes, blocks, and all the other *et ceteras* required for his majesty's fleet; while others again, in a wing of the same building, were employed in finishing single and double canoes; the former for pleasure, the latter for commercial purposes. At the far end of the buildings was erected a blacksmith's forge; and beyond that, in a side room, lay the masts, spars, and rigging of a new schooner. The tools used by the different workmen were very simple, slender, few, and ill-made, and yet the work done by them surprised us.

While in the workshops, Mr. M'Kay took a fancy to a small knot of wood, about the size of a pint-pot, and asked it of the king. His majesty took the bit of wood in his hand, and after looking at it for some time turned round to Mr. M'Kay and said, ''This is a very valuable piece of wood; it is the finest koeye, and what my Erees make their pipes of; but if you will give me a new hat for it, you can have it.'' Mr. M'Kay smiled, adding, ''Your majesty shall have it.'' So the bargain was struck, but Mr. M'Kay fell in love with no more of his majesty's wood. They make their own cloth, cordage, salt, sugar, and whisky.

[39] The king then invited us to dine; and entering a small wretched hovel adjoining the workshop, we all sat down round a dirty little table, on which was spread some viands, yams, taro, cocoa-nuts, pork, bread-fruit, and arrack. The king grew very jovial, ate and drank freely, and pressed us to follow his example. After dinner, he apologized for the meanness of the place, by saying that his banqueting house was tabooed that day. Dinner being over, he brought us to see a large stone building, the only one of the kind on the island, situate at some distance from the other buildings; but he showed no disposition to open the door and let us have a peep at the inside. He said it cost him 2,000 dollars. We were told the royal treasure and other valuables were kept there. Behind the stone building, and near the shore, was lying at anchor an old ship of about 300 tons, with some guns and men on deck—said to be the guard-ship. From this position, we saw sixteen vessels of different sizes, from 10 to 200 tons, all lying in a wretched and ruinous condition along the beach; some on shore, others afloat, but all apparently useless. The day being excessively warm, and

our curiosity gratified, we took leave of his majesty, and staid for the night at the house of a Mr. Brown, an American settler, who had resided on the island for several years.

After passing an agreeable night, we bade adieu to our hospitable landlord, and set out to view the morais, or places of public worship. Of these, Ourourah [40] alone contains fifteen of this description. Each morai is composed of several miserable-looking little huts, or houses. Passing by all the inferior ones, we at length reached the king's morai, or principal one of the place. It consisted of five low, gloomy, and pestiferous houses, huddled close together; and alongside of the principal one stood an image made of wood, resembling a pillar, about 28 feet high, in the shape of the human figure, cut and carved with various devices; the head large, and the rude sculpture on it presenting the likeness of a human face, carved on the top with a black cowl. About thirty yards from the houses, all round about, was a clear spot called the "king's tabooed ground," surrounded by an enclosure. This sacred spot is often rigorously tabooed and set apart for penance. It was while walking to and fro on this solitary place that we saw Tatooirah, the king's eldest son, who was in disgrace. We were prevented from entering within the enclosure. At the foot of this pagot, or pillar, were scattered on the ground several dead animals: we saw four dogs, two hogs, five cats, and large quantities of vegetables, almost all in a state of putrefaction, the whole emitting a most offensive smell. On the death of the king or other great eree, and in times of war, human sacrifices are frequently offered at the shrine of this moloch. The word *taboo* implies interdiction or prohibition from touching the place, person, or thing tabooed; a violation of which is always severely punished, and at the king's morai, with death.

[41] We had scarcely got on board, late in the evening, when a tremendous gale from the land arose and drove the ship out to sea. The fury of the tempest and darkness of the night obliged us to cut cable, and two days were spent in anxious forebodings, ere we got back again into harbour.

On the 27th, all our supplies, according to contract, were safe on board; and from the good conduct of the sailors since our arrival, we began to think matters would go on smoothly for the future; but these hopes were of short duration — the hasty and choleric disposition of the captain destroyed our anticipations. Two of the boats had gone on shore as usual; but on the call for all hands to embark, three of the sailors were missing. The boats, without waiting a moment, pushed off, but had reached the ship only fifteen minutes before two of the three men arrived in an Indian canoe. Notwithstanding the anxiety they manifested, and their assurance that the boat had not been off five minutes before they were on the beach, they were both tied up, flogged, and then put in irons. But this was not all; Emms, the third man, not being able to procure a canoe, had unfortunately to pass the night on shore, but arrived the next morning by sunrise. On arriving alongside, the captain, who was pacing the deck at the time did not wait till he got on board, but jumping into a boat which lay alongside, laid hold of some sugar-canes with which the boat was loaded, and bundled the poor fellow, sprawling and speechless, at [42] his feet; then jumping on deck, kept pacing to and fro in no very pleasant mood; but on perceiving Emms still struggling to get up, he leaped into the boat a second time, and called one of the sailors to follow him. The poor fellow, on seeing the captain, called out for mercy; but in his wrath the captain forgot mercy, and laid him again senseless at his feet, then ordered him to be thrown overboard! Immediately on throwing the man into the sea, Mr. Fox made signs to some Indians, who dragged him into their canoe and paddled off to shore. During this scene, no one interfered; for the captain, in his frantic fits of passion, was capable of going any lengths, and would rather have destroyed the expedition, the ship, and every one on board, than be thwarted in what he considered as ship discipline, or his nautical duties.

In the evening, the Indians brought Emms again to the ship. Here the little fellow implored forgiveness, and begged to be taken on board; but the captain was inexorable, and threatened him with instant death if he attempted to come alongside. Soon after he made his appearance again, but with no better effect. He then asked for his protection, a paper which the American sailors generally take with them to sea. The captain returning no answer to this request, Mr. Fox contrived to throw his clothes and protection overboard unperceived, at the same time making signs to the Indians to convey them to Emms. On receiving the little bundle, he remained [43] for some time without uttering a word; at last, bursting into tears, he implored again and again to be admitted on board, but to no purpose. All hopes now vanishing, the heroic little fellow, standing up in the canoe, took off his cap, and waving it in the air, with a sorrowful heart bade adieu to his shipmates; the canoe then paddled to land, and we saw him no more.

Our supplies being now completed, the king came on board before our departure; and it will appear something surprising that the honest and wealthy monarch, forgetting

the rank and pomp of royalty, should at his parting visit
covet everything he saw with us: he even expressed a wish
to see the contents of our trunks; he begged a handkerchief from me, a penknife from another, a pair of shoes
from a third, a hat from a fourth, and when refused, talked
of his kindness to us on shore; while, on the other hand, he
bowed low when presented with a breastpin, a few needles,
or paper-cased looking-glass, not worth a groat. Even
the cabin-boy and cook were not forgotten by this ''King
of the Isles,'' for he asked a piece of black-ball from the
former, and an old saucepan from the latter. His avarice
and meanness in these respects had no bounds, and we
were all greatly relieved when he bade us farewell and
departed.

Having taken leave of his majesty, I shall now make a
few remarks on the habits, dress, and language of the
natives.

[44] The Sandwich Islanders are bold swimmers, and
expert navigators. They are like ducks in the water. As
soon as we had cast anchor in Karakokooa Bay the natives,
men and women, indiscriminately flocked about the
ship in great numbers: some swimming, others in canoes,
but all naked, although the *Tonquin* lay a mile from the
shore. Few, however, being admitted on board at once
(probably a necessary precaution), the others waited very
contentedly floating on the surface of the water alongside,
amusing themselves now and then by plunging and playing round the ship. After passing several hours in this
way, they would then make a simultaneous start for the
land, diving and plunging, sporting and playing, like so
many seals or fish in a storm all the way. During their
gambols about the ship, we often amused ourselves by
dropping a button, nail, or pin into the water; but such

was their keenness of sight and their agility, that the
trifle had scarcely penetrated the surface of the water
before it was in their possession; nothing could escape
them. On one occasion a ship's block happening to fall
overboard, one of the natives was asked to dive for it
in thirty-six feet of water; but after remaining three
minutes and fifty seconds under water he came up unsuccessful; another tried it and succeeded, after being
under water four minutes and twelve seconds: the blood,
however, burst from his nose and ears immediately after.

Their voyaging canoes are made to ride on the [45]
roughest water with safety by means of a balance or
outrigger shaped like a boat's keel, and attached to the
canoe at the distance of five feet by two slender beams. The
canoe goes fully as well with as without the balance,
skipping on the surface of the water as if no such ap-
pendage accompanied it. When the swell or surge strikes
the canoe on the balance side, the weight of the outrigger
prevents its upsetting, and when on the opposite side
the buoyancy of the outrigger, now sunk in the water,
has the same effect.

The climate here is so very mild and warm that the
natives seldom wear any clothing, and when they do,
it is of their own manufacture, and extremely simple.
The inner bark of different trees (the touta in particular)
is prepared by beating it into a pulp or soft thin web, not
unlike grey paper, called tuppa. The common people
wear it in this raw state, but the better sort paint it with
various colours, resembling printed cotton. Tappa is as
strong as cartridge paper, but not so thick, and can answer
for clothing only in dry climates. The common dress of
the men consists of a piece of this tappa, about ten inches
broad and nine feet long, like a belt, called maro. The

maro is thrown carelessly round the loins, then passed between the thighs, and tied on the left side. The females wear the pow or pau, a piece of tappa similar to the maro, only a little broader, and worn in the same manner; but the queens had on, in addition to the pow, a loose mantle or shawl thrown round [46] the body, called kihei, which consisted of twenty-one folds of tappa; yet when compressed it did not equal in thickness an English blanket. The kihei is generally worn by persons of distinction, but seldom of more than two or three folds, excepting among the higher ranks. Like a Chinese mandarin, a lady here makes known her rank by her dress, and by the number of folds in her kihei.

A custom prevalent here, and which is, I believe, peculiar to these islanders, is, that the women always eat apart from the men, and are forbidden the use of pork. The favourite dish among all classes is raw fish, mashed or pounded in a mortar. Considering their rude and savage life, these people are very cleanly. The houses of all classes are lined and decorated with painted tappa, and the floors overspread with variegated mats. The women are handsome in person, engaging in their manners, well featured, and have countenances full of joy and tranquility; but chastity is not their virtue.

The king's will is the paramount law of the land, but he is represented as a mild and generous soverign, invariably friendly to the whites whom choice or accident has thrown on these islands. To those who behave well the king allots land, and gives them slaves to work it. He protects both them and their property, and is loth ever to punish an evildoer. Near Ourourah we saw eight or ten white men comfortably settled; and upwards of thirty [47] others naked and wild among the natives, wretched unprincipled vagabonds, of almost every nation in Europe, without clothing and without either house or home.

I have already noticed the principal esculent vegetables growing here; there are also some beautiful kinds of wood; that called koeye, of which the war spears or pahooas are made, and sandalwood, are the kinds most highly esteemed among the natives for their hardness and polish. The cocoa-nut, in clumps here and there, forms delightful groves, and these are often frequented by the industrious females for the purpose of manufacturing and painting their tappa—preferring the cool shade and open air to the heat of a dwellinghouse.

At the place where Captain Cook was killed, which we visited soon after our arrival, were still a few old and shattered cocoa-nut trees, pierced with the shot from his ships; and a flat coral rock; at the water's edge, is still pointed out to strangers as the fatal spot where he fell.

The chief weapon used in their warfare is the pahooa or spear, 12 feet long, polished, barbed, and painted. It is poised and thrown with the right hand with incredible force and precision. His majesty ordered fifty men to parade one day, and invited us to see them exercising, and we were certainly much gratified and astonished at their skill in throwing and parrying the weapons.

[48] After going through several manœuvres, the king picked four of the best marksmen out, and ordered one of them to stand at a certain point; the three others at a distance of sixty yards from him, all armed with pahooas, and facing one another. The three last mentioned were to dart their spears at the single man, and he to parry them off or catch them in passing. Each of the three had twelve pahooas; the single man but one. Immediately after taking his position the single man put himself upon

his guard, by skipping and leaping from right to left with
the quickness of lightning: the others, equally on the
alert, prepared to throw.   All eyes were now anxiously
intent; presently one threw his spear, at a short interval
the next followed; as did the third — two at a time next
threw, and then all three let fly at once, and continued to
throw without intermission until the whole thirty-six
spears were spent, which was done in less than three
minutes.   The single man, who was placed like a target
to be shot at, defended himself nobly with the spear he had
in his hand, and sent those of his opponents whistling in
every direction, for he had either to parry them off like a
skilful boxer, or be run through on the spot; but such was
the agility with which he shifted from one position to
another, and managed the spear with his right hand, that
he seemed rather to be playing and amusing himself than
seriously engaged, for twice or thrice he dexterously
seized his opponent's spear at [49] the moment it came in
contact with his own, allowing at the same time the latter
to fly off, and this shifting or exchanging spears is thought
a masterpiece, being the most difficult and dangerous
manœuvre in the whole affair, and it is only an adept that
can attempt it with safety.   When all was over, the man
had received a slight wound on the left arm; but it happens
not unfrequently that he who is thus placed is killed on the
spot; for if he allows the spear to be knocked out of his
hand without catching another, he is almost sure to fall, as
the throwers are not allowed to stop while a pahooa remains with them, and every weapon is hurled with a deadly
intention.

The king is said to be a dexterous pahooa man himself,
and it was his prowess and knowledge in war, and not
his rank, that made him sovereign of these islands.   After

the people had dispersed, the man who had acted so conspicuous a part in the exhibition just described, came to us and offered to risk his life for a handkerchief, at the distance of twenty yards; telling us to select the best marksman among us, with a fowlingpiece either with shot or ball, and he would stand before him, and either win the handkerchief or lose his life! We were not disposed, however, to accept the challenge, but gave the fellow a handkerchief and sent him about his business.

All the islands of this group, excepting one, have [50] acknowledged Tammeatameah as their king, and the jarring interests and feuds of the different islands have at last sunk into a system of union which, if we may judge from appearance, renders this country, under its present government, an earthly paradise, and the inhabitants thereof as free from care, and perhaps as happy, as any in the globe;—but mark! civilized man has now begun to trade on its innocent and peaceful soil: there is an end, therefore, to all primeval simplicity and happiness.

These people speak with a quickness which almost baffles imitation; and in very many instances, the same word is repeated twice. The language is bold and masculine; and, although the accent be clear, is very difficult to be attained by the whites.

We shall now take our leave of the friendly and hospitable natives of these islands. On his majesty leaving the ship, a boat was sent to shore for a few remaining articles; meantime, preparations were made for weighing anchor. The wind from the sea beginning to blow retarded the boat's return; and the delay so nettled our worthy commander, that he gave orders to set sail, and the ship stood out to sea, leaving the boat to follow as she could. The wind soon increasing to a gale, the boat had to struggle with a tempestuous sea for six hours, during which time we expected every minute to witness her destruction. The Falkland Island affair was yet fresh in our [51] minds, and this seemed to equal, if not surpass it in cruelty. At length, however, the ship bore down, and with much difficulty rescued the boat's crew from a watery grave.

[52] CHAPTER IV [11]

Departure from the Sandwich Islands — Bad weather — Live stock destroyed — Columbia River — A boat and crew lost — Captain's conduct towards Mr. Fox — Mouth of the river — Bar and breakers — Cape Disappointment — Point Adams — Narrow escape of the long boat — Sounding the bar — A boat and crew left to perish — The ship in the breakers — Critical situation — Melancholy narrative of Steven Weeks — Search made for the lost boat, and narrow escape — Long boat swamped — Fidelity of the natives — Preparations for leaving the ship — Captain Thorn — The voyage concluded.

On the 1st of March, 1811, we took our departure from the Sandwich Islands; steering direct for Columbia River. The first step taken, after leaving the land, was to liberate those who had been put in irons. Poor fellows! they considered themselves particularly unfortunate, and doubly punished, in not having been partakers of the pleasures which the others had enjoyed on shore. All our thoughts now tended to one point; and the hope of soon terminating a long and irksome voyage made us forget all former misunderstandings, and a few days passed in harmony and good-fellowship, until the 12th, when the weather be-

---

[11] Compare the following account with that of Franchère, particularly notes 36, 37, 40, 41.— Ed.

coming squally and cold, with snow [53] and sleet, the partners wished to serve out some articles of clothing to the passengers, who now began to feel very sensibly the change of climate; but the captain considered the broaching of a bale or box as an encroachment on his authority, and a violation of ship rules, and therefore steadily opposed it. This gave rise to bad blood on both sides. The partners swore they would have such articles as they wanted; the captain swore they should touch nothing. The dispute went to such a height that pistols were resorted to, and all, from stem to stern, seemed for a moment involved in the flame of civil war; but on this, as on a former occasion, Mr. David Stuart and some others interfering brought about a reconciliation. The partners desisted; the captain kept his bales and boxes untouched; and the men froze in the icy rigging of the ship until many of them were obliged to take to their hammocks.

On the 14th, in lat. 37° N. and long. 137° W., a violent gale came on, which increased almost to a hurricane, and lasted four days without intermission, during which we were much puzzled in manœuvring the ship. She had sprung a leak, but not seriously. Sometimes we had to let her scud before the wind; sometimes she lay-to; sometimes under one sail, sometimes under another, labouring greatly; and much anxiety was felt by all on board. During this storm, almost everything on deck was carried off or dashed to pieces; all our live stock were either killed or washed overboard; and so bad was the weather, [54] first with rain, and then with sleet, hail, frost, and snow which froze on the rigging as it fell, that there was no bending either ropes or sails, and the poor sailors were harassed to death. But bad and harassing as this state of things was, it proved to be only the beginning of our troubles, and a prelude to far greater trials. During this gale, we sustained considerable damage in the sails and rigging, besides the loss of our live stock, and other things on board.

On the 22nd of March, we came in sight of land, which, on a nearer approach, proved to be Cape Disappointment, a promontory forming the north side of the Great Oregon or Columbia River. The sight filled every heart with gladness. But the cloudy and stormy state of the weather prevented us seeing clearly the mouth of the river; being then about ten miles from land. The aspect of the coast was wild and dangerous, and for some time the ship lay-to, until the captain could satisfy himself that it was the entrance of the river; which he had no sooner done, than Mr. Fox, the first mate, was ordered to go and examine the channel on the bar. At half-past one o'clock in the afternoon, Mr. Fox left the ship, having with him one sailor, a very old Frenchman, and three Canadian lads, unacquainted with sea service — two of them being carters from La Chine, and the other a Montreal barber. Mr. Fox objected to such hands; but the captain refused to change them, adding that he had none else to spare. Mr. Fox then represented the impossibility of performing the business [55] in such weather, and on such a rough sea, even with the best seamen, adding, that the waves were too high for any boat to live in. The captain, turning sharply round, said — ''Mr. Fox, if you are afraid of water, you should have remained at Boston.'' On this Mr. Fox immediately ordered the boat to be lowered, and the men to embark. If the crew was bad, the boat was still worse — being scarcely seaworthy, and very small. While this was going on, the partners, who were all partial to Mr. Fox, began to sympathize with him, and to intercede with the captain to defer examining the bar till a favourable change took place in the weather. But he was deaf to entreaties, stamped, and swore that a combination was formed to frustrate all his designs. The partners' interference, therefore, only riveted him the more in his determination, and Mr. Fox was peremptorily ordered to proceed. He, seeing that the captain was immoveable, turned to the partners with tears in his eyes and said — ''My uncle was drowned here not many years ago, and now I am going to lay my bones with his.'' He then shook hands with all around him, and bade them adieu. Stepping into the boat — ''Farewell, my friends!'' said he; ''we will perhaps meet again in the next world.'' And the words were prophetic.

The moment the boat pushed off, all hands crowded in silence to take a last farewell of her. The weather was boisterous, and the sea rough, so that we often lost sight of the boat before she got 100 yards from [56] the ship; nor had she gone that far before she became utterly unmanageable, sometimes broaching broadside to the foaming surges, and at other times almost whirling round like a top, then tossing on the crest of a huge wave would sink again for a time and disappear altogether. At last she hoisted the flag; the meaning could not be mistaken; we knew it was a signal of distress. At this instant all the people crowded round the captain, and implored him to try and save the boat; but in an angry tone he ordered about ship, and we saw the ill-fated boat no more.

Mr. Fox was not only an able officer, but an experienced seaman, and a great favourite among all classes on board; and this circumstance, I fear, proved his ruin, for his uniform kindness and affability to the passengers had from the commencement of the voyage drawn down upon his head the ill-will of his captain; and his being sent off on the present perilous and forlorn undertaking, with such awkward and inexperienced hands, whose language he did not understand, is a proof of that ill-will.

The mouth of Columbia River is remarkable for its sand-bars and high surf at all seasons, but more particularly in the spring and fall, during the equinoctial gales: these sand-bars frequently shift, the channel of course shifting along with them, which renders the passage at all times extremely dangerous. The bar, or rather the chain of sand banks, over which the huge waves and foaming breakers [57] roll so awfully, is a league broad, and extends in a white foaming sheet for many miles, both south and north of the mouth of the river, forming as it were an impracticable barrier to the entrance, and threatening with instant destruction everything that comes near it.

The river at its mouth is 4½ miles broad, confined by Cape Disappointment on the north, and Point Adams on the south; the former is a rocky cliff or promontory, rising about 500 feet above the level of the water, and covered on the top with a few scattered trees of stinted growth; the latter a low sandy point, jutting out about 300 yards into the river, directly opposite to Cape Disappointment: the deepest water is near the Cape, but the channel is both narrow and intricate. The country is low, and the impervious forests give to the surrounding coast a wild and gloomy aspect.

After the captain ordered about ship, as already stated, some angry words passed between himself and Mr. Mumford, the second officer, which ended in the latter being ordered below. After passing an anxious night, the return of day only increased the anxiety, and every mind was filled with gloomy apprehensions. In the course of this day, Mr. Mumford resumed his duties, and the ship kept beating off and on till noon, when she cast anchor in fourteen fathoms, about a mile from the breakers; and the weather becoming calm, Mr. M'Kay, Mr. David Stuart, myself, and several others, embarking in the [58] long boat, which was well manned and armed, stood in for the shore, in hopes of being able to effect a landing. On approaching the bar, the terrific chain of breakers, which kept rolling one after another in awful succession, completely overpowered us with dread; and the fearful suction or current became so irresistibly great, that, before we were aware of it, the boat was drawn into them, and became unmanageable: at this instant, Mr. Mumford, who was at the helm, called out, ''Let us turn back, and pull for your lives; pull hard, or you are all dead men''. In turning round, the boat broached broadside to the surf, and was for some time in imminent danger of being engulfed or dashed to pieces; and, although every effort was made, we were for twelve minutes struggling in this perilous situation, between hope and despair, before we got clear, or the boat obeyed the oars, and yet we were still two miles from the shore; and, had it not been for the prompt and determined step taken by Mr. Mumford, the boat and every soul on board of it must have inevitably perished. Notwithstanding our narrow escape, we made a second and third attempt, but without success, and then returned to the ship. The same afternoon, Mr. Mumford was sent more to the south to seek for a channel, but to no purpose. The charts were again examined, and every preparation made for next morning.

On the 25th, early in the morning, Mr. Mumford was again ordered in another direction to go and discover [59] if possible the proper channel, and ascertain the depth of water. After several trials, in one or two of which the boat got again entangled in the breakers, and had a very narrow escape, she at length came into 2½ fathoms of water, and then returned; but the captain seemed to hint that Mr. Mumford had not done so much as he might have done, or in other words, he was dissatisfied; indeed, his mind was not in a state to be satisfied with anything, not even with himself; but his officers, whatever they did, were sure to displease.

The captain now called on Mr. Aikens, the third mate, and ordered him to go and sound in a more northerly direction, and if he found 3½ fathoms water to hoist a flag as a signal. At three o'clock in the afternoon, Mr. Aikens, together with the sailmaker, armourer, and two Sandwich Islanders, embarked in the pinnace, and proceeded to the bar. As soon as the pinnace hoisted the flag agreed upon, the ship weighed anchor and stood in for the channel; at the same time the boat, pulling back from the bar, met the ship about half a mile from the breakers, in eight fathoms, going in with a gentle sea-breeze, at the rate of three knots an hour.

As the ship and boat drew near to each other, the latter steered a little aside to be out of the ship's way, then lay upon her oars in smooth water, waiting to be taken on board, while the ship passed on within twenty yards of them in silence; nor did the people in the boat speak a single word. As soon as the [60] ship had passed, and no motion made to take the boat on board, every one appeared thunderstruck, and Mr. M'Kay was the first that spoke,— "Who," said he, "is going to throw a rope to the boat?" No one answered; but by this time she had fallen astern, and began to pull after the ship. Every one now called out, "The boat, the boat!" The partners, in astonishment, entreated the captain to take the boat on board, but he coolly replied, ''I can give them no assistance.'' Mr. Mumford said it would not be the work of a minute. ''Back a sail, throw a rope overboard,'' cried the partners; the answer was, ''No, I will not endanger the ship.'' We now felt convinced that the boat and crew were devoted to destruction — no advice was given them, no assistance offered, no reasons assigned for risking so cruel a sacrifice of human life — for the place where the boat met us was entirely free from the influence of the breakers, and a long way from the bar. It is impossible, therefore, to account for the cool indifference manifested towards the fated boat and her crew, unless we suppose that the mind of the captain was so absorbed in apprehension, and perplexed with anxiety at the danger which stared him in the face, and which he was about to encounter in a few minutes, that he could not be brought to give a thought to anything else but the safety of the ship.

During this time the ship was drawing nearer and nearer to the breakers, which called our attention [61] from the boat to look out for our own safety; but she was seen for some time struggling hard to follow the ship as we entered the breakers, the sight of which was appalling. On the ship making the first plunge, every countenance looked dismay; and the sun, at the time just sinking below the horizon, seemed to say, ''Prepare for your last.'' Mr. Mumford was now ordered to the mast-head, to point out the channel. The water decreasing from 8 to 2½ fathoms, she struck tremendously on the second reef or shoal; and the surges breaking over her stern overwhelmed everything on deck. Every one who could, sprang aloft, and clung for life to the rigging. The waves at times broke ten feet high over her, and at other times she was in danger

of foundering: she struck again and again, and, regardless
of her helm, was tossed and whirled in every direction, and
became completely unmanageable.   Night now began to
spread an impenetrable gloom over the turbulent deep.
Dark, indeed, was that dreadful night.   We had got about
a mile into the breakers, and not far from the rocks at the
foot of the cape, against which the foaming surges wreaked
their fury unceasingly.   Our anxiety was still further increased by the wind dying away, and the tide still ebbing.
At this instant, some one called out, "We are all lost, the
ship is among the rocks."   A desperate effort was then
made to let go the anchors — two were thrown overboard;
the sails kept flapping for some time: nor was the danger
diminished by learning the fact [62] that the surf dragged
ship, anchors, and all, along with it.   But there is a limit
to all things: hour after hour had passed, and terrific was
the sight; yet our faithful bark still defied the elements,
until the tide providentially beginning to flow — just at a
time when it appeared as if no earthly power could save us
from a watery grave — brought about our deliverance by
carrying the ship along with it into Baker's Bay, snug
within the Cape, where we lay in safety.

Here are two points for consideration; first, the time of
sounding: and, secondly, the time chosen for entering the
breakers.   In respect to both, there was an unwarrantable
precipitation — a manifest want of sound judgment.
We made the land in the middle of a storm, the channel
and coast both unknown to us, and without either pilot or
guide: under such circumstances, it was evident to all that
no boat could live on the water at the time, far less reach
the shore; and our entering the breakers at so late an
hour, the sun at the time not being fifty minutes above the
horizon, the channel also being unexplored, was certainly

a premature and forlorn undertaking: but there existed such disunion — such a spirit of contradiction on board — that the only wonder is how we ever got so far. But I must now inform the reader what became of the boat. In the morning of the 26th, Captain Thorn, Mr. M'Kay, myself, and a few men, left the ship, to take a view of the coast from the top of Cape Disappointment, to try if we could learn any tidings of the [63] boats. We had not proceeded fifty yards, when we saw Steven Weeks, the armourer, standing under the shelter of a rock, shivering and half-dead with cold. Joy for a moment filled our hearts, and running up to the poor fellow, we inquired for his comrades, but could get no satisfactory reply; we then brought him to the ship, and, after giving him some food, resumed our inquiries; but he appeared so overpowered with grief and vexation, that we could scarcely get a word from him; in short, he seemed to reproach us bitterly. "You did it purposely," said he, in great agitation; but after some time, and when we had first told him what we had suffered, he seemed to come round, as if his feelings were soothed by the recital of our dangers; and then he related his melancholy tale, in the following words:—

"After the ship passed us we pulled hard to follow her, thinking every moment you would take us on board; but when we saw her enter the breakers we considered ourselves as lost. We tried to pull back again, but in vain; for we were drawn into the breakers in spite of all we could do. We saw the ship make two or three heavy plunges; but just at this time we ourselves were struck with the boiling surf, and the boat went reeling in every direction; in an instant a heavy sea swamped her — poor Mr. Aikens and John Coles were never seen after. As soon as I got above the surface of the water, I kept tossing about at the

mercy of the waves.   While in this state I saw the two
Sandwich Islanders struggling [64] through the surf to get
hold of the boat, and being expert swimmers they succeeded.
After long struggles they got her turned upon her keel,
bailed out some of the water, and recovered one of the
oars.   I made several attempts to get near them, but the
weight of my clothes and the rough sea had almost exhausted me.   I could scarcely keep myself above water,
and the Owhyhees were so much occupied about the boat,
that they seemed to take no notice of anything else.   In
vain I tried to make signs, and to call out; every effort
only sank me more and more.   The tide had drawn the
boat by this time out to sea, and almost free of the breakers,
when the two islanders saw me, now supporting myself
by a floating oar, and made for me.   The poor fellows
tried to haul me into the boat, but their strength failed
them.   At last, taking hold of my clothes in their teeth,
they fortunately succeeded.   We then stood out to sea
as night set in, and a darker one I never saw.   The
Owhyhees, overcome with wet and cold, began to lose hope,
and their fortitude forsook them, so that they lay down
despairingly in the boat, nor could I arouse them from
their drowsy stupor.   When I saw that I had nothing to
expect from them, I set to sculling the boat myself, and
yet it was with much ado I could stard on my legs.   During
the night one of the Indians died in despair, and the other
seemed to court death, for he lost all heart, and would
not utter a single word.   When the tide began to flow I
was roused by the sense [65] of my danger, for the sound
of the breakers grew louder and louder, and I knew if I got
entangled in them in my exhausted state all was lost; I,
therefore, set to with might and main, as a last effort, to
keep the boat out to sea, and at daylight I was within a
quarter of a mile of the breakers, and about double that

distance short of the Cape. I paused for a moment, 'What is to be done?' I said to myself; 'death itself is preferable to this protracted struggle.' So, turning the head of my boat for shore, I determined to reach the land or die in the attempt. Providence favoured my resolution, the breakers seemed to aid in hurrying me out of the watery element; and the sun had scarcely risen when the boat was thrown up high and dry on the beach. I had much ado to extricate myself from her, and to drag my benumbed limbs along. On seeing myself once more on dry land, I sat down and felt a momentary relief; but this was followed by gloomy reflections. I then got into the boat again, and seeing the poor islander still alive, but insensible, I hauled him out of the boat, and with much ado carried him to the border of the wood, when covering him with leaves I left him to die. While gathering the leaves I happened to come upon a beaten path, which brought me here." Such was Weeks's melancholy story: himself and the Indian being the only survivors of the last boat, it follows that eight men in all lost their lives in entering this fatal river.

[66] In the evening the Sandwich Islander who died in the boat was interred on the beach where the boat came ashore; the other poor fellow was carried to the ship, and afterwards recovered.

On the 27th I was appointed to head a party to go in search of the boat that was lost on the 22nd; but after examining the coast for upwards of forty miles southwards, not a trace of our missing friends was discovered, nor did we ever learn any tidings of them.

We had on this occasion a specimen of Chinooke navigation. While crossing the river in an Indian canoe, on our way back to the ship, we were suddenly overtaken by a storm, and our craft was upset in the middle of the passage. The expertness of the natives in their favourite element was here put to the test. At this time we were upwards of two miles from the shore, while eight persons unable to swim were floating in every direction; coats, hats, and everything else adrift, and all depending on the fidelity of the four Indians who undertook to carry us over; yet, notwithstanding the roughness of the water, and the wind blowing a gale at the time, these poor fellows kept swimming about like so many fishes, righted the canoe, and got us all into her again, while they themselves staid in the water, with one hand on the canoe and the other paddling. In this manner they supported themselves, tossing to and fro, till we bailed the water out of our frail craft, and got under weigh again. Here it was that [67] the Indians showed the skill and dexterity peculiar to them. The instant the canoe rose on the top of a wave, those on the windward side darted down their long paddles to the armpits in the water to prevent her from upsetting; while those on the leeside at the same moment pulled theirs up, but kept ready as soon as the wave had passed under her to thrust them down again in a similar manner, and thus by their alternate movements they kept the canoe steady, so that we got safe to shore without another upset, and with the loss of only a few articles of clothing; but we suffered severely from wet and cold.

During this time the Indians from the village which we had left, seeing our critical situation, had manned and sent off two canoes to our assistance. One of the boats from the ship was also despatched for the same purpose; but all would have proved too late had we not been fortunate enough of ourselves to weather the storm.

The Indians all the time never lost their presence of

mind. Indeed, it was supposed, from the skilful manner in which they acted afterwards, that the sordid rascals had upset us wilfully, in order to claim the merit of having saved us, and therewith a double recompense for their trip. The boat which had put off to our assistance was upset on her return to the ship; and had it not been for the two Indian canoes that followed us, its crew would have all perished.

[68] On the 4th of April the long boat was swamped off Chinooke Point, when ten persons were saved by Comecomly and his people. On this occasion, however, many articles of value were lost, so that every hour admonished us that we stepped on insecure and slippery ground. Every succeeding day was marked by some new and alarming disaster; but a few remarks will now suffice to conclude the account of our voyage, in which we sailed, according to the ship's log, 21,852 miles.

Captain Thorn was an able and expert seaman; but, unfortunately, his treatment of the people under his command was strongly tinctured with cruelty and despotism. He delighted in ruling with a rod of iron; his officers were treated with harshness, his sailors with cruelty, and every one else was regarded by him with contempt. With a jealous and peevish temper, he was easily excited; and the moment he heard the Scotch Highlanders speak to each other in the Scottish dialect, or the Canadians in the French language, he was on his high horse, making every one on board as unhappy as himself; and this brings us down to the period of our departure from the ship, a period to which we all anxiously looked forward, and the satisfaction both felt and expressed was universal, when the general order was read that all the passengers should prepare to land on the following day.

[69] CHAPTER V [12]

Preparations for landing — Site of the new emporium of the west — Astor's representative — Hard work — Huge trees — Natives — Comecomly — Mode of felling trees — Danger — Trying scenes — Three men killed — Three wounded — Party reduced by sickness — Disaffection — Conduct of the deputy — Desertion — Mr. Astor's policy — Climate — Indian rumours — Comecomly's intrigues and policy — Trip to the cascades — Mr. M'Kay and north-west notions — Anecdote — Exploring party to the north — Several persons killed — Hostile threats of the Indians — Potatoes and other seeds planted — New building — Astoria — Departure of the ship — Dangerous situation of the whites — Great assemblage of Indians — People under arms — Blunderbuss accident — Alarming moment — Two strangers arrive — Mr. Thompson at Astoria — M'Dougall's policy — The two great functionaries.

FOR some days, much time was spent in examining both sides of the inlet, with a view of choosing a suitable place to build on. At last it was settled that the new establishment should be erected on the south side, on a small rising ground situate between Point George on the west and Tonquin Point on the east, distant twelve miles from the mouth of the inlet or bar.

[70] On the 12th of April, therefore, the whole party, consisting of thirty-three persons, all British subjects excepting three (eleven Sandwich Islanders being included in that number), left the ship and encamped on shore.

However pleasing the change, to be relieved from a long and tedious voyage, and from the tyranny of a sullen

[12] Compare Ross's description of the building of Astoria with that of Franchère, particularly notes 42, 44, 61.— ED.

despotic captain, the day was not one of pleasure, but of labour. The misfortunes we had met with in crossing the fatal bar had deadened all sensibility, and cast a melancholy gloom over our most sanguine expectations. In our present position, everything harmonized with our feelings, to darken our future prospects. Silent and with heavy hearts we began the toil of the day, in clearing away brush and rotten wood for a spot to encamp on.

The person who now assumed the command was the deputy-agent, Duncan M'Dougall, Esq., an old northwestern, who, in the absence of Mr. Hunt, held the first place in Mr. Astor's confidence. He was a man of but ordinary capacity, with an irritable, peevish temper; the most unfit man in the world to head an expedition or command men.

From the site of the establishment, the eye could wander over a varied and interesting scene. The extensive Sound, with its rocky shores, lay in front; the breakers on the bar, rolling in wild confusion, closed the view on the west; on the east, the country as far as the Sound had a wild and varied aspect; while towards the south, the impervious and magnificent [71] forest darkened the landscape, as far as the eye could reach. The place thus selected for the emporium of the west, might challenge the whole continent to produce a spot of equal extent presenting more difficulties to the settler: studded with gigantic trees of almost incredible size, many of them measuring fifty feet in girth, and so close together, and intermingled with huge rocks, as to make it a work of no ordinary labour to level and clear the ground. With this task before us, every man, from the highest to the lowest, was armed with an axe in one hand and a gun in the other; the former for attacking the woods, the latter for defence against the savage hordes which were constantly prowling about. In the garb of labourers, and in the sweat of our brow, we now commenced earning our bread. In this manner we all kept toiling and tearing away, from sunrise till sunset — from Monday till Saturday; and during the nights we kept watch without intermission.

On our first arrival, the natives of the place appeared very friendly towards us, owing no doubt to some trifling presents which they now and then received from us; but still, circumstances occurred occasionally which indicated treachery, and kept us always on our guard, against the more distant tribes in particular, for their attitude was invariably shy and hostile. Our ill opinion of them proved but too true in the sequel; but we had all along received every assurance of fidelity and protection from Comecomly, [72] the principal chief of the place, and in him we reposed much confidence.

The frame of a coasting vessel, to be named the *Dolly*, was brought out on board the *Tonquin*, and as soon as we had got a spot cleared, the carpenters were set to work, to fit her up for immediate service; but the smallness of her size, of only thirty tons, rendered her useless for any purpose but that of navigating the river.

It would have made a cynic smile to see this pioneer corps, composed of traders, shopkeepers, voyageurs, and Owhyhees, all ignorant alike in this new walk of life, and the most ignorant of all, the leader. Many of the party had never handled an axe before, and but few of them knew how to use a gun, but necessity, the mother of invention, soon taught us both. After placing our guns in some secure place at hand, and viewing the height and the breadth of the tree to be cut down, the party, with some labour, would erect a scaffold round it; this done, four men — for that was the number appointed to each of those huge trees — would then mount the scaffold, and commence cutting, at the height of eight or ten feet from the ground, the handles of our axes varying, according to circumstances, from two and a half to five feet in length. At every other stroke, a look was cast round, to see that all was safe; but the least rustling among the bushes caused a general stop; more or less time was thus lost in anxious suspense. After [73] listening and looking round, the party resumed their labour, cutting and looking about alternately. In this manner the day would be spent, and often to little purpose: as night often set in before the tree begun with in the morning was half cut down. Indeed, it sometimes required two days, or more, to fell one tree; but when nearly cut through, it would be viewed fifty different times, and from as many different positions, to ascertain where it was likely to fall, and to warn parties of the danger.

There is an art in felling a tree, as well as in planting one; but unfortunately none of us had learned that art, and hours together would be spent in conjectures and discussions: one calling out that it would fall here; another, there; in short, there were as many opinions as there were individuals about it; and, at last, when all hands were assembled to witness the fall, how often were we disappointed! the tree would still stand erect, bidding defiance to our efforts, while every now and then some of the most impatient or fool-hardy would venture to jump on the scaffold and give a blow or two more. Much time was often spent in this desultory manner, before the mighty tree gave way; but it seldom came to the ground. So thick was the forest, and so close the trees together, that in its fall it would often rest its ponderous top on some other friendly tree; sometimes a number of them would hang together, keeping us in awful suspense, and giving us double labour to extricate the one from the other, and when [74] we had so far succeeded, the removal of the monster stump was the work of days. The tearing up of the roots was equally arduous, although less dangerous: and when this last operation was got through, both tree and stump had to be blown to pieces by gunpowder before either could be removed from the spot.

Nearly two months of this laborious and incessant toil had passed, and we had scarcely yet an acre of ground cleared. In the mean time three of our men were killed by the natives, two more wounded by the falling of trees, and one had his hand blown off by gunpowder.

But the labour, however trying, we were prepared to undergo. It was against neglect and ill-treatment that our feelings revolted. The people suffered greatly from the humidity of the climate. The Sandwich Islanders, used to a dry, pure atmosphere, sank under its influence; damp fogs and sleet were frequent, and every other day was a day of rain. Such is the climate of Columbia at this season of the year, and all this time we were without tents or shelter; add to this the bad quality of our food, consisting solely of boiled fish and wild roots, without even salt, and we had to depend at all times on the success or good-will of the natives for our daily supply, which was far from being regular; so that one-half of the party, on an average, were constantly on the sick list; and on more than one occasion I have seen the whole party so reduced that scarcely [75] one could help the other, and all this chiefly owing to the conduct of Mr. Astor; first, in not sending out a medical man with the party; and, secondly, in his choice of the great pasha, M'Dougall, whom he placed at the head of his affairs. The sick and the sound both fared alike; the necessities of both were overlooked, while he, himself, was served in state; for a good many articles of provision had been put on shore before the ship sailed.

Our hard labour by day, with the watching during night, had not only reduced our party by sickness to a mere nothing, but raised a spirit of discontent, and plots and plans were set on foot to abandon all, and cross the continent by land. This extravagant resolution was, however, overruled by the more moderate of the malcontents, yet it resulted in a party waiting on M'Dougall with the view of bettering the existing state of things, and opening his eyes to his own situation; but this produced no good effect; it rather augmented the evil: and a second deputation proved equally unsuccessful. At last four men deserted, and had proceeded eighty miles up the river when they were laid hold of by the Indians and kept in a tent; nor would the stern and crafty chief of the tribe deliver them up until he had received a ransom for them.

Yet all this could not open the eyes of M'Dougall, nor was it till he had rashly ventured to provoke all classes, that he began to see clearly that he was standing on the verge of a precipice. Everything at [76] this moment seemed at a stand; the folly and imprudence of the man in power had nearly extinguished all hopes of success. Another party of six men, headed by one of the Americans, deserted, but were brought back the third day by our friendly chief, Comecomly. We had some time ago found out that the sordid hope of gain alone attached this old and crafty chief to the whites.

The desertion of these parties, and the number confined by sickness, began now to admonish the man at the head of affairs that he had probably gone a step too far, and that it is much easier to destroy than restore confidence. He suddenly changed for the better; tents were distributed among the sick, and more attention was paid to their diet; still there was no medical man to attend the sufferers. In this case we surely look in vain for that sagacity and forethought which Mr. Astor was thought to possess. His own interest was involved in the result, and nothing could more clearly prove his reckless indifference for the lives of his people than his not providing a medical man of some kind or other, either for his ship or his infant colony.

But feuds and petty grievances among ourselves, arising chiefly from our minds being soured by hardships, were not the only obstacles we had to contend with; our weakness and forlorn situation began to open our eyes to a sense of common danger, and fear began to exercise its influence, so that unanimity alone could enable us to oppose a [77] common enemy. Rumours from all quarters and suspicious appearances had raised an alarm that the distant tribes were forming some dark design of cutting us off, and reports countenancing this belief were daily brought us by Comecomly and his people. We now established a regular patrol of six men, which diminished our labouring body to a mere nothing, but under such circumstances self-preservation obliged us to adopt every precaution. Comecomly was sent for, and questioned on the occasion; but all we could learn from him was, that the hostile tribes were a very bad people, and ill-disposed towards the whites, and this we had no reason to disbelieve, because Comecomly and his people were the only Indians who had regularly traded with us; consequently, we were anxious to ascertain the cause of this rupture between us and the distant tribes.

We had now begun to pick up a few words of the

language, and were given to understand that the crafty Chinookes, like the cat in the fable, had fomented and nourished the misunderstanding between us and the distant tribes; that they had artfully impressed the latter with the idea that we were hostile towards them, and, by the same crafty policy, assuring us of their enmity. By this stratagem, they kept them from coming near us — thereby monopolizing all the trade themselves, by buying up all the furs, and selling them again to us at double their first cost. As soon, however, as we were convinced of the [78] intrigues of old Comecomly and his people, we set about counteracting them. For this purpose, several parties were sent up the country in different directions, to do away with the unfavourable impressions, and to convince the natives, far and near, of our friendly intentions to all.

On the 2nd of May, Mr. M'Kay, accompanied by Mr. Robert Stuart, in a small canoe, and four men, proceeded up the river to sound the dispositions of the Indians, and to assure them of our good-will towards them; and likewise to gain some information respecting the surrounding country and state of the water. Having proceeded as far as the cascades, a distance of 180 miles, made some presents to the principal men, and convinced all the different tribes they saw of the friendly intentions of the whites, the party returned again at the end of twelve days, reporting most favourably of both natives and country.

Mr. M'Kay had figured in the north-west as an Indian trader — was very active, but whimsical and eccentric. An anecdote will picture the man:— It is a habit among the grandees of the Indian trade to have May-poles with their names inscribed thereon on conspicuous places, not to dance round, but merely to denote that such a person passed there on such a day, or to commemorate some event. For this purpose, the tallest tree on the highest ground is generally selected, and all the branches are stripped off excepting a small tuft at the top.

On Mr. M'Kay's return from his reconnoitring [79] expedition up the river, he ordered one of his men to climb a lofty tree and dress it for a May-pole. The man very willingly undertook the job, expecting, as usual on these occasions, to get a dram; but he had no sooner reached the top than his master, through love of mischief, lighting a fire at the bottom, set the tree in a blaze. The poor fellow was instantly enveloped in a cloud of smoke, and called out for mercy. Water was dashed on the tree; but this only increased the danger by augmenting the smoke, for the fire ran up the bark of the gummy pine like gunpowder, and was soon beyond our reach, so that all hope of saving the man's life was at an end. Descending a little, however, he leaped, in despair, on to a branch of another tree, which fortunately offered him a chance of safety; and there he hung between earth and heaven, like a squirrel on a twig, till another man, at no small risk, got up and rescued him from his perilous situation.

Soon after M'Kay's return from the cascades, Mr. Robert Stuart, myself, and five men, proceeded on an excursion to the north. It was here that we became fully acquainted with the dangerous effects of the Chinooke policy. The Indians, on our approach, flew to arms, and made signs for us to keep at a distance. We halted, and tried to moderate their ferocity by a display of presents; but they would not listen to us. Their forces were collecting fast; every moment's delay increased our danger; and, fearful of being surrounded, we were deliberating on a hasty [80] retreat, when, fortunately, a friendly Indian happened to arrive, by means of whom we got into conversation with the others; and the result was, that they explained and cleared up the matter to our utmost satisfaction, and showed us several piles of furs laid up in store waiting the Chinooke traders; but when they saw and compared the prices we paid with that which the Chinookes were in the habit of giving them, they put their hands on their mouths in astonishment, and strongly urged us to return again, saying they would never more trade with the one-eyed chief. We got back again to the establishment on the fifteenth day; yet, notwithstanding the apparent friendly impression we had made on these sordid and treacherous rogues, we had a very narrow escape in crossing one of the rivers — for a party of them had got before us, taken up a strong position on the opposite bank, and disputed the passage; but, by a little manœuvring, we defeated their intentions. Soon afterwards, however, one of our men was killed by them; and on another occasion, a Mr. M'Kenzie and his whole party, consisting of eight men, were cut to pieces by them.

But we shall now return, for a moment, to notice what was going on at the establishment. On the fourth day after our landing, we planted some potatoes and sowed a few garden seeds, and on the 16th of May we laid the foundations of our first building; but in order to procure suitable timber for the purpose, we had to go back some distance — the wood on [81] the site being so large and unmanageable; and for want of cattle to haul it, we had to carry it on our shoulders, or drag it along the ground — a task of no ordinary difficulty. For this purpose, eight men were harnessed, and they conveyed in six days all the timber required for a building or store of sixty feet long by twenty-six broad. On the 18th, as soon as the foundation was completed, the establishment was named Astoria, in honour of Astor, the projector of the enterprise.

The *Tonquin*, in the prosecution of her voyage along the coast, left Astoria on the 1st of June, and crossed the bar on the 5th, when we saw her for the last time. The captain had landed but a small part of the cargo, intending on his return to put the rest on shore; but with his ship all was lost, and Astoria, in consequence, was left almost destitute of the necessary articles of trade. Mr. M'Kay, as supercargo, went on board with Mr. Lewis and two Canadians; but Mr. Mumford, the second officer, was dismissed and sent on shore. On M'Kay's embarking, he called me aside, and taking me by the hand recommended his son to my care; then adding — ''You see,'' said he, ''how unfortunate we are: the captain, in one of his frantic fits, has now discharged the only officer on board,'' alluding to Mr. Mumford. ''If you ever see us safe back, it will be a miracle.'' So saying, we parted, and he slept on board. The departure of the ship unfolded to us the danger of our situation. It is allowed by all experienced fur-traders, [82] that in forming an establishment among savages, the first consideration is safety; and although we had been aware that the ship's stay protected the embryo settlement, and that her departure would proclaim to all the hostile tribes around our defenceless state, yet was there any preparation made for the event?— None. When the ship left us, not a gun was mounted; not a palisade raised; nor the least precaution taken to secure either life or property. Such was the character of the man whom Mr. Astor placed at the head of his affairs.

The Indians from all quarters now began to assemble in such swarms, that we had to relinquish all labour, and think only of defence. We naturally put the worst con-

struction on so formidable an array of savages in arms.
On the other hand, the arrival of the different tribes might
have been produced by the steps we had lately taken in
regard to the Chinooke policy, of assuring them of our
friendly intentions; but the departure of the ship had
left us so powerless and weak, that we could not help
suspecting their intentions; and our suspicion was
strengthened by the absence of Comecomly and his people,
who had avoided coming near us ever since the arrival of
the strangers. We had frequently sent for the crafty
chief, but he as frequently disappointed us, until he was
given to understand that a large present would be the
reward of his good offices in the present emergency, for we
had reason to believe that now, as on former occasions, he
was very [83] busy in labouring to conceal the truth, or, in
other words, sowing the seeds of alienation, in order that
he and his people might as usual engross all the foreign
trade themselves.

At length Comecomly arrived; necessity compelled us
to dissemble our opinion of his conduct: he was received
with open arms, behaved well, and rendered us essential
services. We now opened a friendly intercourse with
the strangers; traded with each tribe in turn; made
some presents; and they left us, apparently well satisfied with the friendly reception they had experienced,
while we were no less agreeably relieved by their departure.
The guard was reduced, and the people set to work
as usual. Comecomly and his two sons received each a
suit of chief's clothing; nor did they omit to insinuate,
that to their influence and good offices we not only owed
our safety, but were indebted for all the furs obtained from
our distant visitors.

Some days afterwards, however, an awkward circumstance took place, which threatened to involve us again in serious troubles. While in the act of removing some leaf tobacco, an Indian was detected in the act of pilfering — for they are notorious thieves; the tobacco was taken from him, and he was reprimanded for his conduct. "What!" said the fellow, indignantly, "do you say I am a thief?" at the same time drawing his bow. M'Dougall then ordered him to be hand-cuffed and imprisoned, with a sentinel over him, in one of the deep but open pits, out of [84] which a large tree had been dug. In the night, however, he contrived to effect his escape, carrying off not only his irons, but the sentinel's gun along with him. Next day Comecomly, accompanied by a large retinue, arrived at Astoria; the great mufti, as usual, was ushered into the tent of state. Here M'Dougall was showing the Chinooke Tye-yea, among other things, the properties of a blunder-buss, and in so doing made a woful blunder, for off went the piece unexpectedly, shattering a corner of his majesty's robe. The report and the dense smoke issuing from the place proclaimed danger, and the affrighted chief, darting out of the tent without his robe, cap, or gun, began calling to his people, who in a moment, giving the war-whoop and arming themselves, fiercely menaced the whites with destruction. In the mean time one of our sentinels, hearing the report of the gun, and seeing the tent enveloped in a cloud of smoke, and the chief running off at full speed from it, supposed that he had murdered M'Dougall, and fired after him, calling out treason! murder! at the sound of which our people flew to arms; and every man, with his finger on the trigger of his gun, advanced to the spot. M'Dougall and myself, who fortunately knew the circumstances, hastened to run in between the hostile ranks, making signs of peace, and after a tumultuous moment, the mysterious affair was explained without bloodshed; yet long afterwards the chief retained some suspicion that a plot had been formed against his life.

[85] Among the many visitors who every now and then presented themselves, were two strange Indians, in the character of man and wife, from the vicinity of the Rocky Mountains, and who may probably figure in our narrative hereafter. The husband, named Ko-come-ne-pe-ca, was a very shrewd and intelligent Indian, who addressed us in the Algonquin language, and gave us much information respecting the interior of the country.

On the 15th of July, we were rather surprised at the unexpected arrival of a north-west proprietor at Astoria, and still more so at the free and cordial reception given to an opponent. Mr. Thompson, northwest-like, came dashing down the Columbia in a light canoe, manned with eight Iroquois and an interpreter, chiefly men from the vicinity of Montreal. M'Dougall received him like a brother; nothing was too good for Mr. Thompson; he had access everywhere; saw and examined everything; and whatever he asked for he got, as if he had been one of ourselves. Mr. Thompson at once recognised the two strange Indians, and gave us to understand that they were both females. His own visit had evidently no other object but to discourage us — a manœuvre of the North-West policy to extend their own trade at the expense of ours; but he failed. The dangers and difficulties, which he took great pains to paint in their worst colours, did not deter us. He forgot that in speaking to us, he was speaking to north-westers — men as experienced and as cunning as himself. The [86] North-West had penetrated to the west side of the mountains as early as 1804, and had

in 1811 two or three small posts on the waters of the
Columbia, exclusive of the New Caledonia quarter.
Every one knew this, and knowing it, how could we
account for the more than warm and unreserved welcome
Mr. Thompson met with from Astor's representative.
Unless, as some thought at the time, M'Dougall was
trying to pay Mr. Thompson back with his own coin, by
putting on a fair face, so as to dupe him into an avowal of
his real object.   This is more than probable, for in point
of acuteness, duplicity, and diplomatic craft, they were
perhaps well matched.

[87] CHAPTER VI

The ten tribes — Number of warriors — Their laws
   — Chief's arbitrary power — Dress, games, and arms
   of the men — Dress of the women, slaves, and
   basket-making — Lewdness of the women — Food,
   ornaments — The salmon — Superstitious customs —
   Sturgeon — Fathom-fish — Roots and berries — Circulating medium — Econé, or Good Spirit — Ecutoch,
   or Bad Spirit — Etaminua, or priests — Keelalles, or
   doctors — War canoes — Diseases — Winter houses —
   Temporary, or Summer houses — Fleas — Practice of
   flattening the head — Colonization — Wallamitte —
   Cowlitz, or Puget's Sound — Conclusion.

ALL the Indian tribes inhabiting the country about the
mouth of the Columbia, and for a hundred miles round,
may be classed in the following manner:— 1. Chinooks;
— 2. Clatsops;— 3. Cathlamux;— 4. Wakicums;— 5.
Wacalamus;— 6. Cattleputles;— 7. Clatscanias;— 8. Kill-
imux;— 9. Moltnomas;— and, 10. Chickelis; amounting
collectively to about 2,000 warriors. [13]   But they are a

[13] The tribes of the Pacific coast were numerous, and their classification
varies. For the Chinook, Clatsop, Wakiacum, Cathlapotle (Cattleputles),
Tillamook (Killamux), Multnomah, and Chehalis (Chickelis), see Franchère,

commercial rather than a warlike people. Traffic in slaves and furs is their occupation. They are said to be decreasing in numbers. All these tribes appear to be descended from the same stock, live in rather friendly intercourse [88] with, and resemble one another in language, dress, and habits. Their origin, like that of the other aborigines of the continent, is involved in fable, although they pretend to be derived from the musk-rat. Polygamy is common among them, and a man may have as many wives as he pleases, but he is bound to maintain his own children. In war, every man belonging to the tribe is bound to follow his chief; and a coward is often punished with death. All property is sacred in the eye of the law, nor can any one touch it excepting the principal chief, or head Tye-yea, who is above the law, or rather he possesses an arbitrary power without any positive check, so that if he conceive a liking to anything belonging to his subjects, be it a wife or a daughter, he can take it without infringing the law; but he must, nevertheless, pay for what he takes — and their laws assign a nominal value to property of every kind.

The Chinooks are crafty and intriguing, and have probably learned the arts of cheating, flattery, and dissimilation in the course of their traffic with the coasting traders: for, on our first arrival among them, we found guns, kettles, and various other articles of foreign manufacture in their possession, and they were up to all the shifts of bargaining. Nor are they less ingenious than inquisitive; the art they display in the making of canoes, of

notes 39, 40, 45, 52, 53, 65, 67. The other tribes cannot positively be identified, except the Katlamat (Cathlamux), who were a branch of the Upper Chinook, giving name to the town of Cathlamet, Washington. On the subject of the native races of this section, see Thwaites, *Original Journals of Lewis and Clark Expedition* (New York, 1904), under Scientific Data: Ethnology.— ED.

pagods, and of fishing-tackle, and other useful instruments, deserves commendation. They show much skill in carved [89] work, which they finish with the most delicate polish.

The men are generally stout, muscular, and strong, but not tall, and have nothing ferocious in their countenances. Their dress invariably consists of a loose garment, made of the skin of the wood-rat, neatly sewed together and painted, which they wrap round the body like a blanket; nor does the hardy savage, though constantly rustling through the woods, ever wear a shirt, leggings, or shoes. The chief's robe is made of sea-otter skin and other valuable furs. All classes wear the cheapool, or hat, which is made of a tough strong kind of grass, and is of so close a texture as to be water-proof. The crown is of a conic form, terminating generally in a point at the top, and the rim so very broad as to screen the shoulders from the rain. The cheapool is chequered or diversified with the rude figures of different animals, particularly the dog and deer, not painted, but ingeniously interwoven. [14] Their war garments are of two kinds, one is termed clemal, of elk-skin, dressed and worked to the thickness of nearly half an inch, and arrow-proof. The clemal nearly covers the whole body, with an opening left on the right side to allow the arm free action in combat. The other is a kind of vest, made of small round sticks of the size and shape of arrows, twelve inches long: they are laid side to side, and then sewed together, and fixed on the body like a waistcoat. This is arrow-proof also. They carry a circular [90] shield, about eighteen inches in diameter, which is likewise made of the elk-skin; but in addition

---

[14] For information concerning the wood-rat, sea-otter, and chepool, see Franchère, notes 128–130.— ED.

to its thickness it is hardened by fire and painted, and is not only arrow-proof, but proof against the knife and the tomahawk also. Their implements of warfare are guns, bows and arrows, knife, bludgeon, and tomahawk, all of which they use with great dexterity. A Chinooke Indian armed *cap-à-pie* is a most unsightly and hideous being.

When not employed either in war or hunting, the men generally spend their time in gambling. The chief game, chal-e-chal, at which they stake their most valuable property, is played by six persons, with ten circular palettes of polished wood, in size and shape resembling dollars. A mat three feet broad and six feet long is spread on the ground, and the articles at stake laid at one end, then the parties seat themselves, three on each side of the mat, facing one another; this done, one of the players takes up the ten palettes, shuffling and shifting them in his hands, when at a signal given he separates them in his two fists, and throws them out on the mat towards his opponent, and according as the palettes roll, slide, or lie on the mat when thrown, the party wins or loses. This he does three times successively. In this manner each tries his skill in turn, till one of the parties wins. Whole days and nights are spent in this game without ceasing, and the Indians seldom grumble or repine even should they lose all that they possess. During the [91] game the players keep chanting a loud and sonorous tune, accompanying the different gestures of the body just as the voyageurs keep time to the paddle.

Having noticed some of the characteristic manners and customs of the men, I shall now indulge the reader's curiosity with a few remarks on the habits and accomplishments of the fair sex. The women are generally of the middle size, but very stout and flabby, with short necks and shapeless limbs; yet they are well-featured, with something of a smile on the countenance, fair complexion, light hair, and prominent eyes. In addition to the rat-garment used by the men, the women wear a kind of fringed petticoat suspended from the waist down to the knees, made of the inner rind of the cedar bark, and twisted into threads, which hang loose like a weaver's thrums, and keep flapping and twisting about with every motion of the body, giving them a waddle or duck gait. This garment might deserve praise for its simplicity, or rather for its oddity, but it does not screen nature from the prying eye; yet it is remarkably convenient on many occasions. In a calm the sails lie close to the mast, metaphorically speaking, but when the wind blows the bare poles are seen.

Instead of the cedar petticoat, the women of some tribes prefer a breech cloth, similar to the pow of the Owhyhee females, and is nothing more than a piece of dressed deer-skin, six inches broad and four feet long, which, after passing between the thighs, [92] is tied round the waist. Words can hardly express the disgusting unsightliness of this singular female dress. The women, when not employed in their domestic labour, are generally occupied in curing fish, collecting roots, and making mats and baskets; the latter, of various sizes and different shapes, are made of the roots of certain shrubs, which are flexible and strong, and they are capable of containing any liquid. In this branch of industry they excel among Indian tribes. The neatness and good taste displayed in the Chinooke baskets are peculiar to that article, which is eagerly sought after as a curiosity.

The women here are not generally subject to that drudgery common among most other Indian tribes.

Slaves do all the laborious work; and a Chinooke matron is constantly attended by two, three, or more slaves, who are on all occasions obsequious to her will. In trade and barter the women are as actively employed as the men, and it is as common to see the wife, followed by a train of slaves, trading at the factory, as her husband. Slaves are the fruits of war and of trade among the tribes along the sea-coast far to the north, and are regularly bought and sold in the same manner as any other article of property; but I never knew a single instance of a Chinooke, or one of the neighbouring tribes, ever selling his wife, or daughter, or any other member of his family.

Chastity is not considered a virtue by the Chinooke [93] women, and their amorous propensities know no bounds. All classes, from the highest to the lowest, indulge in coarse sensuality and shameless profligacy. Even the chief would boast of obtaining a paltry toy or trifle in return for the prostitution of his virgin daughter.

The females are excessively fond of singing and adorning their persons with the fantastic trinkets peculiar to savages; and on these occasions the slaves are generally rigged out the best, in order to attract attention and procure admirers. All classes marry very young; and every woman, whether free born or a slave, is purchased by her husband.

Children are suckled at the breast till their second or third year, and the mother, in consequence, becomes an old hag at at the age of thirty-five.

The women have also their own amusements. Their chief game, called omintook, is played by two only, with four beaver teeth, curiously marked and numbered on one side, which they throw like dice. The two women being seated on the ground, face to face, like the men at chal-e-chal, one of them takes up the teeth, keeps shaking them in her hands for some time, then throws them down on the mat, counts the numbers uppermost, and repeating the sum thrice, hands the teeth over to the other party, who proceeds in like manner. The highest number wins. At this game, trinkets of various descriptions and value are staked. On a fine day, it is amusing to see a whole camp or village, both men and women, [94] here and there in numerous little bands, gambling, jeering, and laughing at one another, while groups of children keep in constant motion, either in the water or practising the bow and arrow, and even the aged take a lively interest in what is passing, and there appears a degree of happiness among them, which civilized men, wearied with care and anxious pursuits, perhaps seldom enjoy.

These people live by hunting and fishing; but the greater part of their food is derived from the waters. The Columbia salmon, of which there are two species, are perhaps as fine as any in the world, and are caught in the utmost abundance during the summer season: so that, were a foreign market to present itself, the natives alone might furnish 1,000 tons annually. The largest caught in my time weighed forty-seven pounds. Sturgeon also are very abundant, and of uncommon size, yet tender and well flavoured, many of them weighing upwards of 700 pounds, and one caught and brought to us, measured 13 feet 9 inches in length, and weighed 1,130 pounds. There is a small fish resembling the smelt or herring, known by the name of ulichan, which enters the river in immense shoals, in the spring of the year. The ulichans are generally an article of trade with the distant tribes, as they are caught only at the entrance of large rivers. To prepare them for a distant market, they are laid side to side,

head and tail alternately, and then a thread run through
both extremities links them together, in which state they
are dried, smoked, [95] and sold by the fathom, hence
they have obtained the name of fathom-fish. [15] Roots and
berries likewise form no inconsiderable portion of the
native's food. Strawberries are ripe in January. The
wapatoe, a perennial root, of the size, shape, and taste of
the common potato, is a favourite article of food at all
times of the year. This esculent is highly esteemed by
the whites; many other roots and berries are to be had, all
of which grow spontaneously in the low marshy ground. [16]
Fish, roots, and berries, can therefore be had in perfection,
all along the coast, every month in the year. But not a
fish of any kind is taken out of the ocean.

The circulating medium in use among these people is a
small white shell called higua, about two inches long, of a
convex form, and hollow in the heart, resembling in
appearance the small end of a smoking pipe. The higua
is thin, light, and durable, and may be found of all lengths,
between three inches down to one-fourth of an inch, and
increases or decreases in value according to the number
required to make a fathom, by which measure they are invariably sold. Thirty to a fathom are held equal in value
to three fathoms of forty, to four of fifty, and so on. So
high are the higua prized, that I have seen six of 2½ inches
long refused for a new gun. But of late, since the whites
came among them, the beaver skin called enna, has been
added to the currency; so that, by these two articles,
which form the medium of trade, all property is valued, and

---

[15] For the characteristic fish of this coast, see Franchère, notes 88, 124–126.
The *ulichan* is the candlefish, so named because it is fat enough to burn for
illuminating purposes.— ED.

[16] For the wappato root see Franchère, note 87.— ED.

all exchange fixed and [96] determined. An Indian, in buying an article, invariably asks the question, Queentshich higua? or, Queentshich enna? That is, how many higua? or, how many beaver skins is it?

All Indians are more or less superstitious, and we need scarcely be surprised at that trait in their character, when even civilized men respect so many prejudices. Every great chief has one or more pagods or wooden deities in his house, to which, in all great councils of peace or war he presents the solemn pipe, and this is the only religious temple known among them.

They acknowledge a good and a bad spirit, the former named Econé, the latter Ecutoch. The Etaminuàs, or priests, are supposed to possess a secret power of conversing with the Econé, and of destroying the influence of the Ecutoch: they are employed in all cases of sickness to intercede for the dying, that these may have a safe passage to the land of departed spirits. Besides the Etaminua, there is another class called Keelalles, or doctors, and it is usual for women, as well as men, to assume the character of a Keelalle, whose office it is to administer medicine and cure diseases. But the antic gestures, rude and absurd ceremonies gone through by them in visiting the sick, are equally useless and ridiculous, humming, howling, singing, and rattling of sticks, as if miracles were to be performed by mere noise; yet if we forget these useless gesticulations, which may be called the ornamental part, we must [97] allow them to be a serviceable and skilful class of people. Their knowledge of roots and herbs enables them to meet the most difficult cases, and to perform cures, particularly in all external complaints.

The property of a deceased person is generally destroyed, and the near relations cut their hair, disfigure and

lacerate their bodies; nor is this all, at the funeral ceremony strangers are here, as among some oriental nations,
paid to join in the lamentation. All, excepting slaves, are
laid in canoes or wooden sepulchres, and conveyed to some
consecrated rock or thicket assigned for the dead; but
slaves are otherwise disposed of; that is, if he or she dies
in summer, the body is carelessly buried; but if in winter, a
stone is tied about the neck, and the body thrown into the
river, and none but slaves ever touch a slave after death.

When the salmon make their first appearance in the
river, they are never allowed to be cut crosswise, nor
boiled, but roasted; nor are they allowed to be sold without the heart being first taken out, nor to be kept over
night; but must be all consumed or eaten the day they are
taken out of the water; all these rules are observed for
about ten days. These superstitious customs perplexed
us at first not a little, because they absolutely refused to
sell us any unless we complied with their notions, which
of course we consented to do. All the natives along the
coast navigate in canoes, and so expert are they that the
stormiest weather or roughest water never [98] prevents
them from cruising on their favourite element. The Chinook and other war canoes are made like the Birman
barge, out of a solid tree, and are from forty to fifty feet
long, with a human face or a white-headed eagle, as large
as life, carved on the prow, and raised high in front.

If we may judge from appearances, these people are
subject to but few diseases. Consumption and the vene-
real disease are the complaints most common amongst
them; from their knowledge in simples, they generally
succeed in curing the latter even in its worst stages.

In winter they live in villages, but in summer rove about
from place to place. Their houses are oblong, and built

of broad, split cedar-planks, something in the European style, and covered with the bark of the same tree. They are sufficiently large and commodious to contain all the members of a numerous family, slaves included. At the top or ridge pole, an opening gives free passage to the smoke; they have one or more, according to the number of families in each. But I never saw more than four fires, or above eighty persons — slaves and all — in the largest house.

Towards the spring of the year, or as soon as the rainy season is over, all the Indians on the coast break up their winter quarters, and form large square sheds, for the purpose of drying and curing their fish, roots, and berries. Within this huge enclosure they then live in hordes, like so many cattle in a fold; but [99] these sheds are only for temporary purposes; and it must have been on some such occasion that Meares found Wickananish in his "household of 800 persons." [17] They migrate towards the interior sometimes for months together; war and traffic in slaves often call them to a distance; and this may account for the absence of inhabitants about Port Discovery and Desolation Sound when Vancouver was there. [18] But

[17] Captain John Meares, born about 1756, served in the British navy, where he attained the rank of lieutenant. After the Peace of Paris (1783) he entered the merchant service, and founded a commercial house in Macao, China, to trade with the Northwest Coast of North America. In 1786 he made his first voyage thither. Two years later, he formed an establishment at Nootka Sound, and explored the coast to the south — failing, however, to recognize the outlet of the Columbia as the mouth of a great river. In 1789, Meares's establishment at Nootka was demolished by the Spaniards, which led to the diplomatic incident known as the Nootka Sound episode. His book appeared during this controversy — *Voyages made in the years 1788 and 1789 to the N. W. Coast of America* (London, 1791). Meares finally returned to the navy, became commander in 1795, and died in 1809.— ED.

[18] For brief account of Vancouver, see Franchère, note 2. Port Discovery, on the northern coast of Washington, was named for Vancouver's ship. Desolation Sound was farther north in the Gulf of Georgia.— ED.

another cause, and perhaps the best that can be assigned, for their abandoning their winter domiciles as soon as the warm weather sets in, is the immense swarms of fleas that breed in them during that season. You might as well encounter a bee-hive, as approach one of these deserted villages.

Among other fantastic usages, many of the tribes on the coast of the Pacific, and particularly those about Columbia, flatten the heads of their children. No sooner, therefore, is a child born, whether male or female, than its head is put into a press, or mould of boards, in order to flatten it. From the eyebrows, the head of a Chinook inclines backward to the crown; the back part inclining forward, but in a less degree. There is thus a ridge raised from ear to ear, giving the head the form of a wedge; and the more acute the angle, the greater the beauty. [19] The flatness of the head is considered the distinguishing mark of being free born. All slaves are forbidden to bear this aristocratic distinction. Yet I have seen one or two instances to the contrary, where a favourite slave was permitted to flatten the head of a first-born [100] child. No such custom is practised in any part of the interior. But all nations, civilized as well as savage, have their peculiar prejudices. The law of the land compels a South-Sea Islander to pull out a tooth; a northern Indian cuts a joint off his finger; national usage obliges a Chinese lady to deform her feet; an English lady, under the influence of fashion, compresses her waist; while a Chinook lady deforms her head. But Solomon hath said, ''That which is crooked cannot be made straight.''

As tracts suitable for agricultural purposes, may be

---

[19] For the appearance of these flattened heads, see Clark's drawings of the Chinook, in *Original Journals of Lewis and Clark Expedition*.— ED

mentioned several fertile and rich flats on the Columbia, although the country generally presents but a rocky, light, and sandy soil. On the south side, the river is joined, about eighty miles above Astoria, by the Wallamitte, a fine clear stream, 300 miles long, which, with its tributary rivulets, fertilizes one of the finest valleys west of the Rocky Mountains. The Wallamitte was always called by the whites, ''the garden of the Columbia.'' For forty miles the river is navigable for boats of the largest size, to the falls, but there it is barred across by a ledge of rocks, over which the whole body of water descends — a height of 30 feet — in one smooth green sheet. The climate of this valley is salubrious and dry, differing materially from that of the sea-coast; and the heat is sufficiently intense to ripen every kind of grain in a short time.

Descending from the Wallamitte to Puget's Sound, north of the Columbia, where there is a large and [101] convenient sea-port, or harbour, we find here a tract ranking next, perhaps, in an agricultural point of view. The plain is well watered by several fine rivers, and is far more extensive than the valley of the Wallamitte, nor is the soil much inferior; but there is a vast difference in the climate; rain falls near the coast almost incessantly from the beginning of November till April, and the country in other respects is gloomy and forbidding.

But, however inviting may be the soil, the remote distance and savage aspect of the boundless wilderness along the Pacific seem to defer the colonization of such a region to a period far beyond the present generation; and yet, if we consider the rapid progress of civilization in other new and equally remote countries, we might still indulge the hope of seeing this, at no distant time, one of the most flourishing countries on the globe.

The language spoken by these people is guttural, very

difficult for a foreigner to learn, and equally hard to pronounce. To speak the Chinook dialect, you must be a Chinook.

[102] CHAPTER VII

First expedition into the interior — Number of the party — Tongue Point — Canoe swamped — Sailing difficulties — Indian villages — Cedars — First night's encampment — Mount Coffin — Cowlitz — Wallamitte — Columbia Valley — Point Vancouver — Difficulties — The Cascades — Concourse of Indians — General appearance of the country — The portage — Description of the Cascades — The roll of tobacco — Pilfering — Mr. Thompson — Exchange of men — The Long Narrows — Warlike appearance of the Indian cavalry — Button contract — Critical situation of the party — Camp of gamblers — The narrows — Hard work at the carrying place — A day's work — Description of the portage — Number of Indians — Aspect of the country — The plains begin — End of the woods — Want of sleep — Demeanour of the Indians.

NOTWITHSTANDING the departure of the ship, and our reduced numbers, measures were taken for extending the trade; and the return of Mr. Thompson up the Columbia, on his way back to Canada, was considered as affording a favourable opportunity for us to fit out a small expedition, with the view of establishing a trading post in the interior: we were to proceed together, for the sake of mutual protection and safety, our party being too small to attempt anything of the kind by itself. Accordingly, Mr. [103] David Stuart, myself, Messrs. Pillette and M'Lennan, three Canadian voyageurs, and two Sandwich Islanders, accompanied by Mr. Thompson's party and the two strangers, in all twenty-one persons, started from Astoria, at eleven o'clock on the 22nd of July, 1811.

In two clumsy Chinook canoes, laden each with fifteen

or twenty packages of goods, of ninety pounds weight, we embarked to ascend the strong and rapid Columbia; and, considering the unskilfulness of our party generally in the management of such fickle craft, the undertaking was extremely imprudent; but then, being all of us more or less ambitious, we overlooked, in the prospect of ultimate success, both difficulty and danger. After our canoes were laden, we moved down to the water's edge — one with a cloak on his arm, another with his umbrella, a third with pamphlets and newspapers for amusement, preparing, as we thought, for a trip of pleasure, or rather all anxious to be relieved from our present harassing and dangerous situation. The wind being fair and strong, we hoisted sail; but had not proceeded to Tongue Point, a small promontory in the river, not three miles distant from Astoria, when the unfriendly wind dashed our canoes, half-filled with water, on the shore; and, as we were not able to double the Point, we made a short passage across the isthmus, and then, being somewhat more sheltered from the wind, proceeded, but had not got many miles before our progress was again arrested by a [104] still worse accident; for, while passing among the islands and shoals, before rounding Oathlamuck Point, at the head of Gray's Bay, the wind and swell drove us on a sandbank, where we stuck fast — the waves dashing over us, and the tide ebbing rapidly. [20] Down came the mast, sail, and rigging about our ears; and, in the hurry and confusion, the canoes got almost full of water, and we were well drenched: here we had to carry the goods and drag the

[20] For the promontory known as Tongue Point, see Franchère, note 44. Gray's Bay was named for Captain Robert Gray, *op. cit.*, note 1. "Oathlamuck" Point is that now known as Cathlamet Point, in Clatsop County, Oregon. This does not bound Gray's Bay, except as it is the point below which the river widens into great inlets.— ED.

canoes till we reached deep water again, which was no easy task. This disaster occupied us about two hours, and gave us a foretaste of what we might expect during the remainder of the voyage. Cloaks and umbrellas, so gay in the morning, were now thrown aside for the more necessary paddle and carrying strap, and the pamphlets and newspapers went to the bottom. Having, however, got all put to rights again, we hoisted sail once more, passed Puget's Island, and then the great Whill Wetz village, situated on Oak Point, where the river makes a sudden bend to S.S.E.: [21] here, on the south side, the rocks became high and the current strong, and night coming on us before we could reach low ground, we were compelled to encamp on the verge of a precipice, where we passed a gloomy night — drenched with wet, without fire, without supper, and without sleep. During this day's journey, both sides of the river presented a thick forest down to the water's edge — the timber being large, particularly the cedars. The sound, from Cape Disappointment [105] to the head of Gray's Bay, which we passed to-day, is about twenty-five miles in length, and varies from four to seven in breadth.

On the 23rd, after a restless night, we started, stemming a strong and almost irresistible current by daylight. Crossing to the north side, not far from our encampment, we passed a small rocky height, called Coffin Rock, or Mount Coffin, a receptacle for the dead: all over this rock — top, sides, and bottom — were placed canoes of all sorts and sizes, containing relics of the dead, the congregated dust of many ages.

[21] Puget's Island, in the Columbia opposite Cathlamet, Washington, was named when Broughton explored the Columbia (1792), for Peter Puget, lieutenant of Vancouver's vessel, the "Discovery." For Oak Point, see Franchère, note 74. Ross is the only contemporary writer who mentions this Indian village by name.— ED.

Not far from Mount Coffin, on the same side, was the mouth of a small river, called by the natives Cowlitz, near which was an isolated rock, covered also with canoes and dead bodies. This sepulchral rock has a ghastly appearance, in the middle of the stream, and we rowed by it in silence; then passing Deer's Island, we encamped at the mouth of the Wallamitte. [22] The waters of the Columbia are exceedingly high this year — all the low banks and ordinary water-marks are overflowed, and the island inundated. At the mouth of the Wallamitte, commences the great Columbian valley of Lewis and Clarke; but in the present state of flood, surrounded on all sides by woods almost impervious, the prospect is not fascinating. The Indians appeared very numerous in several villages. General course the same as yesterday, S.E.

On the 24th, after a good night's rest, and having [106] made some trifling presents to a principal chief, named Kiasno, [23] we proceeded on our voyage; but had not gone far, when we passed another and larger branch of the Wallamitte — so that this river enters the Columbia by two channels, from the last of which the Columbia makes a gradual bend to the E.N.E.

During this day, we passed the Namowit Village, Bellevue Point, Johnson's Island, and stayed for the night as Wasough-ally Camp, near Quicksand River, which enters the Columbia on the left. [24]

[22] Ross confuses the names of two landmarks; the first should be Mount Coffin (see Franchère, note 48), the second Coffin Rock. The first is an isolated cliff on the Washington bank of the river, the second a rocky islet toward the Oregon side — both used as places of Indian sepulture. For Deer Island, see Franchère, note 75.— ED.

[23] For this chief, see Franchère, note 51.— ED.

[24] The "Namowit" Indians were one tribe of those designated by Lewis and Clark as the "Wappato" Indians; see *Original Journals of Lewis and Clark Expedition,* under Scientific Data: Estimate of Western Indians. For Bellevue

Bellevue Point on the right-hand side of the river, although but low, presents a scene of great beauty, compared to what we had yet seen during the voyage: here the eye is occasionally relieved from the monotonous gloomy aspect of dense woods, by the sight of green spots, clumps of trees, small lakes, and meadows alternately.

On the 25th, early this morning, we arrived at and passed Point Vancouver, so named after the celebrated navigator, and the extreme point of Broughton's survey of the Columbia. [25] From the lower branch of the Walla-mitte to Point Vancouver, the banks of the river on both sides are low; but, as we proceeded further on, a chain of huge black rocks rose perpendicularly from the water's edge: over their tops fell many bold rills of clear water. Hemmed in by these rocky heights, the current assumed double force, so that our paddles proved almost ineffectual; and, to get on, we were obliged to drag ourselves along from point to point, by laying [107] hold of bushes and the branches of overhanging trees, which, although they impeded our progress in one way, aided us in another. After a day of severe toil, we halted for the night. We saw but five Indians all this day; and, for the first time, now came to our camp at night. The ebb and flow of the tide is not felt here. The country, generally, has a wild and savage appearance: course, E.N.E.

On the 26th, it was late this morning before we could

Point, see Franchère, note 55. Johnson's Island was named by Broughton (1792) for the lieutenant of his vessel, the "Chatham;" Lewis and Clark called it Diamond Island; it is now known as Government Island, in Multnomah County, Oregon. Wasougal (Wasough-ally) is a small stream entering the Columbia from the north, in Clark County, Washington. Quicksand River, so named by Lewis and Clark, is the present Sandy, a considerable stream draining the western slope of Mount Hood, and flowing into the Columbia through Multnomah County, Oregon.— ED.

[25] For the location of Point Vancouver, see Francherè, note 55.— ED.

muster courage to embark. The burning sun of yesterday, and the difficulty of stemming the rapid current, had
so reduced our strength that we made but little headway
to-day; and, after being for six hours rowing as many
miles, we stopped, tired and rather discouraged: course,
N.E.

On the 27th, we were again early at work, making the
best of our way against a turbulent and still increasing
current: as we advanced, the river became narrower, the
hills and rocks approaching nearer and nearer to the
river on either side. Here the view was very confined, and
by no means cheering.

We, however, continued our toil till late in the evening,
when, in place of a uniform smooth and strong current, as
usual, the water became confused and ripply, with whirlpools and cross currents, indicating the proximity of some
obstruction. At the foot of a rocky cliff, which we named
Inshoach Castle, [26] we put ashore for the night; nor did
we see a single Indian all day. Mr. Thompson encamped
on one side [108] of the river, and we on the other. General course, to-day, nearly east.

During last night the water rose ten inches. This was
supposed to be occasioned by the tide, although, after
passing Bellevue Point, the influence of tide was not
perceptible on the current. From the mouth of the river
to this place — a distance of a hundred and eighty miles —
there is sufficient depth of water for almost any craft to
pass; even ships of 400 tons might reach Inshoach Castle
had they power to stem the current.

As regards agricultural purposes, Bellevue Point and

[26] The rock that Ross and the Scotch Canadians of his party named "Inshoach Castle," was probably the well-known landmark now called Beacon
Rock, which marks the extent of tidal influence, and may be seen for twenty
miles down the river.— Ed.

the valley of the Wallamitte were the most favourable spots we met with. Generally speaking, the whole country on either side of the river, as far as the eye could reach, presented a dense, gloomy forest. We found, however, a marked improvement in the climate. Here the air is dry and agreeable. Fogs, mists, damp and rainy weather, ceased after we had passed the Wallamitte.

On the 28th, early in the morning, Mr. Thompson crossed over to our camp, and informed us that we were within a short distance of the cascades. We then embarked, and proceeded together. After making some distance with the paddles, we had recourse to the poles, and then to the hauling line, till at length we reached the point of disembarkation.

We had no sooner landed, than a great concourse of Indians assembled at a short distance from us, and, after holding a consultation, came moving on in a [109] body to meet us, or rather, as we thought, to welcome our arrival. The parley being ended, and the ceremony of smoking over, they pointed up the river, signifying that the road was open for us to pass. Embarking again, we pushed on, and passing the Strawberry Island of Lewis and Clarke, we continued for some distance further, and finally put on shore at the end of the portage, or carrying-place, situate on the right-hand side of the river, and at the foot of a rather steep bank. [27] Here the Indians crowded about us in fearful numbers, and some of them became very troublesome. A small present being made to each of the chiefs, or great men, in order to smooth them down a little in our favour, they pointed across the portage, or carrying-place, as much as to say — All is clear; pass on.

[27] For Strawberry Island and the portage of the Cascades, see Franchère, note 112.— ED.

From this point we examined the road over which we
had to transport the goods, and found it to be 1450 yards
long, with a deep descent, near the Indian villages, at the
far end, with up-hills, down-hills, and side-hills, most of
the way, besides a confusion of rocks, gullies, and thick
woods, from end to end.   To say that there is not a worse
path under the sun would perhaps be going a step too far,
but to say that, for difficulty and danger, few could equal
it would be saying but the truth.   Certainly nothing could
be more discouraging than our present situation — obstacles on every side; by land, by water, and from the Indians
— all hostile alike.   Having landed the goods, and secured
the canoe, we commenced the [110] laborious task of
carrying, and by dividing ourselves in the best possible
manner for safety, we managed to get all safe over by sunset.   Not being accustomed myself to carry, I had of
course, as well as some others, to stand sentinel; but seeing
the rest almost wearied to death, I took hold of a roll of
tobacco, and after adjusting it on my shoulder, and holding it fast with one hand, I moved on to ascend the first
bank; at the top of which, however, I stood breathless, and
could proceed no farther.   In this awkward plight, I met
an Indian, and made signs to him to convey the tobacco
across, and that I would give him all the buttons on my
coat; but he shook his head, and refused.   Thinking the
fellow did not understand me, I threw the tobacco down,
and pointing to the buttons one by one, at last he consented,
and off he set at a full trot, and I after him; but just as we
had reached his camp at the other end, he pitched it down a
precipice of two hundred feet in height, and left me to
recover it the best way I could.   Off I started after my
tobacco; and if I was out of breath after getting up the

first bank, I was ten times more so now. During my scrambling among the rocks to recover my tobacco, not only the wag that played me the trick, but fifty others, indulged in a hearty laugh at my expense; but the best of it was, the fellow came for his payment, and wished to get not only the buttons but the coat along with them. I was for giving him — what he richly deserved — buttons of another mould; but peace, in our present situation, was deemed the better [111] policy: so the rogue got the buttons, and we saw him no more.

Before leaving this noted place, the first barrier of the Columbia, we may remark that the whole length of the cascade, from one end to the other, is two miles and a half. We were now encamped at the head or upper end of them, where the whole river is obstructed to the breadth of one hundred or one hundred and twenty feet, and descends in high and swelling surges with great fury for about one hundred yards. Then the channel widens and the river expands, and is here and there afterwards obstructed with rocks, whirlpools, and eddies throughout, rendering the navigation more or less dangerous; but there are no falls in any part of it, either at high or low water, and with the exception of the first shoot, at the head of the cascade, where the water rushes with great impetuosity down its channel, they are, with care and good management, passable at all seasons for large craft, that is boats.

All the Indians we saw about this place were in three small camps or villages, and might number two hundred and fifty or three hundred at most. They call themselves Cath-le-yach-ê-yachs, and we could scarcely purchase from the lazy rascals fish and roots enough for our supper. In dress, appearance, and habits, they differed but little from those about Astoria; but they spoke a different language, although many of them understood and spoke Chinook also. [28]

[112] At first we formed a favourable opinion of them; but their conduct soon changed, for we had no sooner commenced transporting our goods than they tried to annoy us in every kind of way — to break our canoes, pilfer our property, and even to threaten ourselves, by throwing stones and pointing their arrows at us. We were not, however, in a situation to hazard a quarrel with them, unless in the utmost extremity; and it was certainly with great difficulty, and by forbearance on our part, that we got so well off as we did. After finishing the labour of the day, we arranged ourselves for the night. The Indians all assembled again about our little camp, and became very insolent and importunate; they looked at everything, and coveted all they saw. Indeed we were afraid at one time that we would have to appeal to arms; but fortunately, after distributing a few trifling presents among the principal men, they smoked and left us; but we kept a constant watch all night. The only domestic animal we saw among them was the dog.

On the 29th, early in the morning, we prepared to leave the cascades; but the bank being steep, and the current very strong where we had to embark, we did not venture off before broad daylight, and before that time the Indians had crowded about us as usual. Their pilfering propensities had no bounds. The more we gave them the more they expected, and of course the more trouble they gave us; and notwithstanding all our care and kindness [113]

[28] Lewis and Clark called these natives at the Cascades, Clahclellahs, and included them among the generic name of Shahalas, a branch of the Upper Chinook. The tribesmen were a thieving, troublesome lot, as Ross's subsequent narrative will show.— ED.

to them, they stole our canoe axe and a whole suit of clothes, excepting the hat, belonging to Mr. M'Lennan, which we were unable to recover. We had no sooner embarked, however, than Mr. M'Lennan in his usual good-humour, standing up in the canoe, and throwing the hat amongst them, said, ''Gentlemen, there's the hat, you have got the rest, the suit is now complete,'' and we pushed off and left them.

Immediately above the cascade the river resumes its usual breadth, with a smooth and strong current. The day being exceedingly warm, we made but little headway. In the evening we passed a small river on our left, near which we encamped for the night. [29] Here we had promised ourselves a quiet night and sound sleep; but the Indians finding us out partly deprived us of both, as we had to keep watch. They were but few, however, and therefore peaceable. Course this day, N.N.E.

On the 30th we set off early, leaving the five Indians, who slept in our camp last night, sitting by the fire, enjoying a pipe of tobacco. As we proceeded, the country became more bold, rough, and mountainous; but still covered with thick woods and heavy timber. The day being very hot, we encamped early on a very pleasant and thickly-wooded island — course, N.E.

On the 31st, after breakfast, Mr. Thompson and party left us to prosecute their journey, and Mr. Stuart, in one of our canoes, accompanied him as far [114] as the long narrows, nor did he return till late in the afternoon, and then thinking it too late to start, we passed the remainder of the day in camp, enjoying the repose which we had so much need of. The two strangers remained with us.

On Mr. Thompson's departure, Mr. Stuart gave him

[29] Wind River, in Skamania County, Washington.— ED.

one of our Sandwich Islanders, a bold and trustworthy fellow, named Cox, for one of his men, a Canadian, called Boulard. [30] Boulard had the advantage of being long in the Indian country, and had picked up a few words of the language on his way down. Cox, again, was looked upon by Mr. Thompson as a prodigy of wit and humour, so that those respectively acceptable qualities led to the exchange.

On the 1st of August we left our encampment at daylight, but a strong head-wind impeded our progress, and not being able to get on, we put ashore, and encamped at a much earlier hour than we wished. Course, N.E.

On the 2d, at three o'clock in the afternoon, we reached Sandy Bay, at the foot of the narrows. The Indians, being apprised of our coming, had assembled, as might be expected, in great numbers, and presented to us quite a new sight, being all armed *cap-à-pie*, painted, and mounted on horseback. To us in our present situation they were rather objects of terror than of attraction, but we had to put the best face we could on things, so we landed our goods and invited them to smoke with us.

We had not hitherto settled upon any plan, whether [115] to continue our route by water up the long narrows, or undertake the portage by land, both appearing equally difficult and equally dangerous: at last we adopted the latter plan, because it was recommended by the Indians, in whose power we were either way. The plan being now settled, we bargained with the chiefs for the carriage of the goods — ten metal buttons for each piece was the price

---

[30] Michel Boulard had since 1800 been a voyageur with Thompson. In 1806-07 he wintered at Rocky Mountain House, and the following spring crossed the range to Kootenay. The next four winters were spent in the mountains, and he was one of the seven canoe-men who brought Thompson to Astoria in July, 1811. For his later connection with the Astorians, see *post*.— ED.

stipulated, which reduced our stock by exactly two and a half gross: and in less than ten minutes after the whole cavalcade, goods and all, disappeared, leaving us standing in suspense and amazement. While we were in this painful state of anxiety, one man and an Indian were left to guard the canoes, whilst the rest of us, carrying what we could on our backs, followed the Indians on foot to the other end of the portage, where we arrived at sunset, and found, to our great satisfaction, all the property laid together in safety, and guarded by the chiefs. Having paid the Indians what we promised, and a small recompense to the different chiefs, we arranged our little camp for the night, the chiefs promising us their protection. All the Indians now flocked around us, men, women, and children, and spent the whole night in smoking, dancing and singing, while we kept watch in the centre of the ominous circle. During the night, however, notwithstanding the chief's guarantee of protection, we perceived some suspicious movements, which gave us considerable alarm. We had recourse again and again to the chiefs, who at last admitted [116] that there was some indication of danger; but added that they were still our friends, and would do their utmost to protect us. Just at this moment, as we were consulting with the chiefs, several harangues were made in the camp, the smoking ceased, and the women and children were beginning to move off. It was a critical moment; we saw the cloud gathering, but could not dispel it; our fate seemed to hang upon a hair. At last we hit upon a stratagem; we persuaded the chief to come and stop within our little circle for the night, which they did, and from that position they harangued in turn, which had a good effect, and in this manner we passed the night, not forgetting every now and then to give the chiefs some little toy or trifle, to stimulate their exertions in our favour.

Early in the morning of the 3rd, four of us returned to the other end of the portage, and by two o'clock got one of the canoes safe across.   Returning again immediately, we arrived with the other a little after dark; one man still remaining across, taking care of the canoe-tackling and camp utensils.   The Indians all the day kept dancing and smoking, and it was our interest to keep them so employed as much as possible; and no one knew better how to do so than Mr. Stuart, his eye saw everything at a glance, and his mild and insinuating manners won their affections.

As night came on, the Indians were to be seen divided in groups, as if in consultation; but there [117] appeared no sign of unanimity among them; each chief seemed occupied with his own little band, and we learned that they were not all one people, with one interest, or under one control, and this divided state no doubt added greatly to our safety; for wherever we found one chief alone, he invariably pointed to the others as bad men, calling them sho-sho-nez, or inlanders.   Not knowing, however, who were our friends or who our foes, we had to keep a strict watch all night.

At daybreak on the 4th, three of our men crossed the portage for the remainder of the goods, and arrived safely at an early hour, but had enough to do to save their kettles from some scamps they met with on the way.

The length of this dry and sandy portage is nine miles; and when it is taken into consideration that we had to go and come all that distance four times in one day, without a drop of water to refresh ourselves, loaded as we were, and under a burning sun, it will be admitted that it was no ordinary task.   Under any other circumstances but a struggle between life and death, it could never be performed; but it was too much; the effort was almost beyond human strength, and I may venture to say, all circumstances considered, it will never be done again.

The main camp of the Indians is situated at the head of the narrows, and may contain, during the salmon season, 3,000 souls, or more; but the constant inhabitants of the place do not exceed 100 [118] persons, and are called Wy-am-pams; [31] the rest are all foreigners from different tribes throughout the country, who resort hither, not for the purpose of catching salmon, but chiefly for gambling and speculation; for trade and traffic, not in fish, but in other articles; for the Indians of the plains seldom eat fish, and those of the sea-coast sell, but never buy fish. Fish is their own staple commodity. The articles of traffic brought to this place by the Indians of the interior are generally horses, buffalo-robes, and native tobacco, which they exchange with the natives of the sea-coast and other tribes, for the higua beads and other trinkets. But the natives of the coast seldom come up thus far. Now all these articles generally change hands through gambling, which alone draws so many vagabonds together at this place; because they are always sure to live well here, whereas no other place on the Columbia could support so many people together. The long narrows, therefore, is the great emporium or mart of the Columbia, and the general theatre of gambling and roguery.

We saw great quantities of fish everywhere; but what were they among so many: we could scarcely get a score of salmon to buy. For every fisherman there are fifty

---

[31] Ross's designations of Indian tribes differ from those of other travellers in this region. Lewis and Clark called the permanent dwellers at the narrows, Echelutes. Wyampam must be another name for the same tribe — a branch of the Upper Chinooks.— ED.

idlers, and all the fish caught are generally devoured on
the spot; so that the natives of the place can seldom lay
up their winter stock until the gambling season is over,
and their troublesome visitors gone.   All the gamblers,
horse-stealers, [119] and other outcasts throughout the
country, for hundreds of miles round, make this place their
great rendezvous during summer.

The narrows by water are not a great deal longer than
the portage by land.   At the upper end, during low water,
a broad and flat ledge of rocks bars the whole river across,
leaving only a small opening or portal, not exceeding forty
feet, on the left side, through which the whole body of
water must pass.   Through this gap it rushes with great
impetuosity; the foaming surges dash through the rocks
with terrific violence; no craft, either large or small, can
venture there in safety.   During floods, this obstruction,
or ledge of rocks, is covered with water, yet the passage of the narrows is not thereby improved.   Immediately above the rocks, the river resembles a small still
lake, with scarcely any current.

The general aspect of the country around the long
narrows cannot be called agreeable; the place is lone,
gloomy, and the surface rugged, barren, and rocky; yet
it is cheering in comparison with the dense forests which
darken the banks of the river to this place.   At the foot of
the narrows the whole face of nature is changed, like night
into day.   There the woody country ceases on both sides
of the river at once, and abruptly; the open and barren
plains begin.   The contrast is sudden, striking, and
remarkable.   Distance from the cascades to this place
seventy miles.

The great bend or elbow of the Columbia is [120]
formed by the long narrows: here, on the west side, termi-

nates that long, high, and irregular chain of mountains
which lie parallel to the coast, dividing the waters which
flow into the Pacific on the west, from those running into
the Columbia on the east. This range abounds in beaver
and elk, and is often frequented by the industrious hunter.
At the Indian tents we saw several small packages of
beaver, but we purchased none, our canoes being too
small; and, besides, they will always find their way to
Astoria. We have all along, however, impressed on the
natives the object of our visit to their country, and the
value of beaver.

The Indians have been more troublesome, more importunate and forward to-day than at any time since our
arrival among them. They often expressed a wish to see
what we had in our bales and boxes. The chiefs also gave
us to understand that their good offices merited a reward,
and they could not comprehend why people who had so
much as we were not more liberal. We endeavoured to
satisfy their demands, and towards evening the chiefs
were invited to sleep in our camp; but for us there was no
sleep: there is no rest for the wicked.

[121] CHAPTER VIII

Columbia Falls — A canoe swamped — Suspicious be-
haviour of the Indians — Stratagem — Umatallow —
Walla-Walla — Great body of Indians — Harangues —
Indian ceremonies — The great forks — Difference in
the waters — Length of the forks — The British flag —
Mr. Thompson's design — Indian ideas — Salmon —
European articles — Tummatapam — Departure from
the Forks — Indian honesty — Eyakema — Marl-hills
— Dead children — Superstitions — Priest's Rapid —
Rattlesnakes — Appearance of the country — Kewaugh-
chen — Perilous situation of a canoe — The two sisters

— The old Indian — Hunting party — Horses — The
priest — Piss-cows — Sopa — Great assemblage of
Indians — The comet — Oakinacken — Distance from
Astoria — Indian council — Resolve to winter — Some
account of the place — The stolen watch — The priest
dismissed — Voyage concluded — The two strangers —
First building — Division of the party — Lonely winter — The lost party — Indian trade — Mr. Stuart's
adventures.

On the 5th of August, early in the morning, after making
the chiefs a few presents, we proceeded, and had the
singular good luck to get off with the loss of only one
paddle.   As we left the beach, the sullen savages crowded
to the water's edge, and in silence stood and gazed at us,
as if reproaching themselves for their forbearance.   As
we proceeded, the banks [122] of the river were literally
lined with Indians.   Having ascended about seven miles,
we arrived at the falls — the great Columbia Falls, as they
are generally called; but, from the high floods this year,
they were scarcely perceptible, and we passed them without ever getting out of our canoes.   In seasons of low
water, however, the break or fall is about twenty feet high,
and runs across the whole breadth of the river, in an
oblique direction.   The face of the country about this place
is bare, rugged, and rocky, and, to our annoyance, every
point was swarming with Indians, all as anxious to get
to us as we were to avoid them.   Our exertions, and the
want of sleep for the last three nights in succession, almost
stupefied us, and we were the more anxious to find some
quiet resting-place for the night.   We halted a short
distance above the falls, and there encamped.   The
current was strong, and rapid the whole of this day.
Course, north.

On the 6th, after passing a comfortless and almost

sleepless night, owing to the crowd of Indians that had collected about us, we were on the water again before sunrise, stemming a strong and rapid current. About a mile from our last encampment, and opposite to a rocky island, the river Lowhum enters the Columbia on the east side. [32] Its breadth is considerable, but the depth of water at its mouth is scarcely sufficient to float an Indian canoe, and over the rocky bottom it made a noise like thunder. Proceeding from this place, we observed, a short distance ahead, [123] a very large camp of Indians, and in order to avoid them we crossed over towards the left shore; but found the current so powerful, that we had to lay our paddles aside and take to the lines. In this rather dangerous operation, we had frequently to scramble up among the rocks. Soon after, a few Indians volunteered their services to help us, and we found them very useful; but one of them, while conducting the line round a rock, endeavoured to cut it with a stone; he was detected, however, in the act, and just in time to prevent accident. Had the villain succeeded, not only the goods, but in all likelihood some lives would have been lost. The wind springing up, we hoisted sail; but found the experiment dangerous, owing to the rapidity of the current. We encamped at a late hour without seeing a single Indian. Course as yesterday.

On the 7th, early in the morning, we passed the river Day — not broad, but pretty deep, and distant about thirty miles from the river Lowhum. [33] In all directions,

---

[32] The river which Ross calls "Lowhum," had several designations among early travellers. Lewis and Clark call it "Towarnahiooks." All evidently endeavored to give it the Indian name, which was an imitation of the sound made by the falls at its mouth. It is at present known as Des Chutes River.— ED.

[33] Ross later relates the adventures of the pioneer John Day, from whom this river takes its name.— ED.

the face of the country is one wide and boundless plain, with here and there some trifling inequalities, but not a tree nor bush to be seen. General course as yesterday.

On the 8th, after a quiet and comfortable night's rest, we embarked early; and hoisting sail with a fair wind, we scudded along at a good rate till two o'clock in the afternoon, when, all of a sudden, a squall overtook us and broke the mast of one of our canoes, which, in the hurry and confusion of the moment, [124] filled with water, so that we had great difficulty in getting safe to shore.

The day being fine, we set about drying our things, and for that purpose began to spread them out, for every article had got thoroughly soaked; but this task we had no sooner commenced than the Indians flocked about us in great numbers. We therefore soon perceived the impropriety and danger of exhibiting so great a temptation before their eyes. In a few minutes we were almost surrounded by bows and arrows, one volley of which might have extinguished the expedition for ever; and one of the fellows had the audacity to shoot an arrow into one of our bales, as a warning of what might follow. In short, we thought we could read in the savage expression of their countenances some dark design; we therefore immediately commenced loading. Wet and dry were bundled together, and put into the canoes; and in order to amuse for a moment, and attract the attention of the crowd, I laid hold of an axe, and set it up at the distance of eighty yards, then taking up my rifle, drove a ball through it. This manœuvre had the desired effect. While the Indians stood gazing with amazement at the hole in the axe, our people were not idle. We embarked and got off without a word on either side. Having reached a small, snug island near the Suppa river, we put ashore for the night. [34] Course as yesterday.

The 9th, we remained all day encamped drying the goods, and were visited only by the Indians in one canoe, who sold us a fine salmon.

[125] On the 10th, at an early hour, we proceeded on our voyage, and met with no obstacle till the evening, when we arrived at the foot of a long and strong rapid, where we encamped near the mouth of a considerable river called Umatallow, which enters the Columbia here. This river takes its rise in a long range of blue mountains, which runs nearly east and west, and forms the northern boundary of the great Snake nation. Opposite to our encampment, on the west side, is situated a large mound or hill of considerable height, which, from its lonely situation and peculiar form, we called Dumbarton Castle. [35] During this day we saw many Indians, all occupied in catching salmon. Course as usual.

On the 11th we commenced ascending the rapid — a task which required all our skill and strength to accomplish; and paddles, poles, hauling lines, and carrying-straps were in requisition in turn, and yet half the day was consumed ere we got to the top. At the foot of this rapid, which is a mile in length, the river makes a quick bend to the east for about two miles, then comes gradually round again to the north from the head of the rapid. The channel of the river is studded on both sides with gloomy black rocks arranged like colonnades, for upwards of twenty

---

[34] The identification of "Suppa" River is uncertain. The largest affluent of the Columbia between John Day and Umatilla River is that Oregon stream now known as Willow Creek.— ED.

[35] For the Umatilla River, see Franchère, note 141. A large isolated cliff, just below the mouth of the Umatilla, is still called Castle Rock.— ED

miles. Here are some sandy islands also, on one of which we encamped; and a dark and cheerless encampment it was, surrounded and shaded by these gloomy heights.

On the 12th we left our camp early, and in a short [126] time came to the colonnade rocks, which suddenly terminated in two huge bluffs, one on each side of the river, exactly opposite to each other, like monumental columns. The river between these bluffs lies right south and north. [36] The banks of the river then become low with sand and gravel, and the plains open full to view again, particularly on the east side.

Close under the right bluff issues the meandering Walla-Walla, a beautiful little river, lined with weeping willows. It takes its rise in the blue mountains already noticed. At the mouth of the Walla-Walla a large band of Indians were encamped, who expressed a wish that we should pass the day with them. We encamped accordingly; yet for some time not an Indian came near us, and those who had invited us to pass the day with them seemed to have gone away; so that we were at a loss what construction to put upon their shyness. But in the midst of our perplexity we perceived a great body of men issuing from the camp, all armed and painted, and proceeded by three chiefs. The whole array came moving on in solemn and regular order till within twenty yards of our tent. Here the three chiefs harangued us, each in his turn; all the rest giving, every now and then, a vociferous shout of approbation when the speaker happened to utter some emphatical expression. The purport of these harangues was friendly, and as soon as the chiefs had finished they all sat down on the grass in a large circle, when the great calumet of peace

---

[36] The rapid here described, is now known as the Umatilla Rapid; Lewis and Clark designated it as "The Musselshell," from the heaps of those shells spread out upon the banks. The brigade had just passed the present boundary of Oregon, 46° of north latitude.— ED

was produced, and the smoking began. Soon [127] after the women, decked in their best attire, and painted, arrived, when the dancing and singing commenced — the usual symbols of peace and friendship; and in this pleasing and harmonious mood they passed the whole day.

The men were generally tall, raw-boned, and well dressed; having all buffalo-robes, deer-skin leggings, very white, and most of them garnished with porcupine quills. Their shoes were also trimmed and painted red;— altogether, their appearance indicated wealth. Their voices were strong and masculine, and their language differed from any we had heard before. The women wore garments of well dressed deer-skin down to their heels; many of them richly garnished with beads, higuas, and other trinkets — leggings and shoes similar to those of the men. Their faces were painted red. On the whole, they differed widely in appearance from the piscatory tribes we had seen along the river. The tribes assembled on the present occasion were the Walla-Wallas, the Shaw Haptens, and the Cajouses; forming altogether about fifteen hundred souls. [37] The Shaw Haptens and

[37] The Wallawalla Indians are of the Shahaptian stock — one of the great families of the inland Columbians, to which the Nez Percés and Umatilla belong. Usually they were hospitable and well-affected towards the whites. Lewis and Clark especially mention their friendly disposition. Many years later, they became disaffected and joined the Cayuse in acts of hostility. A treaty was made with the Wallawallas in 1855, whereby they surrendered their lands, and retired to the Umatilla reservation, where at the last report (1902) five hundred and sixty-nine were still residing. The "Shaw Haptens" were a kindred race speaking the Shahaptian language.

This appears to be the first mention of the Cayuse tribe, later so prominent in Oregon history. Their language was unlike that of the Wallawalla, so that they are classified as Waülatpuans. Their habitat was the Wallawalla Valley, and south and east of the great bend of the Columbia. Their herds of horses were so numerous that "cayuse" has become a generic term for Indian ponies. These Indians constituted the largest and most powerful tribe of Eastern Oregon. Among them the American Board founded a mission, and it was this tribe that perpetrated the Whitman massacre of 1847. Broken in spirit and numbers by the settlers' avenging warfare, five chiefs were in 1850 surrendered

Cajouses, with part of the Walla-Wallas, were armed with guns, and the others with bows and arrows. The names of the principal chiefs were (in the order of the tribes) Tummatapam, Quill-Quills-Tuck-a-Pesten, and Allowcatt. The plains were literally covered with horses, of which there could not have been less than four thousand in sight of the camp.

On the 13th, we prepared to be off as early as [128] possible; but Tummatapam would not let us go till we had breakfasted on some fine fresh salmon. He told us he would be at the forks before us. We then embarked, and continued our voyage. The banks on both sides of the river, above the Walla-Walla, are low, and the country agreeable. After passing three islands, we arrived at the forks late in the evening, and there encamped for the night. The crowd of Indians assembled at that place was immense, and among the rest was our friend Tummatapam. The Indians smoked, danced, and chanted all night, as usual, while we kept watch in turn.

On the 14th, early in the morning, what did we see waving triumphantly in the air, at the confluence of the two great branches, but a British flag, hoisted in the middle of the Indian camp, planted there by Mr. Thompson, as he passed, with a written paper, laying claim to the country north of the forks, as British territory. [38]

_____

for trial and executed. Five years later, the Cayuse formally ceded their lands and retired to the Umatilla reservation, where three hundred and ninety-one are now (1902) reported. They have abandoned their language for that of the Wallawalla.— ED.

[38] Thompson records (July 9, 1811) "½ a mile to the Junction of the Shawpatin [Snake] River with this the Columbia, here I erected a small Pole, with a half Sheet of Paper well tied about it, with these words on it — Know hereby that this country is claimed by Great Britain as part of its Territories, & that the N W Company of Merchants from Canada, finding the Factory for this People inconvenient for them, do intend to erect a Factory in this Place for the Commerce of the Country around. D. Thompson."— *Henry-Thompson Journals*, p. 748.— ED.

This edict interdicted the subjects of other states from trading north of that station; and the Indians at first seemed to hint that we could not proceed up the north branch, and were rather disposed to prevent us, by saying, that Koo-Koo-Sint — meaning Mr. Thompson — had told them so, pointing at the same time to the south branch, as if to intimate that we might trade there. The chiefs likewise stated that Koo-Koo-Sint had given them such and such things, and among others the British flag, that they should see his commands respected; but that if Mr. Stuart would give them [129] more than Koo-Koo-Sint had done, then he would be the greater chief, and might go where he pleased.

The opposition of the Indians on the present occasion suggested to our minds two things; first, that Mr. Thompson's motive for leaving us at the time he did was to turn the natives against us as he went along, with the view of preventing us from getting further to the north, where the North-West Company had posts of their own; and, secondly, that the tribes about the forks would prefer our going up the south branch, because then we would be in the midst of themselves. But it was our interest then to defeat these schemes, and so completely did we upset Mr. Thompson's plans, that I verily believe had he to pass there again, he would have some difficulty in effecting his purpose. Mr. Thompson's conduct reminds us of the husbandman and the snake in the fable. That he who had been received so kindly, treated so generously, and furnished so liberally by us, should have attempted to incite the Indians against us, in our helpless and almost forlorn state, was conduct which the world must condemn.

At the junction of the two great branches of the Columbia, the country around is open and very pleasant, and seems to be a great resort, or general rendezvous,

for the Indians on all important occasions.   The southeast branch is known by the name of Lewis's River, the
north by that of Clarke's, in honour of the first adventurers.[39]   They are both large rivers, but the north branch is
considerably the larger [130] of the two.   At the junction
of their waters, Lewis's River has a muddy or milk-and-
water appearance, and is warm;   while Clarke's River
is bluish, clear, and very cold.   The difference of colour,
like a dividing line between the two waters, continues for
miles below their junction.   These branches would seem,
from a rough chart the Indians made us, to be of nearly
equal length from the forks — perhaps 700 miles —
widening from each other towards the mountains, where
the distance between their sources may be 900 miles.

All the tributary rivers entering between this and the
falls, a distance of 200 miles, are on the east side.   The
most important fishing place on the Columbia, after the
long narrows, is here, or rather a little below this, towards
the Umatallow.   Yet although the salmon are very fine
and large, weighing from fifteen to forty pounds each,
they are not taken in the immense quantities which
some other countries boast of.   A Columbian fisherman
considers it a good day's work to kill 100 salmon, whereas,
at the Copper-Mine River, a fisherman will kill 1000 a
day;   and a Kamtschatkan, it is said, will kill, with the
same means, 10,000 a day;   but if these countries can
boast of numbers, the Columbia can boast of a better
quality and larger size.

The only European articles seen here with the Indians,

---

[39] Ross is here inaccurate.   The Snake River was called the Lewis; but to
the Columbia above the fork, the explorers never applied the name of Clark —
that was given to the large northern branch still called Clark's Fork of the
Columbia, upon whose upper waters the explorers rested when crossing the
mountains.— ED

and with which they seemed perfectly contented, were guns, and here and there a kettle, or a knife; and, indeed, the fewer the better. They [131] require but little, and the more they get of our manufacture the more unhappy will they be, as the possession of one article naturally creates a desire for another, so that they are never satisfied.

In the afternoon the chiefs held a council, at which Mr. Stuart and myself were present. It was then finally settled that we might proceed up the north branch, and that at all times we might count upon their friendship. This being done, Tummatapam came to our tent, smoked a pipe, and took supper with us; and as he was going off, Mr. Stuart presented him with a suit of his own clothes, which highly pleased the great man. The Indians having retired, we set the watch for the night as usual.

Tummatapam is a middle-aged man, well featured, and of a very agreeable countenance; and what is still better, he is, to all appearance, a good man, was very kind to us, and rendered us considerable service; but the other two chiefs appeared to take precedence of him in all matters of importance.

On the 16th, we left the forks and proceeded up the north branch, which to the eye is as broad and deep here as below the forks. About twelve miles up, a small river entered on the west side, called Eyakema. The landscape at the mouth of the Eyakema surpassed in picturesque beauty anything we had yet seen. [40] Here three Walla-Walla Indians overtook us on horseback, and to our agreeable surprise delivered us a bag of shot which we had left by mistake at our encampment of last night —

---

[40] The Yakima (Eyakema) River enters the Columbia from the east, about ten miles above the Snake. It is a large tributary, draining the eastern slope of the Cascade Range. Lewis and Clark called it the Tapteet. The Northern Pacific Railway follows the valley of the Yakima for some distance.— ED.

a convincing [132] proof that there is honesty among Indians; and if I recollect well, a similar circumstance, attesting the probity of the Walla-Wallas, occurred when Lewis and Clarke passed there in 1805. [41] We saw but few Indians to-day, and in the evening we encamped without a night watch, for the first time since we left Astoria. General course, north.

On the 17th, we were paddling along at daylight. On putting on shore to breakfast, four Indians on horseback joined us. The moment they alighted, one set about hobbling their horses, another to gather small sticks, a third to make a fire, and the fourth to catch fish. For this purpose, the fisherman cut off a bit of his leather shirt, about the size of a small bean; then pulling out two or three hairs from his horse's tail for a line, tied the bit of leather to one end of it, in place of a hook or fly. Thus prepared, he entered the river a little way, sat down on a stone, and began throwing the small fish, three or four inches long, on shore, just as fast as he pleased; and while he was thus employed, another picked them up and threw them towards the fire, while the third stuck them up round it in a circle, on small sticks; and they were no sooner up than roasted. The fellows then sitting down, swallowed them — heads, tails, bones, guts, fins, and all, in no time, just as one would swallow the yolk of an egg. Now all this was but the work of a few minutes; and before our man had his kettle ready for the fire, the Indians were already eating their breakfast. [133] When the fish had hold of the bit of wet leather, or bait, their teeth got entangled in it,

---

[41] It was on the return journey (May 1, 1806) that three Wallawalla overtook Lewis and Clark, with a steel trap which they had travelled a day's journey to restore.— ED.

so as to give time to jerk them on shore, which was to us a new mode of angling; fire produced by the friction of two bits of wood was also a novelty; but what surprised us most of all, was the regularity with which they proceeded, and the quickness of the whole process, which actually took them less time to perform, than it has taken me to note it down.

Soon after passing the Eyakema, a long range of marl hills interrupts the view on the east side of the river. Here two dead children were presented to us by their parents, in order that we might restore them to life again, and a horse was offered us as the reward. We pitied their ignorance, made them a small present, and told them to bury their dead. As we advanced along the marl hills, the river inclined gradually to the N.W. After a good day's work, we stopped for the night near a small camp of Indians, who were very friendly to us. Here and there were to be seen, on small eminences, burial-places. The dead are interred, and a few small sticks always point out the cemetery.

On the 18th, we reached the end of the marl hills. Just at this place the river makes a bend right south for about ten miles, when a high and rugged hill confines it on our left. Here the increasing rapidity of the current gave us intimation that we were not far from some obstruction ahead; and as we advanced a little under the brow of the hill, a strong [134] and rocky rapid presented itself in the very bend of the river. Having ascended it about half way, we encamped for the night.

Here a large concourse of Indians met us, and after several friendly harangues, commenced the usual ceremony of smoking the pipe of peace: after which they passed the night in dancing and singing. The person who stood foremost in all these introductory ceremonies, was a tall, meagre, middle-aged Indian, who attached himself very closely to us from the first moment we saw him. He was called Ha-qui-laugh, which signifies doctor, or rather priest; and as this personage will be frequently mentioned in the sequel of our narrative, we have been thus particular in describing him. We named the place ''Priest's Rapid,'' after him.

The name of the tribe is Ska-moy-num-acks; they appear numerous and well affected towards the whites. From the Priest's Rapid, in a direct line by land to the mouth of the Umatallow, the distance is very short, owing to the great bend of the river between the two places.

The Priest's Rapid is more than a mile in length, and is a dangerous and intricate part of the navigation. The south side, although full of rocks and small channels, through which the water rushes with great violence, is the best to ascend.

On the 19th, early in the morning, we started, but found the channel so frequently obstructed with rocks, whirlpools, and eddies, that we had much difficulty [135] in making any headway. Crossing two small portages, we at length, however, reached the head of it, and there encamped for the night, after a very hard day's labour, under a burning sun. From the head of the Priest's Rapid, the river opens again due north.

The ground here is everywhere full, covered with flat stones, and wherever these stones lie, and indeed elsewhere, the rattlesnakes are very numerous. At times they may be heard hissing all around, so that we had to keep a sharp look-out to avoid treading on them; but the natives appeared to have no dread of them. As soon as one appears, the Indians fix its head to the ground with a small forked stick round the neck, then extracting the fang or poisonous part, they take the reptile into their hands, put it into their bosoms, play with it, and let it go again. When any one is bitten by them, the Indians tie a ligature above the wounded part, scarify it, and then apply a certain herb to the wound, which they say effectually cures it.

On the 20th we left the Priest's Rapid, and proceeded against a strong ripply current and some small rapids, for ten miles, when we reached two lofty and conspicuous bluffs, situate directly opposite to each other, like the piers of a gigantic gate, between which the river flowed smoothly. Here we staid for the night, on some rocks infested with innumerable rattlesnakes, which caused us not a little uneasiness during the night. From this place due [136] east, the distance, in a direct line, to the marl hills left on the 18th is very short. At the southern angle of this flat is situated the Priest's Rapid, which we left this morning. Course, north.

Early on the 21st, we were again on the water. The country on the east side is one boundless rough and barren plain; but on the west, the rocks, after some distance, close in to the water's edge, steep and rugged, and the whole country behind is studded with towering heights and rocks, giving the whole face of the country, in that direction, a bleak, broken, and mountainous appearance. We saw but few natives to-day, but those few were very friendly to us. Towards evening we put ashore for the night, at a late hour. General course, north.

On the 22nd we left our camp early, and soon reached the foot of a very intricate and dangerous rapid, so full of

rocks that at some little distance off the whole channel of
the river, from side to side, seemed to be barred across, and
the stream to be divided into narrow channels, whirlpools,
and eddies, through which we had to pass. At the
entrance of one of these channels, a whirlpool caught one
of the canoes, and after whirling her round and round
several times, threw her out of the channel altogether
into a chain of cascades, down which she went, sometimes
the stem, sometimes stern foremost. In this critical manner
she descended to the foot of the rapids, and at last stuck
fast upon a rock, when, after much trouble and danger,
we succeeded in throwing [137] lines to the men, and
ultimately got all safe to shore. Here we encamped for
the night, and spent the remainder of the day in drying the
goods, mending the canoe, and examining the rapid.

On the 23rd we again commenced ascending, and
found on the right-hand side a neck of land, where we
made a portage: from thence we towed ourselves among
the rocks, from one to another, until we reached the head
of the rapid, and a most gloomy and dismal rapid it was.
Both sides of the river at this place is rocky, and in no part
of the Columbia is the view more confined. A death-like
gloom seems to hang over the glen. This rapid, which
is called Ke-waugh-tohen, after the tribe of Indians
inhabiting the place, who call themselves Ke-waugh-
tohen-emachs, is about thirty miles distant from the
Priest's Rapid. [42]

Having got clear of the rapid early in the day, we
proceeded on a smooth current for some little distance,

[42] This is the Gualquil Rapid, one hundred and ten miles above the mouth
of Snake River. The Kewaughtohenemachs are mentioned only by Ross;
they were probably a Pisquow tribe. For a description of the Columbia above
the entrance of the Snake, see Symons, *Upper Columbia River* (Washington,
1882.)—ED.

when the river makes a short bend nearly west. Here, on the south side, were observed two pillars on the top of an eminence, standing erect side by side, which we named the Two Sisters. [43] They proved to be of lime- stone, and at a little distance very much resembled two human figures. From the Two Sisters, the river turns to the north again, where once more we had a sight of the open country. Nature, in these gloomy defiles just passed through, wears the dreary aspect of eternal winter. On the west, the hills are clothed with woods; but on the east side, the plains are bleak and barren. On a [138] beautiful green spot, near a small Indian camp, we put ashore and passed the night. Here the priest, for the reader must know he had still followed us, introduced us to a friendly Indian, called Ma-chy-keu-etsa, or the Walking Bear. This gray-headed, little, old man made us comprehend that he had seen eighty-four winters or snows, as he expressed himself — he looked very old, but was still active, and walked well.

On the 24th we embarked early, and soon reached the mouth of Pisscow's river, a beautiful stream, which empties itself into the Columbia, through a low valley, skirted on each side by high hills. Its mouth, in the present high state of the water, is eighty yards broad. [44] Here the

---

[43] Column Bluffs is the usual designation of this point on the river, about ten miles above Gualquil Rapid. According to an Indian legend, two wicked women who lived here were accustomed to kill those who passed. The Indians begged the Great Spirit to destroy them, and he, answering their prayer, sent an immense bird which picked out their brains and turned them into stone.— ED.

[44] Lewis and Clark called this river Wahnaacha, after the tribe of Pisquow Indians of that name who dwelt along its banks. Wenatchee and Pischous are both used to designate the stream at the present time. It takes its rise in the Wenatchee Mountains and flows southeastward, emptying into the Columbia one hundred and forty-eight miles from the mouth of the Snake. The Great Northern Railway follows its course.— ED.

Indians met us in great numbers, and vied with each other in acts of kindness. Sopa, the chief, made us a present of two horses, and others offered some for sale. We purchased four, giving for each one yard of print and two yards of red gartering, which was so highly prized by them that horses from all quarters were brought to us; but we declined buying any more, not knowing what to do with them. Our six horses were now delivered over in charge to the priest, who was to proceed with them by land.

The higher we ascend the river, the more friendly and well disposed are the aborigines towards us. Sopa invited us to pass the day with him, which we did, and were highly gratified to see the natives hunt the wild deer on horseback. They killed several [139] head of game close to our camp, and we got a two days' supply of venison from them. Sopa and his tribe kept smoking, dancing, and singing the whole night, and at every pause a loud and vociferous exclamation was uttered, denoting that they were happy now. The whites had visited their land, poverty and misery would no longer be known amongst them; we passed the night without keeping watch.

On the 25th we left Pisscows, and proceeded on our voyage, passing another small river, named Intyclook, and from thence to Oak Point, at the foot of a steep crag, where we passed the night. [45]

Early in the morning of the 26th we left our encamp-

[45] Oak Point, mentioned so frequently in accounts of Columbian exploration, was near Astoria — Franchère, note 74. The one here referred to must be near the mouth of the Entiatqua (Entiyatecoom) River, known to the Canadian voyageurs as Point de Bois. The Entiatqua, which Ross calls Intyclook, is a small stream about a hundred feet wide, flowing into the Columbia from the west, fifteen miles above the Pischous.— ED

ment, but the stream becoming more and more rapid, we advanced but slowly, and towards evening had a good deal of pulling or hauling to ascend Whitehill rapid, where the river, almost barred across by a ledge of low flat rocks, makes several quick bends. The west side is mountainous and gloomy to the water's edge. Encamping at the head of the rapid, we passed a quiet night, nor did a single Indian trouble us. [46] Here we saw the ibex, the white musk goat, and several deer, [47] and supped on a half devoured salmon, which a white-headed eagle had very opportunely taken out of the river. Course, north.

On the 27th we started early, and about ten o'clock passed a small but rapid stream, called by the natives Tsill-ane, which descended over the rocks in white broken sheets. [48] The Indians told us it took [140] its rise in a lake not far distant. From Tsill-ane, the hills on the west side receded, and the river became smooth. Meeting with some Indians, we put ashore, and the priest, with his horses, joining us soon after, we passed the night together. Here we got some salmon, roots, and berries from the Indians, which proved a very seasonable supply. The Indians were very friendly, communicative, and intelligent.

On the 28th, after despatching the priest with his

---

[46] Between Oak Point and White Hill Rapid the west bank is a continuous volcanic bluff about two thousand feet high and striped with different-colored strata — white, gray, black, and dark brown. The rapid was doubtless named from the white hills on the eastern side.— ED.

[47] Concerning these animals, see Franchère, note 172.— ED.

[48] This is the Chelan River, which empties into the Columbia from the northwest, about one hundred and eighty-five miles above the Snake. It is but two and a half miles long, is the outlet of a considerable lake of the same name, and has a fall of two hundred and fifty feet. Just above its mouth was the principa village of the Chelan tribe, a branch of the Salish. A military post was established on this lake (1880), but not long after was removed to Spokane.— ED.

charge, we left our camp and pursued our voyage against a strong current. The country on both sides was open, and the banks of the river low, yet many rapid places detained us long, and this detention was increased by a strong head-wind, which so fatigued us that we halted early. On our way to-day, we saw many deer and some beavers swimming about, but they were very shy.

On the 29th we reached the foot of a short but strong rapid, where the river abruptly veers round to east. Opposite to this rapid enters a tributary stream, which the Indians call Buttle-mule-emauch, or Salmon-fall River. [49] It is less than the Pisscows, shallow, and full of stones, having its source near the foot of some lofty mountain not far distant. After making a discharge, we got over the rapid, and encamped for the night. Here the Indians assembled in friendly crowds, according to their usual habit — presented us with abundance of salmon, offered many horses for sale, and were in all other respects exceedingly [141] kind. Here also they invited us to remain, to build, and to winter among them: they said their country abounded in beaver, nor should we want for provisions.

On the 30th, just as we were pushing off from the shore early in the morning, a large band of Indians, all mounted on horseback, arrived at our camp: we immediately put about to receive them, which was no sooner done than harangue after harangue, smoking, and speechifying commenced; and after one party, another arrived, so that we were absolutely obliged to remain the whole day where we were.

From the strangers we learned that there were whites

---

[49] Ross also calls this the Meathow River, and Methow is at present the usual appellation. The rapids just below the mouth have been named Ross Rapids, probably in honor of our author.— ED.

before us, but a long way off. The Indians showed us a gun, tobacco, and some other articles, which they said had been purchased from the whites ahead, which confirmed the report. We therefore at once suspected that it must be a party of the North-Westerns; and here Mr. Stuart, for the first time, began to think of finding a suitable place to winter in.

On the 31st, we parted early from our friendly visitors, and shaping our course in an easterly direction along the bend of the river, we pushed on for about nine miles till we reached the mouth of a smooth stream called Oakinacken, which we ascended for about two miles, leaving the main Columbia for the first time, and then pitched our tents for the night. A great concourse of Indians followed us all [142] day, and encamped with us. After acquainting them with the object of our visit to their country, they strongly urged us to settle among them. For some time, however, Mr. Stuart resisted their pressing solicitations, chiefly with the view of trying their sincerity; but, at last consenting, the chiefs immediately held a council, and then pledged themselves to be always our friends, to kill us plenty of beavers, to furnish us at all times with provisions, and to ensure our protection and safety.

During this afternoon we observed, for the first time, about 20° above the horizon, and almost due west, a very brilliant comet, with a tail about 10° long. The Indians at once said it was placed there by the Good Spirit — which they called Skom-malt-squisses — to announce to them the glad tidings of our arrival; and the omen impressed them with a reverential awe for us, implying that we had been sent to them by the Good Spirit, or Great Mother of Life.

On the 1st of September, 1811, we embarked, and descending the Oakinacken again, landed on a level spot, within half a mile of its mouth. There we unloaded, took our canoes out of the water, and pitched our tents — which operation concluded our long and irksome voyage of forty-two days.

The mouth of the Oakinacken is situate 600 miles up the Columbia, and enters it through a low level plain, a mile wide. This plain is surrounded on all sides by high hills, so that in no direction does the view extend far.

[143] The source of the Oakinacken is 280 miles due north, and in its course south the stream runs through three lakes: near its junction with the Columbia, it is hemmed in on the east by a sloping range of high rocky hills, at the foot of which the two rivers meet. On the south bank of the Oakinacken, half a mile from its mouth, was the site pitched upon for the new establishment.

The general aspect of the surrounding country is barren and dreary. On the west the hills are clothed with thick woods — a dense forest: on the south and east, the scene is bare; but to the north the banks of the river were lined with the willow and poplar, and the valley through which it meanders presents a pleasing landscape.

Here it may be remarked, that all the tributary rivers from this place to the falls, a distance of 200 miles, enter on the right-hand, or west, side of the Columbia, having their sources in the lofty range of mountains which terminates at the great narrows, as noticed by me on the 4th of August; so that from this point, or rather a few miles below this, the Columbia runs south to the narrows; nor is the distance from this place to the Pacific, in a direct line due west by land, far off. If we can rely on Indian report, it is not 150 miles. [50]

[50] The distance is really about one hundred and twenty-five miles. For a brief history of Okanagan post, see Franchère, note 71.— ED.

Soon after the tent was pitched, the priest arrived with his horses all safe. In the course of the day, Mr. Stuart missed his time-piece, which had been stolen out of the tent: a general search was made, and [144] the watch was found, by hearing it strike, although concealed under the dry sand in the face of the bank. The theft was traced to the holy man, the priest, which circumstance greatly lessened the high opinion we had formed of him. On this discovery being made, he was paid for his services and dismissed.

This little incident taught us that, however strong might be the friendly professions of the natives, it was still necessary to guard against their pilfering propensities.

In the account of our voyage, I have been silent as to the two strangers who cast up at Astoria, and accompanied us from thence; but have noticed already, that instead of being man and wife, as they at first gave us to understand, they were in fact both women — and bold adventurous amazons they were. In accompanying us, they sometimes shot ahead, and at other times loitered behind, as suited their plans. The stories they gave out among the unsuspecting and credulous natives, as they passed, were well calculated to astonish as well as to attract attention. Brought up, as they had been, near the whites — who rove, trap, and trade in the wilderness — they were capable of practising all the arts of well-instructed cheats; and, to effect their purpose the better, they showed the Indians an old letter, which they made a handle of, and told them that they had bent sent by the great white chief, with a message to apprize the natives in general that gifts, consisting of goods and implements of all kinds, were forthwith [145] to be poured in upon them; that the great white chief knew their wants, and was just about to supply them with everything their hearts could desire; that the

whites had hitherto cheated the Indians, by selling goods
in place of making presents to them, as directed by the
great white chief. These stories, so agreeable to the
Indian ear, were circulated far and wide; and not only
received as truths, but procured so much celebrity for the
two cheats, that they were the objects of attraction at every
village and camp on the way: nor could we, for a long
time, account for the cordial reception they met with from
the natives, who loaded them for their good tidings with
the most valuable articles they possessed — horses,
robes, leather, and higuas; so that, on our arrival at
Oakinacken, they had no less than twenty-six horses,
many of them loaded with the fruits of their false reports.

As soon as we could get the distant tribes, who had
come to welcome our arrival, dismissed, we commenced
erecting a small dwelling-house, sixteen by twenty feet,
chiefly constructed of drift wood, being more handy and
easier got than standing timber; but, while the building
was in a half-finished state, Messrs. Pillet and M'Lennan,
with two men, were dispatched to Astoria, as had been
agreed upon. Mr. Stuart, with Montigny and the two
remaining men, set off on a journey towards the north, or
head waters of the Oakinacken, intending to return in the
course of a month; while I was to remain alone at [146]
the establishment till Mr. Stuart's return; my only
civilized companion being a little Spanish pet dog from
Monterey, called Weasel.

Only picture to yourself, gentle reader, how I must
have felt, alone in this unhallowed wilderness, without
friend or white man within hundreds of miles of me, and
surrounded by savages who had never seen a white man
before. Every day seemed a week, every night a month.
I pined, I languished, my head turned gray, and in a brief

space ten years were added to my age.   Yet man is born
to endure, and my only consolation was in my Bible.

The first thing I did after my friends left me, was to
patch up the house a little, and put the few goods I had,
so tempting to Indians, into a kind of cellar which I made
in the middle of the house.   This done, I set to in earnest
to learn the Indian language, and wrote vocabulary after
vocabulary;   and although the task was a hard one, I
soon found, from my progress, that perseverance would
overcome many difficulties.

The novelty of white men, and particularly of a white
man alone, drew crowds of inquisitive Indians about the
place.   I mixed with them, traded with them, and at last
began to talk with them, and from a constant intercourse
soon came to understand them;   but still the evenings
were long, and the winter dreary.   Every night before
going to bed I primed my gun and pistol anew, and
barricaded the door of my lonely dwelling;   and the
Indians, [147] friendly inclined, always withdrew from
the house at dusk;   yet they had often alarms among
themselves, and often gave me to understand that enemies,
or ill-disposed Indians, were constantly lurking about;
and whenever they began to whoop or yell in the night,
which they frequently did, I of course partook of the
alarm.

One night I was suddenly awakened out of my sleep
by the unusual noise and continual barking of Weasel,
running backwards and forwards through the house. Half
asleep, half awake, I felt greatly agitated and alarmed. My
faithful gun and pistol were at hand, for they lay always at
my side in bed; but then all was dark, I could see nothing,
could hear nothing but the barking of Weasel, which was
continually growing louder and louder.   I then thought

there must be somebody in the house; for I was ready to put the worst construction on appearances. In this perplexing dilemma I got my hand, with as little noise as possible, to the muzzle of my gun, and gradually drawing out the ramrod, tried, with my right arm stretched out, to stir up the embers, so that I might see; but here again a new danger presented itself; I was exposing myself as a mark to a ball or an arrow, without the chance of defending myself, for the light would show me to the enemy before I could see my object; but there was no alternative, and something must be done. Between hope and despair I managed to stir up the ashes, so that I could see little Weasel running [148] to and fro to the cellar-door. I concluded that the enemy must be skulking in the cellar. I then, but not without difficulty, got a candle lighted. Holding the candle in my left hand, I laid hold of my pistol. With the lynx-eye and wary step of a cat ready to pounce on its prey, I advanced rather obliquely, with my right arm stretched out at full length holding the cocked pistol, till I got to the cellar-door, the little dog all the while making a furious noise; when, lo! what was there but a skunk sitting on a roll of tobacco! The shot blew it almost to atoms, and so delicately perfumed everything in the house that I was scarcely able to live in it for days afterwards; but that was not all, the trivial incident was productive of very bad consequences. Several hundreds of Indians being encamped about the place at the time, no sooner did they see the light, or hear the shot, than they all rushed into the house, thinking something serious had happened. So far, however, there were no great harm; but when they beheld two rolls of tobacco and two small bales of goods, it appeared such wealth in their eyes that they could scarcely recover from the surprise. These tempting articles I had endeavoured all along to keep as much as possible out of their sight, and dealt them out with a sparing hand, and as long as the Indians did not see them in bulk all went well; but after the overwhelming exhibition of so much property there was no satisfying them. They became importunate [149] and troublesome for some time, and caused me much anxiety. The time fixed for Mr. Stuart's return had now arrived, and I most anxiously looked for him every hour. Often had I reason to curse the intrusion of the skunk into my house. After some time, however, things settled down again to their usual level, and good order and good feelings were again renewed between us.

October had now passed by and November also, but no Mr. Stuart came, and various reports were circulated by the Indians as to his fate; and I myself now began to despair of his return. The delay of Mr. Stuart's party had a visible effect on the conduct of the Indians; they became more bold, neglected their hunting, and loitered about the place, as if in expectation of some sudden change. Strange Indians were every day swelling the camp; they held councils, too; altogether they were a changed people.

Seeing this unfavourable change fast spreading among the Indians, in consequence of Mr. Stuart's delay, I set about counteracting it. I assembled all the chiefs and other great men, and after smoking the pipe of friendship, told them not to be uneasy at Mr. Stuart's absence; that I could easily account for it; that finding the country rich in furs as he went along, and the Indians peaceable and

. well disposed, he had most probably gone off to the white men's land for more goods, and would be back early with a rich supply and many people, so that [150] all their wants would be satisfied; that those who hunted best would get most; that they had better exert themselves in hunting and procuring furs; that their success would entitle them to the favour of Mr. Stuart and the great white chief; and that I would not fail to represent their conduct in the fairest light. This harangue had the desired effect. The Indians set to hunting in earnest, and kept bringing in furs regularly, and in other respects behaved exceedingly well during the whole of the winter.

Thus I wished to make them believe what I did not believe myself, because in my critical situation safety required it. But to return to Mr. Stuart: December now was passed, and the new year of 1812 ushered in; but still there was no account of the absent party. January passed, and likewise February, but no Mr. Stuart; nor was it till the 22nd of March that little Weasel announced, early in the morning, the approach of strangers, and I was rejoiced to meet again at my lonely dwelling my long-expected friends all safe and well.

During Mr. Stuart's absence of 188 days I had procured 1550 beavers, besides other peltries, worth in the Canton market 2,250*l.* sterling, and which on an average stood the concern in but 5½*d*, a piece, valuing the merchandize at sterling cost, or in round numbers 35*l.* sterling; a specimen of our trade among the Indians!

Here follows Mr. Stuart's account of his journey: [151] —"After leaving this place," said he, "we bent our course up the Oakinacken, due north, for upwards of 250 miles, till we reached its source; then crossing a height of land fell upon Thompson's River, or rather the south branch of

Fraser's River, [51] after travelling for some time amongst a powerful nation called the She Whaps. The snow fell while we were here in the mountains, and precluded our immediate return; and after waiting for fine weather the snows got so deep that we considered it hopeless to attempt getting back, and, therefore, passed our time with the She Whaps and other tribes in that quarter. [52] The Indians were numerous and well disposed, and the country throughout abounds in beavers and all other kinds of fur; and I have made arrangements to establish a trading post there the ensuing winter. On the 26th of February we began our homeward journey, and spent just twenty-five days on our way back. The distance may be about 350 miles."

[152] CHAPTER IX

Anxieties at Astoria — Indians depart — A schooner built — The *Dolly's* first trip — Criminal curiosity — The powder keg — The schooner condemned — Mr. Astor's cargoes — His policy — Remarks on the North-West coast — Unwelcome rumours — Calpo's statement — Rumours renewed — Hard cases — Joe Lapierre — Kasiascall's account of the *Tonquin* — Strange Indian — Kasiascall's conduct — His character — His design on Astoria — Remarks.

HAVING in the preceding chapters given a detailed

---

[51] This river was discovered by the explorer Thompson (for whom see Franchère, note 61). It has two large branches, a northern and an eastern, which unite at Lake Kamloops, one hundred and fifty miles directly north of the Okanagan post; the united stream then flows southwest for about ninety miles and unites with the Fraser. Thompson, thinking that he was upon the Columbia, descended its northern branch to the forks.— ED.

[52] The Shushwaps (She Whaps) are a branch of the Salishan family and closely allied in language and habits to the tribes about Okanagan post. They were also called Atnahs (strangers), a name given them by the Carrier Indians, farther to the northwest. They formerly occupied the country along the Thompson and its branches, but by 1900 they were reduced to fifty-four persons.— ED.

account of our first expedition into the interior, we propose in the present briefly to notice the state of things at Astoria after our departure, and the fate of the *Tonquin*.

No sooner had we left the establishment in July last, than the natives became more and more hostile and annoying to the whites at Astoria, so that under the impression of danger, all other labour being suspended, the hands and minds of all were employed both day and night in the construction and pallisading of a stronghold for self-defence; but after various alarms the savage horde, without making any hostile demonstration more than usual, took their departure [153] from the place, leaving the whites once more in the enjoyment of peace and tranquillity.

In the fall of the year, a schooner, of twenty-five tons, to be named the *Dolly*, the frame of which had come out in the *Tonquin*, was built at Astoria. This vessel was intended only for the coast trade; but in the present instance was placed as a guard-ship in front of the infant establishment. She was found, however, to be too small for the coast trade, and even unfit for tripping up and down the river; and from her unwieldiness, not so safe as either open boats or canoes. The people were also awkward and unskilful, as might be expected, having never been accustomed to such duties. In the very first trip up the river, she had well nigh fallen into the hands of the Indians: getting becalmed one day a little above the mouth of the Wallamitte, with only four men on board, curiosity drew a crowd of Indians about her, and once on board it was no easy matter to get them off again. Curiosity led to theft: every one began to help himself, and to take whatever he could lay his hands upon. The pillage was begun, when the interpreter boldly and opportunely

called out that he was going instantly to set fire to a keg
of powder, and would blow all up into the air, unless
they left the ship that moment: the Indians got frightened;
those who had canoes jumped into them, made for shore
with the hurry of despair; others jumped overboard,
and in an instant the vessel was cleared of her troublesome
visitors, and let go before [154] the current. It will be
recollected that Mr. Aikins, the officer who had come out
to take command of the *Dolly*, was, with several others,
unfortunately drowned on the bar. Having made two
or three trips up the river, she was condemned, and laid
aside altogether as useless.

It is a true saying, that the wisest of us is not always
wise. In appointing so small a vessel as the *Dolly* to a
station so dangerous, was manifested a total ignorance
of the character of the natives on the coast. Mr. Astor
ought to have known that even well appointed large and
armed ships often ran great hazards there, some of that
class having been taken and pillaged by the hostile savages
of that quarter.

The American traders, with their usual spirit of enterprize, had long carried on a lucrative business on the
north-west coast; they knew well, and none knew better
than Astor himself, what was necessary and suitable for
that market; but we had got nothing of this kind. Instead of guns, we got old metal pots and gridirons; instead
of beads and trinkets, we got white cotton; and instead of
blankets, molasses. In short, all the useless trash and
unsaleable trumpery which had been accumulating in his
shops and stores for half a century past, were swept
together to fill his Columbia ships. That these cargoes
were insured need not be told; sink or swim, his profits
were sure.

But these we might have overlooked, had we not [155] felt aggrieved in other matters closely connected with the general interest.   The articles of agreement entered into, and the promises of promotion held out, when the company was formed, were violated, and that without a blush, by the very man at the head of the concern,— that man who held its destinies in his hand.   This perhaps may be rendered a little more intelligent, by stating, that according to the articles of co-partnership made at New York, two of the clerks were to be promoted to an interest in the concern, or, in other words, to become partners, after two years' service, and on that express condition they joined the enterprize; but what will the reader say, or the world think, when it is told that a young man who had never seen the country was, by a dash of the pen, put over their heads, and this young man was no other than Mr. Astor's nephew.   Although a little out of place, we shall just mention another circumstance which may show how deeply and how sincerely Mr. Astor was interested in the success and prosperity of his Columbia colony. When the war broke out between Great Britain and the United States, the Boston merchants sent out, at a great expense, intelligence of the event to their shipping on the north-west coast, and applied to Astor for his quota of that expense, as he too had people and property there at stake.   What was his reply?   ''Let the United States' flag protect them.''   Need it then be told that we were left to shift for ourselves.   So much did Mr. Astor care about our safety.

[156] But from this disagreeable subject we turn to another still more so, and that is the fate of the unfortunate *Tonquin*, which ship, it will be remembered, left Astoria in June last.

On the 5th of August, Calpo, [63] a friendly Chinook Indian, informed M'Dougall that it was current among the Indians that the *Tonquin* had been destroyed by the natives along the coast, and this was the first tidings the Astorians had of her fate: the report had spread quickly and widely, although we remained ignorant of the fact; for not many days after we had arrived at Oakinacken, a party of Indians reached that place, on their return from the Great Salt Lake, as they called it, and gave us to understand by signs and gestures that a large ship, with white people in it, had been blown up on the water; and, in order the better to make us comprehend the subject, they threw up their arms in the air, blew with the mouth, and made the wild grimace of despair, to signify the explosion. On our part all was conjecture and suspense, unwilling as we were to believe what we did not wish to be true; but the more we reflected, the more we were disposed to believe the report, from the well-known fact that Mr. Astor's choice of a captain was most unfortunate: in this instance, he seemed to have wanted his usual sagacity; and this was the first rock on which his grand enterprize had split. A man who could deliberately leave, as we have already seen, nine of his fellow-creatures to perish on the Falkland Islands; [157] who could throw one of his sailors overboard, at the Island of Woahoo; who could offer the Indians at Owhyhee a reward for the head of one of his own officers; who could force from his ship four of his men in a storm, to perish at the mouth of the Columbia; who could witness unmoved, from his own deck, three of his men left to perish on Columbia bar; and, to cap the climax of cruelty, we might, however disagreeable, mention another circumstance. On the 11th of

[63] For an account of this Indian, see Franchère, note 46.— ED.

February, 1811, while sailing on the high seas, a man named Joe Lapierre fell from the mainmast-head overboard, the ship at the time going eight knots — a boat was instantly lowered: in the mean time a hen-coop, binnacle, and some boards were thrown into the water, but he failed to get hold of anything, and soon fell a good mile or more astern. When picked up he was in a state of insensibility, and the crew made all possible haste to reach the ship; but, as they were approaching, the captain, in a peremptory tone, ordered them back to pick up the hen-coop, binnacle, and boards, before they came alongside, or put the man on board. The boat obeyed orders, went back again, picked up all, and returned to the ship at the end of fifty-two minutes — yet life was not quite extinct, for, after applying the usual remedies of salt, warm blankets, and friction, Lapierre revived.

But to return to the subject of Calpo's report — the conduct of Captain Thorn throughout, coupled with the fact of his having left Astoria without a [158] single officer on board his ship, led strongly to the conclusion that all was not right, and that the reports in circulation might ultimately prove true. The facts above stated I myself witnessed — fifty others witnessed them also: they cannot be denied nor gainsaid — yet such was the man who enjoyed Mr. Astor's unbounded confidence.

Various and conflicting were the reports that had from time to time reached Astoria respecting the fate of the *Tonquin*; yet all agreed in the main point — that is, in her destruction. She had also passed, by some months, the time of her expected return, so that there remained but little doubt of her fate; yet, subsequently to Calpo's statement, nothing transpired to add to our fears for a month or two, although during that time various individuals and parties had been employed to trace out the true story of her fate.

On the 12th of October, however, three Chinooks were fitted out, and set off with the determination not to return until they should reach the place where it was reported she had been cut off, or obtain certain accounts respecting her. These men had not, however, proceeded far, before they were met by a strange Indian, on his way to Astoria with the unwelcome news of the *Tonquin's* tragical end: so the Chinooks turned about, and accompanied the stranger back to Astoria, where they arrived on the eighth day; and here the strange Indian made his report, which we shall give in his own words:—[54]

[159] "My name is Kasiascall, but the Chinooks and other Indians hereabout call me Lamazu. I belong to the Wick-a-nook tribe of Indians near Nootka Sound. I have often been on board ships. The whites call me Jack. I understand most of the languages that are spoken along the coast. I can speak some Chinook, too. I have been twice at this place before; once by land and once by sea. I saw the ship *Tonquin*; Captain Thorn was her commander. I went on board of her at Woody Point harbour in June last. We remained there for two days. We then sailed for Vancouver's Island; and just as we had got to it, a gale of wind drove us to sea, and it was three days before we got back again. The fourth morning we cast anchor in Eyuck Whoola, Newcetu Bay. There we remained for some days; Indians going and coming, but not much trade. One day the Indians came on board in great numbers, but did not trade much,

---

[54] Compare Franchère's account of the destruction of the "Tonquin" with this of Ross. The village was Newity or New Whitty. Nootka Sound is on the west coast of Vancouver Island, in latitude 49° 50' north.—|ED.

although they had plenty of skins. The prices offered did not please the Indians; so they carried back their furs again.   The day following the chiefs came on board, and as usual asked the captain to show them such and such things, and state the lowest price, which he accordingly did.   They did not, however, trade, but pressed the captain for presents, which he refused.   The chiefs left the ship displeased at what they called stingy conduct in the captain, as they were accustomed to receive trifling presents from the traders on the coast.

"In the evening of the same day, Mr. M'Kay and [160] myself went on shore, and were well received by the chiefs, and saw a great many sea-otter skins with the Indians.   We both returned to the ship the same evening. Next day the Indians came off to trade in great numbers. On their coming alongside, the captain ordered the boarding-netting to be put up round the ship, and would not allow more than ten on board at a time; but just as the trade had commenced, an Indian was detected cutting the boarding-netting with a knife in order to get on board. On being detected, he instantly jumped into one of the canoes which were alongside, and made his escape.   The captain then, turning round, bade the chiefs to call him back.   The chiefs smiled and said nothing, which irritated the captain, and he immediately laid hold of two of the chiefs, and threatened to hang them up unless they caused the delinquent to be brought back to be punished.   The moment the chiefs were seized, all the Indans fled from the ship in consternation.   The chiefs were kept on board all night with a guard over them. Food was offered them, but they would neither eat nor drink.   Next day, however, the offender was brought to the ship and delivered up, when the captain ordered him to be stripped and tied up, but did not flog him. He was then dismissed. The chiefs were also liberated, and left the ship, refusing with disdain a present that was offered them, and vowing vengeance on the whites for the insult received.

"Next day not an Indian came to the ship; but in [161] the afternoon an old chief sent for Mr. M'Kay and myself to go to his lodge. We did so, and were very kindly treated. Mr. M'Kay was a great favourite among the Indians; and I have no doubt that the plot for destroying the ship was at this time fully arranged, and that it was intended, if possible, to save M'Kay's life in the general massacre. But not finding this practicable without the risk of discovery, he, as we shall soon learn, fell with the rest. When we were on shore we saw the chiefs, and they seemed all in good humour, and asked me if the captain was still angry; and on being assured that they would be well treated and kindly received by him if they went on board, they appeared highly pleased, and promised to go and trade the following day. Mr. M'Kay returned to the ship that evening, but I remained on shore till the next morning. When I got on board, Mr. M'Kay was walking backwards and forwards on deck in rather a gloomy mood, and considerably excited; himself and the captain having, as he told me, had some angry words between them respecting the two chiefs who had been kept prisoners on board, which was sorely against M'Kay's will.

"As soon as I got on deck, he called me to him. 'Well,' said he, 'are the Indians coming to trade to-day?' I said, 'They are.' 'I wish they would not come,' said he again; adding, 'I am afraid there is an under-current at work. After the captain's late conduct to the chiefs, I do not

like so sudden, so flattering a change.   There is treachery
in the case, or they [162] differ from all other Indians I
ever knew.   I have told the captain so — I have also
suggested that all hands should be on the alert when the
Indians are here; but he ridicules the suggestion as groundless. So let him have his own way.' M'Kay then asked me
my opinion.   I told him it would be well to have the
netting up.   He then bid me go to the captain, and I
went; but before I could speak to him, he called out,
'Well, Kas, are the Indians coming to-day?' I said I
thought so.   He then asked — 'Are the chiefs in good
humour yet?'   I said I never saw them in better humour.
'I humbled the fellows a little; they'll not be so saucy
now; and we will get on much better,' said the captain.
At this moment M'Kay joined us, and repeated to the
captain what he had just stated to me.   The captain
laughed; observing to M'Kay, 'You pretend to know a
great deal about the Indian character: you know nothing
at all.'   And so the conversation dropt.

''Mr. M'Kay's anxiety and perturbation of mind was
increased by the manner in which the captain treated his
advice; and having, to all appearance, a presentiment
of what was brooding among the Indians, he refused
going to breakfast that morning, put two pair of pistols
in his pockets, and sat down on the larboard side of the
quarter-deck in a pensive mood.   In a short time afterwards, the Indians began to flock about the ship, both
men and women, in great crowds, with their furs; and
certainly I myself thought that there was not the least
danger, particularly as the [163] women accompanied the
men to trade; but I was surprised that the captain did not
put the netting up.   It was the first time I ever saw a ship
trade there without adopting that precaution.   As soon

as the Indians arrived, the captain, relying no doubt on the apparent reconciliation which had taken place between M'Kay and the chiefs on shore, and wishing perhaps to atone for the insult he had offered the latter, flew from one extreme to the other, receiving them with open arms, and admitting them on board without reserve, and without the usual precautions. The trade went on briskly, and at the captain's own prices. The Indians throwing the goods received into the canoes, which were alongside, with the women in them; but in doing so, they managed to conceal their knives about their persons, which circumstance was noticed by one of the men aloft, then by myself, and we warned the captain of it; but he treated the suggestions, as usual, with a smile of contempt, and no more was said about it; but in a moment or two afterwards, the captain began to suspect something himself, and was in the act of calling Mr. M'Kay to him, when the Indians in an instant raised the hideous yell of death, which echoed from stem to stern of the devoted ship, the women in the canoes immediately pushed off, and the massacre began. The conflict was bloody but short. The savages, with their naked knives and horrid yells, rushed on the unsuspecting and defenceless whites, who were dispersed all over the ship, and in five [164] minutes' time the vessel was their own. M'Kay was the first man who fell, he shot one Indian, but was instantly killed and thrown overboard, and so sudden was the surprise that the captain had scarcely time to draw from his pocket a clasp-knife, with which he defended himself desperately, killed two, and wounded several more, till at last he fell dead in the crowd. The last man I saw alive was Stephen Weeks, the armourer. In the midst of the carnage, I leapt overboard, as did several other Indians, and we were taken up by the women in the canoes, who were yelling, whooping, and crying like so many fiends about the ship; but before I had got two gun-shots from the ship, and not ten minutes after I had left her, she blew up in the air with a fearful explosion, filling the whole place with broken fragments and mutilated bodies. The sight was terrific and overwhelming. Weeks must have been the man who blew up the ship, and by that awful act of revenge, one hundred and seventy-five Indians perished, and some of the canoes, although at a great distance off, had a narrow escape. The melancholy and fatal catastrophe spread desolation, lamentation, and terror throughout the whole tribe.

"Scarcely anything belonging to the ship was saved by the Indians, and so terrifying was the effect, so awful the scene, when two other ships passed there soon afterwards, not an Indian would venture to go near them. I knew that the *Tonquin* belonged to the whites at Columbia, I was eighteen days on [165] board of her, and had started long ago with the tidings of her tragical end; but falling sick, I was prevented from coming sooner. There might have been twenty-four days between the time the *Tonquin* left the Columbia and her destruction by the Indians."

Thus ended the sad story of Kasiascall, a story which we at the time believed to be perfectly true; but not many days after, some Indians belonging to the same quarter reached Astoria also, and gave a somewhat different version of the affair, particularly as regarded Kasiascall himself, and what convinced us that he had acted a treacherous part, was the fact, that on hearing that the other Indians were coming, he immediately absconded, and we saw him no more. These Indians confirmed

Kasiascall's story in every respect as regarded the destruction of the ill-fated *Tonquin*; but persisted in assuring us that he was not on board at the time, and that he was privy to the whole plot. They said, that before that affair he had caused the death of four white men, and that, early in the morning of the *Tonquin's* fatal day, he had induced the captain, through some plausible artifice, to send a boat with six men to shore, and that neither he nor the six men were on board at the time of her destruction. That in the evening of the same day, Kasiascall himself headed the party who went, and brought the six unfortunate men, after the ship was blown up, to the Indian camp, where they were first tortured with savage cruelty, and then all massacred in the most inhuman manner.

[166] We have now brought the tragical story of the fated *Tonquin* nearly to a close. Wise men profit by experience, listen to counsel, and yield to circumstances. Captain Thorn, on the contrary, looked upon every suggestion as an attempt to dictate to him, despised counsel, and treated advice with contempt. Had he profited either by the errors or misfortunes of others, or had he listened to the dictates of common prudence, and used the means he had at command, the savages along the coast, numerous and hostile as they are, would never have obtained the mastery, nor taken the *Tonquin*. We lament the fate of her unfortunate crew and commander. Captain Thorn had many good qualities — was brave, had the manners of a gentleman, and was an able and experienced seaman; but his temper was cruel and overbearing,— and his fate verifies the sacred decree, that "he shall have judgment without mercy, that hath showed no mercy."

The destruction of the *Tonquin* left Astoria defenceless and almost hopeless, and might have proved fatal to the enterprise; but, whilst these scenes were yet fresh in the minds of the Astorians, and augmented the gloom occasioned by their harassing and perilous situation, the timely arrival of M'Kenzie, with the first division of Mr. Hunt's party, overland, made them for a moment forget that their friends of the *Tonquin* were no more. This seasonable addition to their numbers, with the daily expectation of others — for the main party had not yet arrived — [167] hushed, for a time, the threatening tone of the Indians, and relieved the whites from that incessant watching which prudence and a regard to safety obliged them to adopt, ever since the first rumour of the *Tonquin's* fate had reached their ears. The subject of the land expedition we shall reserve for the next chapter, concluding the present with a few cursory observations on the conduct of that perfidious wretch, Kasiascall.

After absconding from Astoria, as already stated, he lurked for some time among the neighbouring tribes, trying to stir them up to betray the whites, and take Astoria. He had laid several plans for the purpose; and, being desperate and daring himself, he had, on the 5th of December, with twenty or thirty others of like character, approached the establishment on the south side, through the woods, till within sight of the back gate, with the intention of examining the place, in order to make the attack sure the following morning; but, providentially, his treason was baulked by one of those fortunate incidents which sometimes intervene to save the innocent; for, that very evening, the Astorians, as good luck would have it, had collected some Indians, who, with the whites, made a display at the back gate, with the intention

of proceeding next morning to the chase, to hunt up
some wild hogs which were roaming at large in the woods;
and were, as we were well informed afterwards, seen
by Kasiascall and his party as they were making their
approaches [168] to the fort. They, supposing from
the armed array that their own atrocious designs had
been discovered, immediately took to flight, leaving,
in the hurry, a gun, a quiver full of arrows, and some
other things behind; so that, in all probability, to this
circumstance alone the place owed its preservation,
and the whites their lives. How precarious is the life
of an Indian trader, if we take into consideration the
habits of the country and the spirit of the people he has
to live among — a people who feel no remorse in using
the instruments of death — a people who delight in
perfidy! Perfidy is the system of savages, treachery
and cunning the instruments of their power, and cruelty
and bloodshed the policy of their country.

[169] CHAPTER X [55]

Land expedition — Hunt and M'Kenzie — Montreal
recruits — La Chine — Devout farewell — Mackina in
1810 — Fur traders of the South — Frolic parties —
Comparison between the South and North — Arrival
at St. Louis — Recruiting service — Yankees — Canoe-
men — Delays at St. Louis — Difficulties — Mr. Miller
— The Missouri — Canadian voyageurs — Winter
quarters — Mr. Hunt revisits St. Louis — M'Kenzie —
Mr. Astor's policy — The Yankees desert — Winter
quarters broken up — Rocky Mountains — Pilot knobs
— New scenes — Columbia River — The horses

[55] For notes on the following persons and places mentioned in this chapter,
see Bradbury's *Travels*, volume v of our series: Hunt, note 2; McKenzie, note 4;
Crooks, note 3; Missouri Fur Company, note 149; Miller, note 72; Nadowa,
note 5; McClellan, note 72.— ED.

abandoned — Take to canoes — The canoes abandoned — Trappers — Mr. Miller — Party on foot — Hardships — Starvation — Conflicting councils — Gloomy prospects — Property *en cache* — The party divided — Three men perish — M'Kenzie's speech — He arrives at Astoria — Mr. Crooks and others left behind — Mr. Hunt's arrival at Astoria — Voyage concluded.

WE have already mentioned the departure of the land expedition from Montreal, and now propose to follow up its history, through its zig-zag windings and perils, to Columbia, the place of its destination.

The gentleman appointed to head the adventurous party was Mr. Wilson Price Hunt, a citizen of the United States — a person every way qualified for the arduous undertaking. Had Mr. Astor been as fortunate [170] in his choice of a marine commander to conduct his expedition by sea as he was in that of his land expedition, a very different result would have ensued.

Mr. Hunt was also accompanied on this journey by Mr. Donald M'Kenzie, another partner, who had formerly been in the service of the North-West Company. This gentleman had already acquired great experience in the Indian countries, was bold, robust, and peculiarly qualified to lead Canadian voyageurs through thick and thin. Mr. Astor placed great confidence in his abilities, perseverance, and prudence. Under, therefore, two such leaders as Hunt and M'Kenzie, he had, in fact, everything to hope and little to fear.

The trumpet of enterprize was, therefore, no sooner sounded at the office of the new company for recruits, than crowds of blustering voyageurs, of all grades and qualities, flocked thither to enroll themselves under the banner of this grand undertaking. Money was tempting,

and Jean Baptiste has ever been fond of novelty. The
list of adventurers therefore might have been filled up in
an hour; but a different line was pursued. M'Kenzie
was too sagacious and wary to be taken in by appearances;
he drew a line of distinction, and selected those only who
had already given proofs of capacity. The picking and
choosing system, however, gave great offence to many;
consequently, those who had been rejected put every
iron in the fire, out of pure spite, to discourage those
[171] already engaged, or about to engage; and the money
once expended, little persuasion was required to effect
their purpose.

Mr. M'Kenzie, from his knowledge of the Canadian
character, wished to engage at once a sufficient number
for the enterprize, so that no subsequent delays might
interrupt their progress; and this was generally allowed
to be the better plan, as we shall have occasion to notice
hereafter. But Mr. Hunt — grave, steady, and straightforward, himself — detested the volatile gaiety and ever-
changing character of the Canadian voyageurs, and gave
a decided preference to Americans, and the mongrel
Creoles of the south, who, as he alleged, might be got on
the route, either at Mackina or St. Louis; and this was
the plan ultimately adopted: so that no more Canadian
voyageurs were taken than were barely sufficient to
man one large canoe. These men, however, were
voyageurs of the first class, whose well-tried experience
on the lakes, rivers, and frozen regions of the north,
made them anticipate the pleasures of a holiday voyage
on the waters of the south — hardy veterans, who thought
of nothing but to toil and obey. Such were the men —
second to no canoe-men in Canada — that joined the
expedition at Montreal. The party now assembled in

high spirits, and after bidding a dozen adieux to their friends and companions, embarked at La Chine on the 5th of July. On arriving at St. Anne's, the devout voyageurs, according to usual custom, expressed a wish to go on shore to make [172] their vows at the holy shrine before leaving the island. There, prostrated on the ground, they received the priest's benediction; then embarking, with pipes and song, hied their way up the Ottawa or Grand River for Mackina, which place they reached on the seventeenth day.

Michilimackina, or Mackinaw, was their first resting-place after leaving La Chine; and here they had again to recommence the recruiting service, as at Montreal — with this difference, however, that the Montreal men are expert canoe-men, the Mackina men expert bottle-men. That Canadians in general drink, and sometimes even to excess, must be admitted; but to see drunkenness and debauchery, with all their concomitant vices, carried on systematically, it is necessary to see Mackina.

Here Hunt and M'Kenzie in vain sought recruits, at least such as would suit their purpose; for in the morning they were found drinking, at noon drunk, in the evening dead drunk, and in the night seldom sober. Hogarth's drunkards in Gin Lane and Beer Alley were nothing compared to the drunkards of Mackina at this time. Every nook and corner in the whole island swarmed, at all hours of the day and night, with motley groups of uproarious tipplers and whisky-hunters. Mackina at this time resembled a great bedlam, the frantic inmates running to and fro in wild forgetfulness; so that Mr. Hunt, after spending several weeks, could only pick up a few disorderly Canadians, already ruined in mind and body; whilst [173] the cross-breeds and Yankees kept aloof, viewing the expedition, as an army views a forlorn hope, as destined to destruction. Mr. Hunt now saw and confessed his error in not taking M'Kenzie's salutary advice to engage more voyageurs at Montreal, but regretted most of all the precious time they had lost to no purpose at Mackina, and therefore set about leaving it as soon as possible.

But before we take our leave of a place so noted for gallantry and gossiping, we may observe that it was, at the date of this narrative, the chief rendezvous of the Mackina Fur Company, and a thousand other petty associations of trappers and adventurers, all in some way or other connected with the Indian trade. Here then Mackina was the great outfitting mart of the south — the centre and head-quarters of all those adventurers who frequented the Mississippi and Missouri waters in search of furs and peltries.

These different parties visit Mackina but once a year, and on these occasions make up for their dangers and privations among the Indians by rioting, carousing, drinking, and spending all their gains in a few weeks, sometimes in a few days; and then they return again to the Indians and the wilderness. In this manner these dissolute spendthrifts spin out, in feasting and debauchery, a miserable existence, neither fearing God nor regarding man, till the knife of the savage, or some other violent death, despatches them unpitied.

In the fur trade of the north many have attained [174] to a competency, not a few to independence, and many have realized fortunes after a servitude of years; but in the slippery and ruinous traffic of the south many fortunes have been lost, and an awful sacrifice made of human life; so that of all the adventurers engaged, for half a century past, in the fur trade of that licentious quarter, few, very few indeed, ever left it with even a bare competency.

At Mackina, Mr. Crooks, formerly a trader on the Missouri, joined the expedition as a partner. The odds and ends being now put together, and all ready for a start, the expedition left Mackina on the 12th of August, and crossing over the lake to Green Bay, proceeded up Fox River, then down to Prairie du Chien by the Wisconsin, [56] and from thence drifted down the great Mississippi to St. Louis, where they landed on the 3rd of September.

No sooner had the St. Louis papers announced the arrival of Astor's expedition at that place, than the rendezvous of Hunt and M'Kenzie teemed with visitors of all grades, anxious to enlist in the new company. Pleased with the flattering prospect of soon completing their number, they commenced selecting such countenances as bespoke health and vigour; but, alas! few of that description was to be found in the crowd.

The motley group that presented itself could boast of but few vigorous and efficient hands, being generally little better, if not decidedly worse, than those lounging about the streets of Mackina, a [175] medley of French Creoles, old and worn-out Canadians, Spanish renegades, with a mixture of Indians and Indian half-breeds, enervated by indolence, debauchery, and a warm climate.

---

[56] This route, travelled by Marquette and Jolliet in 1673 was from a well-established Indian and French waterway between the Great Lakes and the Mississippi. The Fox River (of Wisconsin) was ascended from Green Bay to the present site of Portage, Wisconsin; a portage path of a mile and a half in length was followed (in floods, the intervening swamp was overflowed, and Wisconsin River waters emptied into the Fox), and the Wisconsin was descended to its junction with the Mississippi, at Prairie du Chien.— ED.

Here, again, Mr. Hunt's thoughts turned to Canada; and in the bitterness of disappointment he was heard to say, "No place like Montreal for hardy and expert voyageurs!" Several Yankees, however, sleek and tall as the pines of the forest, engaged as hunters and trappers; but here again another difficulty presented itself, the sapient Yankees, accustomed to the good things of St. Louis, must have their dainties, their tea, their coffee, and their grog. This caused a jealousy; the Canadians, who lived on the usual coarse fare of the north, began to complain, and insisted on receiving the same treatment which the hunters and trappers had,— such is the force of example; and dissatisfaction once raised is not so easily allayed again. To adjust these differences, Mr. Hunt adopted an expedient which, in place of proving a remedy, rather augmented the evil. Thinking it easier, or at all events cheaper, to reduce his own countrymen, being but few in number, to the Canadian pot-luck, rather than pamper Jean Baptiste with luxurious notions, he issued his orders accordingly, that all denominations should fare alike; but Jonathan was not to be told what he was to eat, nor what he was to drink. Finding, however, Mr. Hunt determined to enforce the order, the new comers shouldered their rifles to a man, and, in the [176] true spirit of Yankee independence, marched off with their advance in their pockets, and the expedition saw them no more; and not only that, but they raised such a hue-and-cry against the parsimonious conduct of the new enterprize, that not a man could be afterwards got to engage; and this state of things the other traders, and particularly the Missouri Fur Company, turned to their advantage, by representing to the people the horrors, the dangers, and privations that awaited our adventurous friends; that if they were fortunate enough to escape being scalped by the Indians, they would assuredly be doomed, like Nebuchadnezzar, to eat grass, and never would return to tell the sad tale of their destruction.

While Mr. Hunt's affairs thus seemed almost at a stand, a new impulse was given to the expedition by the timely acquisition of another partner, a Mr. Miller, who had been a trader up the Missouri, had considerable experience among Indians along the route to be followed, and was a great favourite with the people at St. Louis. As soon, therefore, as Mr. Miller joined the expedition, people from all quarters began again to enlist under the banner of the new company. Canoemen, hunters, trappers, and interpreters were no longer wanting, and the number of each being completed, the expedition left St. Louis, after a vexatious delay of forty-eight days.

On the 21st of October the expedition started [177] in three boats, and soon after reached the mouth of the Missouri, up which the party proceeded. Our Canadian voyageurs were now somewhat out of their usual element. Boats and oars, the mode of navigating the great rivers of the south, were new to men who had been brought up to the paddle, the cheering song, and the bark canoe of the north. They detested the heavy and languid drag of a Mississippi boat, and sighed for the paddle and song of former days. They soon, however, became expert at the oar, and Mr. Hunt, who was somewhat partial to the south men, was forced to acknowledge that their merits were not to be compared to the steady, persevering, habits of the men of the north. Yet the progress was but slow, scarcely averaging twenty-one miles a day, so that it was the 16th of November before they reached the Nodowa, a distance of only 450 miles up the Missouri, and there, from the coldness of the weather and lateness of the season, they were obliged to winter.

Mr. M'Kenzie, accustomed, during the days of the North-West, to start from Montreal and reach the mouth of Columbia river, or Great Bear's Lake,the same season, did not much like this slow travelling, and had his advice been acted on, the expedition, in place of wintering at the Nodowa, would have wintered on the waters of the Columbia.

Here it was that Mr. M'Lellan, another partner, joined the expedition. This gentleman was one of the first shots in America, nothing could escape his [178] keen eye and steady hand; hardy, enterprizing, and brave as a lion: on the whole, he was considered a great acquisition to the party.

After settling the winter quarters, Mr. Hunt returned to St. Louis, which place he reached on the 20th of January, 1811, and before he joined his wintering friends at the Nodowa River again, it was the 17th of April.

During Mr. Hunt's visit at St. Louis, orders arrived, among other instructions, from Mr. Astor, that the sole command of the expedition should be vested in him alone, although hitherto it was intrusted to Hunt and M'Kenzie. This underhand proceeding of Astor's gave umbrage to the other partners, and particularly to M'Kenzie, and added new difficulties to Mr. Hunt's situation, by throwing the whole responsibility of the enterprize upon him alone; but such was Astor, that no confidence could be placed in his arrangements; his measures, like the wind, were ever changing.

During Mr. Hunt's absence, several changes had taken place in the wintering camp; some of the men had deserted, others again, under various pretences shook themselves

clear of the ill-omened undertaking, and even after Mr.
Hunt's return, several more turned their backs and walked
off, without the least compunction, and all those who so
unceremoniously and treacherously left the expedition,
excepting one, were Americans. Mr. Hunt, in his eager-
ness to press forward, was perfectly worn out with anxiety.

[179] On the 22d of April, however, the adventurers
broke up their camp, or winter quarters, and bent their
course up the strong and rapid current of the Missouri,
no less formidable in itself, than dangerous on account of
the numerous savage hordes that infest its banks.

On the 14th of September the party reached the heights
of the Rocky Mountains, safe and in good spirits, after
many hairbreadth escapes, and drew near to the Pilot
Knobs, or *Trois Tetons*, that great landmark, so singular
and conspicuous, near which is the romantic source of
Louis River, or the great south branch of the Columbia.[57]
From the Nodowa to the Pilot Knobs occupied them one
hundred and forty-five days.

The Pilot Knobs, so cheering to our wayfaring friends,
proved but the beginning of their real troubles: for, after
various projects and plans, it was resolved, on the 18th
of October, to abandon their hitherto serviceable and
trusty horses, and they were, therefore, turned loose, to
the number of one hundred and eighty, and the party
embarking in fifteen crazy and frail canoes, undertook

---

[57] The Three Tetons are the most noted historic peaks in the Rocky Mountains. The topography of the country is such that the highest peak, Grand
Teton (13,691 feet) can be seen from a great distance and has long served as a
landmark to trappers and pioneers. Unlike the mountains of that region, the
Tetons are not hemmed in by foothills, but rise in bold relief from the surrounding plateau — the Grand Teton towering seven thousand feet above Jackson
Lake, at its base. The range is but sixty miles long and lies some twenty-five
miles southwest of Yellowstone Lake. It is crossed by Teton Pass, about
twenty miles south of Grand Teton.— Ed.

to descend the rugged and boiling channels of the head
waters of the great south branch of the Columbia. Having
proceeded about 350 miles, they were at last compelled
to abandon the project of navigating these bold and
dangerous waters; but not before one of their best
steersmen was drowned, and they were [180] convinced
as to the impracticability of proceeding by water.

At this time, two small and separate parties, consisting
in all of twelve persons, were fitted out as trappers to hunt
the beaver, and, to the astonishment of all, Mr. Miller,
in one of his headstrong fits, turned his back on the expedition abruptly, and became a trapper also.

The canoes being now abandoned altogether, various
plans were thought of; two or three parties were sent out
as scouts, to try and fall in with Indians, provisions being
now so scarce that the most gloomy apprehensions were
entertained. These parties, however, saw but few
Indians, and those few were destitute themselves. At
this time a starving dog that could hardly crawl along
was a feast to our people, and even the putrid and rotten
skins of animals were resorted to in order to sustain life.
Whilst these parties were exhausting themselves to little or
no purpose, another party attempted to recover the horses,
which had been so thoughtlessly and imprudently left
behind; but they returned unsuccessful, after a week's
trial and hunger. A fifth party was despatched ahead to
explore the river, and they also returned with the most
gloomy presage — all failed, and all fell back again on
the cheerless camp, to augment the general despondency;
the party now, as a last resource, set about depositing
and securing the goods and baggage, by putting them in
caches; this done, the party finally separated [181] into
four bands, each headed by a partner, and the object of one

and all was, to reach the mouth of the Columbia by the best and shortest way. That part of the country where they were was destitute of game, and the provisions of the whole party taken together were scarcely enough for two days' journey. At that season of the year, the Indians retire to the distant mountains, and leave the river till the return of spring, which accounts for their absence at this time.

We have already stated that one man, named Clappine, had been drowned — another of the name of Prevost had become deranged through starvation, and drowned himself — and a third, named Carrier, lingered behind and perished; these fatal disasters happened in the parties conducted by Messrs. Hunt and Crooks. M'Kenzie and his party were more fortunate: as soon as the division of the men and property took place, that bold North-Wester called his little band together,— "Now, my friends," said he, "there is still hope before us; to linger on our way, to return back, or to be discouraged and stand still, is death — a death of all others the most miserable; therefore, take courage; let us persevere and push on ahead, and all will end well; the foremost will find something to eat, the last may fare worse." On hearing these cheering words, the poor fellows took off their caps, gave three cheers, and at once shot ahead. They kept as near the river as possible, and got on wonderfully well, until they came into the [182] narrow and rugged defiles of the Blue Mountains: there they suffered much, and were at one time five days without a mouthful to eat, when, fortunately, they caught a beaver; and on this small animal and its skin, scarcely a mouthful to each, the whole party had to subsist for three days. At this time some of them were so reduced that M'Kenzie himself had to carry on his own back two of his men's blankets, being a strong and robust man, and long accustomed to the hardships and hard fare of the north. He alone, of all the party, stood the trial well; and, by still cheering and encouraging his men on, he brought them at length to the main waters of the Columbia, at Walla-Walla, a little below the great forks; from thence they descended with the current to the long-looked-for Astoria, where they arrived safe and sound on the 10th of January, 1812.

Mr. Hunt and the other parties still lingered behind; and from the severe trials and privations which M'Kenzie, who was reckoned the boldest and most experienced adventurer in the expedition, suffered, fears were entertained as to the safety of the other parties, more particularly as many gloomy reports had reached Astoria; some saying that they had been killed by the Indians, others that they had died of hunger in the mountains; but at last, on the 15th of February, the joyful cry of white men approaching, announced at Astoria the glad tidings of Mr. Hunt's arrival.

The emaciated, downcast looks and tattered garments [183] of our friends, all bespoke their extreme sufferings during a long and severe winter. To that Being alone who preserveth all those who put their trust in Him, were in this instance due, and at all times, our thanksgiving and gratitude.

[184] CHAPTER XI

Doings at Astoria — Three parties on foot — Their object — M'Lellan's resolution — Hostile attack at the Long Narrows — Mr. Reed — Two Indians shot — Heroic conduct of M'Lellan — Difficulties adjusted — Advance of the party — Remarks — Arrival at Oakinacken — Departure again for Astoria — Scene at Umatallow — Mr. Crooks's adventures and suffering — Yeck-a-tap-am — Umatallow left — Merit rewarded — Arrival of the party at Astoria — The ship *Beaver* there also.

As the spring advanced, various resolutions were passed, and preparations made in furtherance of the views of the concern for the current year. In the prosecution of these plans, three parties were set on foot for the interior; one, consisting of three men, under Mr. Reed, for New York, overland; another, under Mr. Farnham, for the goods left *en cache* by Mr. Hunt on his journey; and a third, to be conducted by Mr. Robert Stuart, for Oak-inacken, with supplies for that post. [58]

On the 22nd of March, all these parties, consisting of seventeen men, left Astoria together, under the [185] direction of Mr. Stuart. On the departure of the party, Mr. M'Lellan, following the example of his colleague, Mr. Miller, abruptly resigned, and joined the party for New York. This gentleman possessed many excellent qualities, but they were all obscured and thrown into the shade by a fickle and unsteady mind.

---

[58] For a sketch of Stuart, see Bradbury's *Travels*, volume v of our series, note 119.

Russell Farnham of Massachusetts came to Astoria on the "Tonquin." He left with Captain Hunt on the brig "Pedlar," was landed at Kamchatka, journeyed overland to Hamburg, and sailed thence to New York. When the American Fur Company resumed operations after the War of 1812-15, he was foremost in endeavoring to establish posts on the Missouri River. In 1831 he had charge of the trade in the country of the Sauk and Fox Indians, and died at St. Louis, October 30, 1832.— ED.

Everything went on smoothly till the party reached the long narrows; that noted resort of plunderers, where few can pass without paying a heavy tax; but there, while in the act of making the portage, the party being unavoidably divided, they were furiously attacked by a strong party of Indians. Mr. Reed, bearer of the express for New York, was knocked down in the scuffle, and severely wounded; and had not M'Lellan, with a bravery and presence of mind peculiar to himself, leaped dexterously over a canoe, he would have been felled to the ground; but his agility saved him, and in all probability saved the whole party, for he instantly shot the man who aimed the blow, then drawing a pistol from his belt, shot him who had assailed Reed dead at his feet; then clapping his hand to his mouth, in the true Indian style, he gave the war-whoop, fired his rifle, and the Indians fled. During the critical scuffle, the despatches were carried off by the savages, and a few other articles of but little value. The firing and the war-whoop summoned in a moment all the whites together, and the Indians, being panic-struck at M'Lellan's heroic conduct, retired rather disconcerted, [186] giving Mr. Stuart and his party time to collect their property, embark, and depart.

They had not proceeded far, however, when the Indians assembled again in battle array, and taking up a position some distance ahead, appeared determined to dispute the passage. But Mr. Stuart was on the alert, and took up his station on a rock some distance from the shore, and from the savages also; when, after a momentary suspense, and many wild flourishes and threats on the part of the Indians, a parley ensued, and Mr. Stuart had the good fortune to negociate a peace. Six blankets and a few trifling articles satisfied the Indians, or at least they preferred them to the doubtful issue of a second attack.

As soon, therefore, as they had received the stipulated oblation for their dead, they retired, and our friends pursued their journey without any further molestation; but for some days and nights after, our party kept a good look-out.

Mr. Stuart, although brave and prudent, erred in attempting to pass the portage in the night; that stealthy proceeding revealed their fears or weakness, and was, in all probability, the cause of the whole disaster. Mr. Reed gradually recovered, but the despatches were lost; so that there was an end to the expedition overland. Mr. Reed and his men therefore accompanied Mr. Stuart, as did Mr. Farnham and the *cache* party; it not being considered prudent to divide. The party now continued their route together, and arrived safe at Oakinacken on the 24th [187] of April. Here they remained for five days, when the party left for Astoria, in four canoes, carrying off with them 2500 beaver skins. Mr. David Stuart and two of our men accompanied the party down, leaving at Oakinacken only myself, Mr. Donald M'Gillis, and one man.

On their way down, one morning a little after sunrise, while near the Umatallow River, where a crowd of Indians were assembled together, they were hailed loudly in English to "come on shore." The canoes instantly closed together, and listened with some anxiety to hear the words repeated. They had no sooner done so than the voice again called out to "come on shore." To shore the canoes instantly steered; when, to the surprise of all, who should be there, standing like two spectres, but Mr. Crooks and John Day, who, it will be remembered, had been left by Mr. Hunt among the Snake Indians the preceding autumn; but so changed and emaciated were they, that our people for some time could scarcely recognise them to be white men; and we cannot do better here than give their story in their own words. The following is, therefore, Mr. Crooks's account of their adventures and their sufferings:—

"After being left by Mr. Hunt, we remained for some time with the Snakes, [59] who were very kind to us. When they had anything to eat, we ate also; but they soon departed, and being themselves without provisions, of course they left us without any. [188] We had to provide for ourselves the best way we could. As soon, therefore, as the Indians went off, we collected some brushwood and coarse hay, and made a sort of booth or wigwam to shelter us from the cold; we then collected some firewood; but before we got things in order, John Day grew so weak that when he sat down he could not rise again without help. Following the example of the Indians, I dug up roots for our sustenance; but not knowing how to cook them, we were nearly poisoned. In this plight, we unfortunately let the fire go out, and for a day and night we both lay in a torpid state, unable to strike fire, or to collect dry fuel. We had now been a day without food, or even water to drink, and death appeared inevitable. But Providence is ever kind. Two straggling Indians happening to come our way, relieved us. They made us a fire, got us some water, and gave us something to eat; but seeing some roots we had collected for food lying in a corner, they gave us to understand that they would poison us if we ate them. If we had had a fire, those very roots would have been our first food, for we had nothing else to eat; and who can tell but the hand of a kind and

---

[59] For a brief description of the Snake Indians, see Bradbury's *Travels,* note 123.— ED.

superintending Providence was in all this? These poor fellows staid with us the greater part of two days, and gave us at their departure about two pounds of venison. We were really sorry to lose them.

"On the same day, after the Indians had left us, a very large wolf came prowling about our hut, when [189] John Day, with great exertions and good luck, shot the ferocious animal dead; and to this fortunate hit I think we owed our lives. The flesh of the wolf we cut up and dried, and laid it by for some future emergency, and in the mean time feasted upon the skin; nor did we throw away the bones, but pounded them between stones, and with some roots made a kind of broth, which, in our present circumstances, we found very good. After we had recovered our strength a little, and were able to walk, we betook ourselves to the mountains in search of game; and, when unsuccessful in the chase, we had recourse to our dried wolf. For two months we wandered about, barely sustaining life with our utmost exertions. All this time we kept travelling to and fro, until we happened, by mere chance, to fall on the Umatallow River; and then following it, we made the Columbia about a mile above this place, on the 15th day of April, according to our reckoning. Our clothes being all torn and worn out, we suffered severely from cold; but on reaching this place, the Indians were very kind to us. This man," pointing to an old grey-headed Indian, called Yeck-a-tap-am, "in particular treated us like a father. After resting ourselves for two days with the good old man and his people, we set off, following the current, in the delusive hope of being able to reach our friends at the mouth of the Columbia, as the Indians gave us to understand that white men had gone down there in the winter, which we supposed must have been Mr. Hunt and his party.

[190] ''We had proceeded on our journey nine days, without interruption, and were not far from the falls, which the Indians made us comprehend by uttering the word 'tumm,' which we understood to mean noise or fall;[60] when one morning, as we were sitting near the river, gazing on the beautiful stream before us, the Indians in considerable numbers collected around us, in the usual friendly manner: after some little time, however, one of them got up, and, under pretence of measuring the length of my rifle with his bow, took it in his hands; another in the same manner, and at the same moment, took John Day's rifle from him. The moment our guns were in their possession, the two Indians darted out of the crowd to some distance, and assuming a menacing attitude, pointed them at us; in the same instant, all the others fled from us and joined the two who had carried off our guns. All began to intimate to us by signs, in the most uproarious and wild manner, that some of their people had been killed by the whites, and threatened to kill us in turn. In this critical conjunction, John Day drew his knife, with the intention of rushing upon the fellows to get hold of his gun; but I pointed out to him the folly of such a step, which must have instantly proved fatal to us, and he desisted.

''The Indians then closed in upon us, with guns pointed and bows drawn, on all sides, and by force stripped us of our clothes, ammunition, knives, and everything

---

[60] Lewis and Clark state that the Indians designated the great falls of the Columbia by the words ''Timm,'' so pronounced as to represent the fall of a distant cataract.— ED.

else, leaving us naked as the day we were [191] born, and,
by their movements and gestures, it appeared evident
that there was a disposition on their part to kill us; but
after a long and angry debate, in which two or three old
men seemed to befriend us, they made signs for us to be
off: seeing the savages determined, and more of them
still collecting, we slowly turned round, and went up the
river again, expecting every moment to receive a ball or
an arrow. After travelling some little distance, we
looked back and saw the savages quarrelling about the
division of the booty; but fearing pursuit, we left the
river and took to the hills. All that day we travelled
without tasting food, and at night concealed ourselves
among the rocks — without fire, food, or clothing. Next
day we drew near to the river, and picked up some fish-
bones at a deserted Indian encampment; with these we
returned to the rocks again, and pounding them with
stones, tried to eat a little, but could not manage to swallow
any: that night also we hid ourselves among the rocks,
but at last we resolved to keep by the river, and, as it
seemed impossible to avoid death, either by the Indians or
starvation, to brave all dangers in the attempt to reach
our good old friend Yeck-a-tap-am — and Providence
still guarded us.

"Soon after we arrived at the river, we unexpectedly
fell on a small Indian hut, with only two old people and a
child in it: we approached with hesitating and doubtful
steps, but on entering the solitary wigwam, the poor inmates were more [192] frightened than ourselves; and,
had they had timely notice of our approach, they would
have certainly fled. The good people, however, gave us
fish, broth, and roots to eat; and this was the first food
we had tasted, and the first fire we had seen, for four days

and four nights. Our feet were severely cut and bleeding, for want of shoes; yet we lost no time, but set off, and arrived here three days ago, and our good old friend, Yeck-a-tap-am, received us again with open arms, and gave us these skins to cover our nakedness, as ye now see.

"The good old man then killed a horse, which his people cut up and dried for us, and with that supply we had resolved to set out this very day and retrace our steps back again to St. Louis overland, and when you came in sight we were just in the act of tying up our little bundles; regretting, most of all, that we had no means of recompensing our good and faithful friend Yeck-a-tap-am."

Mr. Crooks having concluded his narrative, Mr. Stuart called the old man to him, and clothed him from head to foot for his friendly services. Mr. Crooks and his fellow-sufferer then cordially shaking hands with Yeck-a-tap-am, the party pushed off, and continued their voyage. On arriving at the place where Crooks had been robbed, the party put on shore; but the Indians, having notice of their approach, fled to the interior; so that they had no opportunity of either recovering the guns or inquiring into the affair.

[193] From the long narrows the party met with no interruption, but continued their route till they reached Astoria, on the 12th of May, where Crooks and all the party were greeted with a hearty welcome; and what made the meeting more joyous was the safe arrival, three days previous, of the Company's ship *Beaver* from New York, with a supply of goods, and a reinforcement of men.

[194] CHAPTER XII

General meeting of the partners — Resolutions passed — Departure of the parties for the interior — Mr. Clarke — The cascades — Wyampam, or the Long Narrows — Situation of the party — Loss of time — Mr. M'Kenzie — A stroll through the Indian camp — Mr. Clarke's alarms — Command transferred — Reed's rifle recovered — A robber in irons — The five shots — Yeck-a-tap-am rewarded — Mr. Stuart's departure for St. Louis — Second division — Summer trip to She Whaps — Boullard and his squaw — Mr. Stuart's arrival at Oakinacken — Departure for She Whaps — Winter operations at Oakinacken — Visits — Travelling scenes — A night in the snow — Jacque and his powder-horn — Mr. Stuart's account of his journey — Arrival at Walla Walla.

ALL parties being now at their posts, for the first time a meeting of the partners was convened, at which the following resolutions, among others, were passed — "That Mr. David Stuart proceed to his post at Oakinack-en, explore the country northward, and establish another post between that and New Caledonia: [61] That Mr. M'Kenzie winter on the Snake country; recover the goods left in *cache* there by Mr. Hunt; and report on the state

---

[61] Simon Fraser, on his first expedition west of the Rocky Mountains (1805), gave the name "New Caledonia" to the region of Stuart and upper Fraser rivers, whose numerous lakes, lying among the bold and craggy mountains, reminded him of the Scotch highlands. The following year, accompanied by John Stuart, he farther explored the country and established St. James post, on Stuart River. For some time the boundaries of New Caledonia were indefinite, but its southern limit was always over two hundred miles north of Okanagan post. After it was erected into a district of the Hudson's Bay Company, it extended from 51° 30′ to 56° north latitude and from 124° 10′ west longitude to the Rocky Mountains. Fort Alexandria (established 1821), on Fraser River, one hundred and seventy miles north of Fort Okanagan, became the principal trading post of the district.— ED.

of the country: That Mr. Clarke [62] winter at Spokane, as an intermediate [195] post, between Mr. Stuart on the north and Mr. M'Kenzie on the south, in order to oppose and keep in check the North-West Company established there: That Mr. Robert Stuart proceed to St. Louis across land, with despatches for Mr. Astor:[63] That all these several parties, for mutual safety, advance together as far as the forks, or entrance of the great south branch." It was likewise settled at this council, "That Mr. Hunt should accompany the ship *Beaver* to the Russian settlements on his coasting trip." These preparatory steps being taken, the several parties, numbering sixty-two persons, left Astoria for the interior on the 29th of June.

This was the first formidable and regular party that left Astoria, which seemed to impart to the concern a character of permanency and success, and was conducted by Mr. Clarke, the brightest star in the Columbian constellation, as Mr. Astor expressed himself — for to him, by mutual consent, was conceded the important command.

On their progress, no interruption impeded the party till they reached the cascades, where the Indians were rather troublesome, and shot a few arrows at the canoes as they passed; but on the party landing all was submission; the portage was made; and the party advanced at a rapid rate till they reached the long narrows: that intricate and gloomy pass is constantly infested with gambling Indians of the vilest character.

Here, as usual, the thievish subjects of Wyampam assembled in numbers, and showed a formidable and

---

[62] Concerning John Clarke, see Franchère, note 81.— ED.

[63] For further information regarding the St. Louis party, see Bradbury's *Travels*, note 119.— ED.

[196] determined front.   To one used to their gasconading threats, there was nothing in all this to intimidate; but to Mr. Clarke, although a man of nerve on most occasions, the sight was overwhelming. He stood appalled, and almost speechless. In short, he looked upon all as irretrievably lost. To advance, to retreat, or to stand still with safety, seemed to him equally hopeless. Guards and patrols were stationed round the tempting bales of goods, and days and nights wasted in useless harangues and parleys, without result. Mr. Clarke's lofty tent, pitched in the centre of the arena, as a beacon on the top of a hill shining afar, was guarded on every side by trusty Sandwich Islanders; while the rest, forming the circumvallation, had to protect all within.   This state of things continued for several days and nights, until Mr. M'Kenzie and Mr. David Stuart, taking a voluntary stroll for upwards of two miles through the Indian camp, proved by their safe return that the alarm and fears of Mr. Clarke were utterly groundless, and urged him to press forward, as every moment's delay only increased the danger.

Mr. Clarke, however, viewed their situation as desperate, and the thought of advancing as utterly hopeless. Mr. M'Kenzie then told him that he could wait no longer, but would proceed with his own party alone; Mr. Stuart said the same. To this threat, Mr. Clarke replied, that if they could pass he could pass also, but would not answer for the consequences. Mr. M'Kenzie replied that he would [197] answer for them, and therefore took upon himself the command, and immediately ordered the tents to be struck and the party to advance. The party advanced accordingly, and by adopting judicious arrangements got through the suspicious pass without molestation or loss.

Before we proceed further, however, we may here mention that whilst M'Kenzie and Stuart were on their ramble through the Indian camp, they saw in a corner of one of the chief's lodges the rifle which had been taken from Mr. Reed when he was wounded, and they were resolved at all hazards to recover it.

As soon, therefore, as all were safe above the narrows, M'Kenzie took eight men, well armed, with him, and went direct to the chief's lodge; then stationing four of his men at the door, he, himself, went in with the other four, and demanded the stolen rifle; but the chief denied that he had it, or that it was in his lodge. Mr. M'Kenzie, however, insisted that it was there, and said he was determined to have it; and seeing that fair means would not avail he drew his dagger, and began to turn over and cut up everything that came in his way, until at last the rifle was discovered, when M'Kenzie upbraided the chief for falsehood and dishonesty, took the rifle, and with his party made for the door of the lodge. The Indians were now assembling together in crowds; but before they had time to decide on any step, M'Kenzie and his men were out of their reach, [198] carrying the rifle with them. The business was well timed, for had they delayed some minutes longer in the lodge, it is hard to say what the consequences might have been. Early in the morning our party proceeded on their journey; passed the falls, and encamped for the night near the spot where Mr. Crooks and John Day had been robbed on their forlorn adventures down the river.

The Indians, however, flocked round our party as if nothing had happened, and among the rest the ruffian who took John Day's rifle was recognised. He was immediately laid hold of and secured in one of the canoes.

Mr. Crooks's rifle was alone recovered. Some were for hanging the offender, others were for cutting his ears off; but after keeping him a prisoner for two days, he was set at liberty without any further punishment; and, under all circumstances, that was perhaps the wisest course. Before he went off, however, Mr. M'Lellan, to show him the effect of fire-arms in the hands of the whites, set up a piece of board, with a white spot on it, only two inches in diameter, and in three successive shots, at a hundred yards distance, with his rifle he pierced the bull's eye; then stopping up the holes of two of the shots, put a hazel-nut in the third, and broke it with two successive shots at the same distance.

On passing the Umatallow, Yeck-a-tap-am was not forgotten, Mr. Crooks giving him a chief's coat in return for the kindness shown to the latter while in distress.

[199] On the 29th of July, all the parties arrived safe at Walla-Walla; here they were to separate, and here it was that Mr. Robert Stuart, after staying for two days with Tummeatapam, and purchasing ten horses, the number requisite for his journey overland, took his departure for St. Louis. The party consisted of Mr. Stuart, Benjamin Jones, Andrè Vallar, Francis Le Clerc, and Mr. Crooks and Mr. M'Lellan. The two latter gentlemen relinquished all connection with the concern, and joined the party for St. Louis. This little, bold, and courageous party bade adieu to their associates, and commenced their perilous undertaking on the 31st of July. In the mean time, the main party struck off at the forks, leaving M'Kenzie and Clarke on their way up the Snake River, or south branch, to their respective destinations. We shall, for the present, accompany Mr. David Stuart to his wintering ground, and back again to this place,

where the parties agreed to meet in the following June. The histories of the other parties shall be recounted hereafter, each in its proper place.

From the forks, Mr. Stuart and his party, ascending the north branch, continued their voyage, and arrived at Oakinacken on the 12th of August. Here it will be remembered that when the party left this on the 28th of April for Astoria, I remained at Oakinacken, having only Mr. M'Gillis and one man, named Boullard, with me. On the 6th of May I started with Boullard and an Indian, with sixteen horses, on a trading excursion, and following Mr. [200] Stuart's route of last winter, reached the She Whaps on Thompson's River, the tenth day, and there encamped at a place called by the Indians Cumcloups, near the entrance of the north branch. [64] From this station I sent messages to the different tribes around, who soon assembled, bringing with them their furs. Here we stayed for ten days. The number of Indians collected on the occasion could not have been less than 2,000. Not expecting to see so many, I had taken but a small quantity of goods with me; nevertheless, we loaded all our horses — so anxious were they to trade, and so fond of tobacco, that one morning before breakfast I obtained one hundred and ten beavers for leaf-tobacco, at the rate of five leaves per skin; and at last, when I had but one yard of white cotton remaining, one of the chiefs gave me twenty prime beaver skins for it.

[64] This is Fort Kamloops, also known as Fort Thompson. It was built by David Thompson (1810) at the junction of the northern and the eastern branches of Thompson River, a few miles from Lake Kamloops and one hundred and fifty miles north of Okanagan post. It became the centre of the Thompson River district of the Hudson's Bay Company. In 1841 the agent, Black, was murdered in the fort by some Indians, and his successor had the stockade removed across the river to the south side. It is now a town on the Canadian Pacific Railroad, and in 1890 had a population of fifteen hundred.— ED.

Having now finished our trade, we prepared to return home; but before we could get our odds-and-ends ready, Boullard, my trusty second, got involved in a love affair, which had nearly involved us all in a disagreeable scrape with the Indians. This was the very man Mr. Stuart got from Mr. Thompson in exchange for Cox, the Owhyhee. He was as full of latent tricks as a serpent is of guile. Unknown to me, the old fellow had been teasing the Indians for a wife, and had already an old squaw at his heels, but could not raise the wind to pay the whole purchase-money. With an air of effrontery he asked me to unload one of my horses to satisfy the demands of the [201] old father-in-law, and because I refused him, he threatened to leave me and to remain with the savages. Provoked at his conduct, I suddenly turned round and horsewhipped the fellow, and, fortunately, the Indians did not interfere. The castigation had a good effect: it brought the amorous gallant to his senses — the squaw was left behind. We started; but were frequently impeded on our journey by the sudden rise of the rivers. As we were often obliged to swim our horses, our packs of beaver got now and then wet, but without sustaining any serious injury; and on the 12th of July we reached home, well pleased both with our trade and the reception we had met with from the Indians. On this trip we had frequent opportunities of paying attention to the aspect and topography of the country through which we passed.

On the 25th of August, Mr. Stuart, with his men and merchandise, left Oakinacken to winter among the She Whaps, appointing me, as a recompense for my successful voyage to Cumcloups, to the post of Oakinacken. Although not hitherto formally appointed, I had virtually been in charge of it since its first establishment. Having escorted Mr. Stuart for seventy miles, I returned to prepare my own post for the winter operations. After spending all the autumn in trading excursions, according to the custom of the country, I resolved on the 2nd of December to pay a visit to Mr. John Clarke, at Fort Spokane, which place we reached on the fourth day. [65] Spokane lies [202] due east from Oakinacken — distant about 150 miles. The face of the country is rocky and barren.

I had never seen Mr. Clarke before; but certainly a more affable, generous, and kind gentleman in his own house could not be met with.

During the three days I remained with him, I had frequent opportunities of observing the sly and underhand dealings of the competing parties, for the opposition posts of the North-West Company and Mr. Clarke were built contiguous to each other. When the two parties happened to meet, they made the amplest protestations of friendship and kindness, and a stranger, unacquainted with the politics of Indian trade, would have pronounced them sincere; but the moment their backs were turned, they tore each other to pieces. Each party had its manœuvreing scouts out in all directions, watching the motions of the Indians, and laying plots and plans to entrap or foil each other. He that got most skins, never minding the cost of the crime, was the cleverest fellow; and under such tutors the Indians were apt disciples. They played their tricks also, and turned the foibles and wiles of their teachers to their own advantage.

Leaving Spokane Fort, we turned towards home again. In the evening of the 13th, not far from home, as we were ascending a very steep hill, at the top of which is a vast

---

[65] An account of Spokane Fort is given in Franchère, note 85.— ED.

plain, I and my man had to walk, leaving our horses to
shift for themselves, and climb up as they could; and so
steep and intricate [203] were the windings that I had to
throw off my coat, which, together with my gun, I laid on
one of the pack-horses. The moment we reached the
top, and before we could gather our horses or look about
us, we were overtaken by a tremendous cold snowstorm;
the sun became instantly obscured, and the wind blew a
hurricane. We were taken by surprise. I immediately
called out to the men to shift for themselves, and let the
horses do the same. Just at this moment I accidentally
came in contact with one of the loaded horses, for such
was the darkness that we could not see three feet ahead;
but, unfortunately, it was not the horse on which I had
laid my coat and gun. I instantly cut the tyings, threw
off the load, and mounting on the pack-saddle, rode off
at full speed through the deep snow, in the hopes of
reaching a well-known place of shelter not far off; but
in the darkness and confusion I missed the place, and at
last got so benumbed with cold that I could ride no
farther; and, besides, my horse was almost exhausted.
In this plight I dismounted and took to walking, in order
to warm myself. But no place of shelter was to be found.
Night came on; the storm increased in violence; my
horse gave up; and I myself was so exhausted, wandering
through the deep snow, that I could go no further. Here
I halted, unable to decide what to do. My situation
appeared desperate: without my coat; without my gun;
without even a fire-steel. In such a situation I must
perish. At [204] last I resolved on digging a hole in the
snow; but in trying to do so, I was several times in danger
of being suffocated with the drift and eddy. In this
dilemma I unsaddled my horse, which stood motionless

as a statue in the snow. I put the saddle under me, and the saddle-cloth, about the size of a handkerchief, round my shoulders, then squatted down in the dismal hole, more likely to prove my grave than a shelter. On entering the hole I said to myself, "Keep awake and live; sleep and die." I had not been long, however, in this dismal burrow before the cold, notwithstanding my utmost exertions to keep my feet warm, gained so fast upon me that I was obliged to take off my shoes, then pull my trousers, by little and little, over my feet, till at last I had the waistband round my toes; and all would not do. I was now reduced to the last shift, and tried to keep my feet warm at the risk of freezing my body. At last I had scarcely strength to move a limb; the cold was gaining fast upon me; and the inclination to sleep almost overcame me. In this condition I passed the whole night; nor did the morning promise me much relief; yet I thought it offered me a glimpse of hope, and that hope induced me to endeavour to break out of my snowy prison. I tried, but in vain, to put on my frozen shoes; I tried again and again before I could succeed. I then dug my saddle out of the snow, and after repeated efforts, reached the horse and put the saddle on; but could not myself get into the saddle. [205] Ten o'clock next day came before there was any abatement of the storm, and when it did clear up a little I knew not where I was; still it was cheering to see the storm abate. I tried again to get into the saddle; and when I at last succeeded, my half-frozen horse refused to carry me, for he could scarcely lift a leg. I then alighted and tried to walk; but the storm broke out again with redoubled violence. I saw no hope of saving myself but to kill the horse, open him, and get into his body, and I drew my hunting-knife

for the purpose; but then it occurred to me that the body
would freeze, and that I could not, in that case, extricate
myself. I therefore abandoned the idea, laid my knife
by, and tried again to walk, and again got into the saddle.
The storm now abating a little, my horse began to move;
and I kept wandering about through the snow till three
o'clock in the afternoon, when the storm abated altogether;
and the sun coming out, I recognised my position. I
was then not two miles from my own house, where I
arrived at dusk; and it was high time, for I could not
have gone much farther; and after all it was my poor
horse that saved me, for had I set out on foot, I should
never, in my exhausted condition, have reached the house.

How my men weathered the storm we shall presently
see. Two of them got home a little before myself, but
much frost-bitten. The other two had not made their
appearance yet; but some Indians were instantly despatched in search of them; and [206] one was found
that night; the other not till the next day. He was
carried home almost in a dying state, but ultimately
recovered. One of the horses was found dead; all the
rest were recovered, but the load which I had thrown off
the horse which I rode was totally destroyed by the
wolves. Such a destructive storm had not been felt
in these parts for many years previous. An Indian,
with his whole family, consisting of seven persons,
perished by it; two more were severely frost-bitten, and
more than twenty horses were lost.

On the 20th of December, just six days after my return
from Spokane, I set out with one man on a visit to Mr.
Stuart, at the She Whaps, and arrived at Cumcloups on
the last day of the year; soon after, Mr. Stuart reached
his wintering place. The North-West, jealous of that

quarter, followed hard at his heels, and built alongside of him. So that there was opposition there as well as at Mr. Clarke's place, but without the trickery and manœuvring. M. La Rocque, the North-West clerk in charge, [66] and Mr. Stuart, were open and candid, and on friendly terms. The field before them was wide enough for both parties, and, what is more, they thought it so; consequently they followed a fair and straightforward course of trade; with Mr. Stuart I remained five days, and in coming home I took a near and unknown route, in order to explore a part of the country I had not seen before; but I chose a bad season of the year to satisfy my curiosity: we got [207] bewildered in the mountains and deep snows, our progress was exceedingly slow, tedious, and discouraging. We were at one time five days in making as many miles, our horses suffered greatly, had nothing to eat for four days and four nights, not a blade of grass appearing above the snow, and their feet were so frightfully cut with the crust on the snow that they could scarcely move, so that we were within a hair's breadth of losing every one of them.

One evening, the fuel being damp, we were unable to kindle a brisk fire. In this predicament, I called on Jacques to give me a little powder, a customary thing in such cases; but in place of handing me a little powder, or taking a little out in his hand, wise Jacques, uncorking his horn, began to pour it out on the heated coal. It instantly exploded, and blew all up before it, sending Jacques himself sprawling six feet from where he stood, and myself nearly as far, both for some time stunned and senseless, while the fire was completely extinguished.

We, however, received no injury beyond the fright, though Jacques held the horn in his hand when it was

---

[66] For a brief biography of Larocque, see Franchère, note 90.— Ed.

blown to atoms. On recovering, we were not in the
best humour, and sat down for some time in gloomy
mood; cold, however, soon admonished us to try again;
but it was midnight before we could get a fire lighted and
ourselves warmed, and we passed a disagreeable night
without sleep or food. We hastened next morning from
this unlucky encampment, [208] and getting clear of
the mountains, we descended into a low and pleasant
valley, where we found the Indians I had been in search
of, and something both for ourselves and our horses to
eat. At the Indian camp we remained one day, got the
information we required about the country, procured some
furs, and then, following the course of the Sa-milk-a-meigh
River, [67] got to Oakinacken at the forks; thence we
travelled almost day and night till the 24th of January,
when we reached home again. On this journey we met
with several cross purposes, and suffered a good deal
from both cold and hunger, so that I got heartily tired
of visiting. During my absence, Mr. M'Gillis managed
matters at the post very well. Several other trading
trips took place in the course of the spring, and these,
with the ordinary routine business of the place, kept our
hands full till the hour of embarkation arrived. In the
course of the last year I had travelled in various directions
through the country, 3,355 miles.

On the 13th of May, Mr. Stuart, with his men and
furs, arrived from the She Whaps. In reference to his
post, he remarked, ''I have passed a winter nowise
unpleasant, the opposition, it is true, gave me a good deal
of anxiety when it first arrived, but we agreed very well,

[67] Similkameen is the present name of this river. It rises in the Cascade
Mountains not far from the boundary line, and flows southeast into the Okanagan.— ED.

and made as much, perhaps more, than if we had been enemies. I sent out parties in all directions, north as far as Fraser's River, and for two hundred miles up the south branch. The accounts from all quarters were most satisfactory. [209] The country is everywhere rich in furs, and the natives very peaceable. The She Whaps will be one of the best beaver posts in the country, and I have now brought a fine stock of valuable furs with me."

After remaining at Oakinacken for ten days, to get the furs packed and pressed, Mr. Stuart and myself, with the men and furs, set out for Walla Walla, the place of general rendezvous settled upon last summer, where we arrived on the 30th of May; the other parties not having yet come in.

[210] CHAPTER XIII

Mr. Clarke — Stragglers — Hard travelling — Cox's pilgrimage — Visit to Spokane — Trade — Mr. Pillet — Mr. Farnham — Cootanais and Flatheads — M'Lennan — Plunge in the lake — Adventures — Outposts — Catatouch chief — Curiosity — Fracas — Introduction of civilization — Commotion — M'Kenzie — Great Snake River — Caches robbed — Canadian wanderers — Character of the Shahaptains — Visit to Spokane — M'Tavish — Account of the war — Winter travels — M'Kenzie at Astoria — New resolves — M'Kenzie's return to his post — Indian chiefs — Bold enterprize — Property recovered — Chiefs and their horses — Stratagems — Indians outwitted — Plotting — Friendly Island — Conference — Marauding propensities — Treaty of peace — System changed — Plentiful market — The island abandoned — Arrival at Walla Walla — Commotions among the savages — Tummeat-apam — Arrival at Astoria.

WE now come to the history of Mr. Clarke and his party, whom we left at the forks in August last, on his way to his winter-quarters at Spokane. Having proceeded up the South-branch, or Louis River, for about fifty miles, he reached the Catatouch band, at the mouth of the Pavilion River. [68] The Catatouches are a small and friendly tribe of the great Nez Percé nations, and the lowest of them on the South-branch. [69] This spot terminated Mr. Clarke's voyage by water. From thence his route lay across land to the Spokane River, distant [211] about 170 miles. Leaving his canoes under the care of the friendly Catatouch chief, he purchased horses from the Indians for the transportation of his goods.

Mr. Clarke had four clerks with him, Messrs. Pillet, Farnham, M'Lennan, and Cox. He had also more men and merchandize than any of the other parties, as it was supposed he would have most to do in opposing a formidable opposition.

Having purchased a sufficient number of horses, he left the Pavilion on the 10th of August, and set out on his journey by land. He had not proceeded far, however, when he got into some little difficulties with his people. They had started together; but before they had been two hours on the march, some of them lagged so far behind that the motley cavalcade outstretched a mile in length; while Mr. Clarke, like a general at the head of an army, had to keep riding backwards and forwards to keep together the broken line of stragglers, the greater part of whom being on foot, and having to keep up with horses, over a barren and sandy plain, in the hot and

---

[68] The Palouse River—Drewyer's River of Lewis and Clark. Palouse is probably an Indian word, although it has been connected with the French word ''pelouse,'' in that it flows through a rolling, bunch-grass country, the most fertile in eastern Washington. It empties into the Snake eighty-five miles from the Columbia, and is its only important tributary on the northern side.— ED.

[69] Concerning the Nez Percés, see Franchère, note 145.— ED.

sultry weather of a Columbia summer, had a task too
severe, perhaps, even for the best travellers.

The most refractory of the rear-guard was Mr. Cox —
the little Irishman, as he was generally called. [70] Mr.
Clarke riding back ordered him, in an angry tone, to
quicken his steps. "Give me a horse," said Cox, "and
I'll ride with yourself at the head." At this reply Mr.
Clarke raised his whip — some say he [212] put his
threats in execution — and then rode off. Be that as it
may, Cox slunk off and took to the mountains; the party
moved on, and Cox remained behind. The sixth day
the party arrived at Spokane. Indians were then sent
out in all directions; but it was the seventh day after the
party had reached its destination before Cox made his
appearance. The Indians had picked him up in a most
destitute and forlorn condition on the thirteenth day of
his wayward pilgrimage; his clothes all torn, his feet bare,
and his belly empty. When I was there in the winter, Cox
had hardly recovered yet. Mr. Clarke's mode of trading
might do for a bourgeois; but it was not fit for a clerk.
What was considered moderate at Spokane would be
denounced as exorbitant at Oakinacken. Mr. Clarke
was extravagant; but to be called by the Indians a
generous chief was his greatest glory.

Mr. Clarke established himself at the corner of the
opposition post; and being formerly a North-Wester
himself, he was up to the rigs of his opponents. The
Indians were assembled, long speeches were made,
and mighty things were promised on both sides, but
never fulfilled. As soon as Mr. Clarke had got himself
and property under shelter, following the North-West
system, he gave a grand ball to his men, and appointed

[70] For an account of Cox, see Franchère, note 84.— ED.

three or four of the most conceited and blustering fellows
in his party to be a guard, such as the Sioux and other
savage nations employ as instruments of tyranny [213]
in the hands of despotic chiefs. These fellows wore
feathers in their caps, the insignia of their office. To
challenge, fight, and bully their opponents, stand at the
heels of their bourgeois, to be ready at a wink to do
whatever he commands them, is their duty; and they
understand it well. All these preliminary steps being
taken, Mr. Clarke set about establishing outposts, to
compete with his opponents and keep them in check.

Mr. Pillet, with some men and a supply of goods, was
sent to the Cootanais to oppose Mr. Mantour on the part
of the North-West.[71] Mr. Pillet travelled a great deal,
and turned his time to good account. Both were zealous
traders, and they could fight a duel as well as buy a
skin, for they carried pistols as well as goods along with
them. They therefore fought and traded alternately,
but always spared the thread of life, and in the spring
parted good friends.

Mr. Farnham was fitted out for the Selish, or Flathead
tribe [72]— crossed with them the Rocky Mountains —

---

[71] The original Kootenay post was established by Thompson in July, 1807,
on the Columbia River (called by him Kootenay) just below lower Columbia
Lake. He wintered here in 1808-09 and 1809-10.

In 1808, Finan McDonald, a member of Thompson's party, built a post at the
southern end of the loop in the Kootenay River, in the northwest corner of the
present state of Montana, five miles south of the boundary line. This became
an important North West fort. McDonald remained until late in 1811, when
Montour was placed in charge.

Nicholas Montour was in 1804 a clerk in the employ of the North West
Company at Fort de Prairie. From 1811 to 1816 he was active on the Columbia,
moving about between Fort Kootenay, Spokane, and Okanagan, with head-
quarters at Spokane after 1814. See Coues, *Henry-Thompson Journals*, ii,
pp. 606, 672–675, 757.— ED.

[72] For a description of the Salishan Indians, see Franchère, note 145.— ED.

visited the head waters of the Missouri — saw much of the country, and made a good trade. Farnham was a bustling, active, and enterprizing fellow.

Both the Cootanais [73] and Selish tribes live and range along the foot of the mountains, often crossing them, and have frequent encounters with the Blackfeet, by whom they have suffered greatly of late years; the Blackfeet being too numerous for them. [74]

[214] Mr. M'Lennan was stationed at the Pointed Hearts, or Sketch-hugh Lake. [75] In going to his destination, he was rather unlucky, for his canoe upset in crossing the lake, and swamped his goods; but he swam like a fish, got the two men he had with him into the canoe again, then kept diving like a seal, although the weather was cold and the water deep, till he recovered the most of his property: his exertions on this occasion astonished every one who knew the difficulties of the task. M'Lennan was hardy as steel, and bold as a lion: he made a very good and a very cheap trade, and was altogether a favourite among the Indians.

Spring now drawing nigh, Mr. Clarke got in all his outposts and scouts, and left Spokane, with thirty-two

[73] The Kootenai or Flatbows wandered between the northern forks of the Columbia and the Rocky Mountains. Possibly they were the Tushepaws of Lewis and Clark. They were unrelated to any of the surrounding peoples, and resembled more the Indians east of the Rocky Mountains.— ED.

[74] The Blackfeet Indians are treated in Bradbury's *Travels*, note 120.— ED.

[75] Lake Cœur d'Alêne (Pointed Heart) is at the head of Spokane River, about twenty-five miles southeast of Spokane Falls. It is a small lake fed by the Cœur d'Alêne and St. Joseph rivers, flowing from the Bitter Root Mountains. There are two theories regarding the origin of the name — one, that the Indians living there were so sharp at bargaining that the fur-traders named them Cœur d'Alênes, "Awl-Hearts," or "Pointed Hearts;" the other, that among the first traders was a Canadian of so close and niggardly a disposition that the Indians applied an epithet to him which the interpreter translated "Cœur d'Alêne," and the name became fixed upon the Indians.— ED.

horses loaded with furs, on the 25th of May: a confidential
man, named Pion, a newly-promoted clerk, with three
men, was left in charge of the post.   The party performed
the journey across land to the Pavilion in six days, and
found the canoes, which had been left there in charge of
the Catatouch chief, all safe.

The most trivial incidents sometimes prove instructive,
and may in their consequences afford an important lesson.
As soon as Mr. Clarke arrived at the Pavilion, and
found his canoes safe, pleased at the conduct of the chief,
he made him a present of some ammunition and tobacco;
this done, they set about packing up the different articles
in order to embark, and among others two silver goblets
[215] belonging to Mr. Clarke himself, who took this
opportunity of showing them to the chief, and expatiated
on their high value;   then pouring a little wine into one
of them made the chief drink out of it, telling him when
done that he was a greater man now than ever he was
before.   The chief was delighted, and turning the goblet
over and over in his hands, and looking at it with intense
interest, handed it over to the next great man, and he to
another, and so on till, like the pipe of peace, it had
gone round the whole circle.   The precious curiosity
was then laid by, and the Indians retired.

Next morning, however, the pearl of great price was
gone!   everything in and about the camp was turned
topsy-turvy in search of the silver goblet, but to no
purpose: all business was now suspended — the goblet
must be found.   At last it was conjectured the Indians
must have stolen it;   and Mr. Clarke, with fury in his
countenance, assembled the whole Catatouch camp,
and made known his loss — the loss of his silver goblet!
he coaxed, he flattered, he threatened to bring down

vengeance upon the whole tribe for the loss of his goblet,
and, in his wrath and vexation, denounced death upon
the offender should he be discovered. The poor Indians
stood gazing in amazement; they sympathized with him,
pitied him, and deplored his loss, and promised to do
their utmost to find the goblet: with this solemn declaration they went off, the whole tribe was called together,
the council sat, and soon afterwards they [216] returned
in a body, like messengers of peace, bringing the glad
tidings to Mr. Clarke that the silver goblet was found;
at the same time the chief, stepping forward and spreading
out his robe, laid the precious vessel before him. ''Where
is the thief?'' vociferated Mr. Clarke. The chief then
pointed to a fellow sitting in the ring as the criminal.
''I swore,'' said Mr. Clarke, ''that the thief should die,
and white men never break their word.'' The fellow
was told of his fate; but he kept smiling, thinking himself,
according to Indian custom, perfectly safe; for the moment
the stolen article is returned to the rightful owner, according to the maxims of Indian law, the culprit is exonerated.
Mr. Clarke, however, thought otherwise, and, like Herod
of old, for the sake of his oath considered himself bound
to put his threat into execution, and therefore instantly
commanded the poor, unsuspecting wretch to be hung
up — and hung he was accordingly; and the unhallowed
deed was aggravated by the circumstance of their taking
the poles of his own lodge to make the gallows.

The Indians all the time could not believe that the
whites were in earnest, till they beheld the lifeless body.
The deed was, however, no sooner committed than Mr.
Clarke grew alarmed. The chief, throwing down his
robe on the ground, a sign of displeasure, harangued his
people, who immediately after mounted their fleetest

horses, and scampered off in all directions to circulate the news and assemble the surrounding [217] tribes, to take vengeance on the whites. In the mean time, leaving the enraged Indians to follow their inclination, the canoes were thrown into the water, loaded, and down the current Mr. Clarke and his men pushed their way day and night till they reached the Walla Walla, where they arrived safe on the 4th of June; and here we shall leave them for the present, while we detail M'Kenzie's winter adventures. Fortunately for the whites, the defunct Indian was a person of very low degree, even in the estimation of the Indians themselves, being an outcast without friends or relatives, which made them less bent on revenge, but not the less disposed to annoy, as we shall have occasion to notice hereafter.

Mr. M'Kenzie and party before mentioned accompanied Mr. Clarke up the South-branch as far as the Pavilion: here Clarke and his party forked off for Spokane in August, leaving M'Kenzie to prosecute his voyage up the same river till he reached the very centre of the Great Shahaptain, or Nez Percé nation, where he established himself for the winter. [76] By way of clearing up some points not very intelligible to many, we may here mention that the Great Snake River, Louis River, South-branch, Shahaptain River, and Nez Percé River, are all one and the same stream, with different denominations.

As soon as M'Kenzie had got his goods safe under cover, he sent off Mr. Reed, at the head of a small party, to bring the *caches* of goods left by Mr. Hunt to his own post. On his way, he picked up seven of [218] the

---

[76] On his map, Ross located McKenzie's post on the Snake at the mouth of Reed's River, the present Boisé River. Fort Boisé, a Hudson's Bay post, was afterwards established there.— ED.

Canadians belonging to the trapping parties fitted out by Mr. Hunt on his land expedition: these were, Dubreuil, Carson, the gunsmith, Delaunay, St. Michel, Turcotte, Landrie, and La Chapelle, the blacksmith. Some of these fellows, despairing of ever reaching the Columbia, and no doubt thinking the *caches* would be lost, went, accompanied by a band of the Snakes, and rifled several of them; and what they did not take was destroyed by the rains, the wolves, and other animals: some, however, had not been touched, and these Mr. Reed and his party carried off with them to M'Kenzie's post, which place they reached at the end of thirty-five days.

On questioning the wanderers, the true story of the *cache* robbery came out; for M'Kenzie learned from Turcotte and La Chapelle, that, having lost their horses by a marauding party of Blackfeet, and being otherwise destitute, they, in company with Landrie, meditated a descent upon the *caches* in order to supply their wants, and took the Snakes along with them as a safeguard; with their share of the spoil they purchased more horses, then following the Snakes to the Buffalo, they were again surprised by the Blackfeet, lost their horses and everything else, and were left as poor, if not poorer, than before. Filled with remorse, they promised to live honest men the rest of their lives.

M'Kenzie now began to learn the true character of the Indians about him. Their occupations were [219] war and buffalo-hunting. Their country did not abound in furs, nor would men accustomed to an indolent and roving life submit to the drudgery of killing beavers. They spurned the idea of crawling about in search of furs; ''Such a life,'' they said, ''was only fit for women and slaves.'' They were, moreover, insolent and independent. I say independent, because their horses procured them guns and ammunition; the buffaloes provided them with food and clothing; and war gave them renown. Such men held out but poor prospects to the fur-trader; so that M'Kenzie soon got sick of them, and weary of the place. He then equipped the seven Snake wanderers, and sent them out to trap beaver; but they had to go to the mountains, and on their way thither the Indians annoyed them, stole their traps, and frightened them back again to the post. M'Kenzie then resolved to abandon that post, and proceed further up the river; but before taking this step, he went over to Spokane to visit Mr. Clarke; and while there, Mr. John George M'Tavish, a partner of the North-West Company, arrived with a strong reinforcement of men and goods from the east side of the mountains, bringing an account of the war between Great Britain and the United States. [77] On receiving this unwelcome news, M'Kenzie hastened back to his post; but instead of removing further up, as he had contemplated, he put his goods in *cache*, and set off with all his men for Astoria, where he arrived on the 15th of January 1813.

[220] M'Kenzie was dismayed on reaching Astoria to find that the *Beaver* had not returned. M'Dougall and M'Kenzie, weighing circumstances, concluded that all was hopeless. The North-West Company now strong in numbers and well supplied with goods; the *Tonquin* lost, and the *Beaver* not returned, nor any account of her; add to these untoward circumstances, the declaration of war. In this gloomy state of things, M'Kenzie and M'Dougall were of opinion that prompt measures should be adopted for abandoning the undertaking altogether,

---

[77] A biography of McTavish will be found in Franchère, note 90.— ED.

and that ways and means should be concerted to remove the furs and goods at Astoria into the interior, to be out of the way in case of British ships of war entering the river.

On the 2nd of February, M'Kenzie turned his face towards the interior; and in two canoes, with eighteen men, pushed on to his post, having letters from M'Dougall pointing out the actual state of things, and informing Messrs. Clarke and Stuart of the resolution entered into between himself and M'Kenzie for abandoning the enterprize early in the spring. Messrs. Stuart and Clarke, however, viewed things in a different light, and condemned the proposed step as premature.

On his way up, Mr. M'Kenzie met two North-West canoes sweeping down the current. In these were M'Tavish, two clerks, and twenty men, on their way to the mouth of the Columbia, to meet the far-famed ship *Isaac Todd*, destined for that [221] part. On the twenty-second day after leaving Astoria, Mr. M'Kenzie arrived at his post on the Shahaptain River; but was mortified to find his *cache* robbed.

The Indians indicated their guilt by their shyness, for scarcely one of them came to visit the trader. M'Kenzie therefore summoned the chiefs, and they appeared, expecting no doubt to receive something. When they were all seated, he opened the business of the *cache*, and demanded the goods; adding, that if they were given up, friendship would again be restored. But they all, with one accord, denied having any knowledge of, or hand in, the pillage or robbery. They admitted the fact of the robbery, but denied that they were in any way accessory to it. They regretted the misconduct of their young men; but the goods were now gone, and

they could do nothing; and so the conference ended.
Seeing that the chiefs would not assist to recover the
stolen property, and that every hour's delay lessened
the chance of regaining it, M'Kenzie at once resolved
on a bold and hazardous step; namely, to dash into the
heart of the Indian camp, and recover what he could.
Accordingly next morning, after depositing in a safe
place the few articles he had brought with him, he and
his little band, armed *cap-à-pie*, set out on foot for the
camp. On their approach, the Indians, suspecting
something, turned out in groups here and there, also
armed. But M'Kenzie, without a moment's hesitation,
or giving them time to reflect, [222] ordered Mr. Seaton, [78]
who commanded the men, to surround the first wigwam
or lodge reached with charged bayonets, while he himself
and Mr. Reed entered the lodge, ransacked it, turning
everything topsy-turvy, and with their drawn daggers
cutting and ripping open everything that might be
supposed to conceal the stolen property. In this manner
they went from one lodge to another till they had searched
five or six with various success, when the chiefs demanded
a parley, and gave M'Kenzie to understand that if he
desisted they would do the business themselves, and
more effectually. M'Kenzie, after some feigned reluc-
tance, at last agreed to the chief's proposition. They
then asked him to withdraw; but this he peremptorily
refused, knowing from experience that they were least
exposed in the camp; for Indians are always averse to
hostilities taking place in their camp, in the midst of their
women and children. Had the Indians foreseen or been
aware of the intention of the whites, they would never have

[78] Concerning Seton, see Franchère, note 81.— ED.

allowed them within their camp. But they were taken by surprise, and that circumstance saved the whites. However, as soon as the chiefs undertook the business, M'Kenzie and his men stood still and looked on. The chiefs went from house to house, and after about three hours time they returned, bringing with them a large portion of the property, and delivered it to M'Kenzie, when he and his men left the camp and returned home, bearing off in triumph the fruits of their valour; and well pleased [223] with their hairbreadth adventure; an adventure not to be repeated. And under all circumstances, it was at the time considered the boldest step ever taken by the whites on Columbian ground.

This dispute with the Indians led to others; and if the whites got the upper hand in the late affair, the Indians were determined to be even with them in another way — for not a single horse would they sell, and on horse-flesh M'Kenzie and his men had to depend. On this head various conferences took place between the parties, and higher prices than usual were tendered; but the chiefs were inexorable. They had resolved either to drive the whites off their country altogether, or make them pay the most extravagant prices. The object of the whites in delaying their departure was to procure horses, which would be absolutely required in the event of Messrs. Stuart and Clarke acceding to the views of M'Dougall and M'Kenzie; but the Indians, free and independent as the air they breathed or the wind that blew, could not brook the restraint which the whites were always affecting to exercise over them. After some little time, all intercourse between the parties was at an end; not an Indian was to be seen about M'Kenzie's camp, except by stealth in the night, to beg, curry favour, or carry reports, yet five of these secret spies were always kept in pay by M'Kenzie to watch the motions of the Indians, and through them he knew every move in the hostile camp.

At this time one of the spies reported that the [224] Indians had plotted together to starve M'Kenzie into terms, or drive him off altogether. M'Kenzie, on his part, had recourse to a stratagem to bring them to terms. Both were on the alert. When the whites had nothing to eat, the articles usually paid for a horse were tied up in a bundle; that done, M'Kenzie, with ten or twelve of his men, would sally forth with their rifles to the grazing grounds of the horses, shoot the fattest they could find, and carry off the flesh to their camp; leaving the price stuck upon a pole alongside the head of the dead horse.

This manœuvre succeeded several times, and annoyed the Indians very much; some of them lost their best horses by it. Then it was that they combined to attack the whites in their camp. This news was brought M'Kenzie by one of his hired spies, and was confirmed by the fact of an Indian offering to sell a horse for powder and ball only. From various other suspicious circumstances, there remained but little doubt in the minds of the whites but that there was some dark design in agitation. In this critical conjuncture, M'Kenzie again eluded their grasp by ensconcing himself and his party in an island in the middle of the river. There they remained, in a manner blockaded by the Indians; but not so closely watched but that they appeared every now and then with their long rifles among the Shahaptain horses; so that the Indians grew tired of their predatory excursions, and therefore sent a messenger to M'Kenzie. A parley ensued between the main land [225] and the island; the result of which was, that the Indians agreed to sell horses to the whites at the usual price — the whites, on their part, to give up their marauding practices.

Notwithstanding this formal treaty, the whites did not put implicit faith in their Indian allies, nor deem it prudent to leave the island; but the trade in horses went on briskly, and without interruption, M'Kenzie getting all his wants supplied. He bought, besides, an extra reserve of eighty horses for contingencies, which he sent off to Spokane; and on the return of his men he left the island, apparently on good terms with the Indians, and reached the Walla Walla, to join his associates, on the 1st of June.

When we reached the Walla Walla on the 30th of May, as already mentioned, we were at a loss to account for the unusual movement and stir among the Indians, who seemed to be assembling from all quarters in great haste. The mystery was, however, soon cleared up when Mr. Clarke joined us, and related the affair of the silver goblet at the Catatouch camp. What did Stuart and M'Kenzie say? What could any man say? The reckless deed had been committed, and Clarke's countenance fell when the general voice of disapprobation was raised against him. The Indians all along kept flying to and fro, whooping and yelling in wild commotion. At this time, Tummeatapam came riding up to our camp at full speed. "What have you done, my friends?" called out the old and agitated chief. "You have spilt blood on our lands!" [226] Then pointing to a cloud of dust raised by the Indians, who were coming down upon us in wild confusion —"There, my friends, do you see them? What can I do?" The chief did not dismount, but wheeling round his horse again, off he went like a shot, leaving us to draw a salutary inference from the words "What can I do?"— meaning, no doubt, that we had better be off immediately. Taking the hint, we lost no time. Tents were struck; some had breakfasted, some not — kettles and dishes were all huddled together and bundled into the canoe, and, embarking pell-mell, we pushed with all haste from the inauspicious shore. We pushed our way down the current, passing the falls, the narrows, and the cascades, without the least interruption, and arrived safe at Astoria on the 14th day of June. And here we shall leave the party to recount to each other their various exploits, while we take up the thread of Mr. Stuart's adventures from Columbia to St. Louis.

[227] CHAPTER XIV [79]

Mr. Stuart — Snake River — Trappers — Joyous meeting — Trappers' resolution — Crow Indians' troubles — Horses change masters — Mr. Stuart on foot — M'Lellan left alone — Hardships of the party — Famine — Le Clerc's horrid proposition — The old bull — The old horse — Pilot-knobs — Winter quarters — Unwelcome visitors — Change of quarters — Spring — Travelling at random — An Otto Indian — River Platte — Two traders — News of the war — The Missouri — The old horse given for an old canoe — St. Louis — Mr. Astor — Wallamitte — Falls — Scenery — Habits of the Col-lap-poh-yea-ass tribes — Concourse of savages — M'Dougall's letter — M'Kenzie's stratagem — Indian disappointment — The ship *Beaver* — Coasting voyage — Mr. Astor's policy — Captains — Their instructions — Mr. Hunt baulked in his plans — The Boston merchants — Mr. Astor's conduct — Difficulties of Mr. Hunt's situation — The ship *Albatross* — All the parties at headquarters.

WHEN we left Mr. Stuart on the 31st of July last, he

---

[79] For notes on the following persons and places mentioned in this chapter, see Bradbury's *Travels*, volume v of our series: Hoback, Rezner, and Robinson, note 65; Crow Indians, note 121; Arapaho Indians, note 120; Oto Indians, note 42.— ED.

had then just mounted his horse on his journey across land for St. Louis; we now propose keeping him company, and will make such remarks during his perilous route as barren, wild, and savage hordes may from time to time suggest.

From Walla Walla the party journeyed onwards, first over the open plains, and next across the Blue [228] Mountains, till at length they fell on the Great Snake River, along which they occasionally continued their route for many days without any interesting occurrence till the 20th of August, when they, by mere chance, stumbled on Mr. Miller, and three of the beaver-trappers, Hoback, Resner, and Robinson, fitted out by Mr. Hunt.

It will be remembered that Mr. Miller abruptly left Mr. Hunt and party to join one of the trapping parties. The joy manifested by both parties at meeting was, as might be expected, the most cordial and lively. They swore that they had met to part no more till they parted in that land which had given them birth. So Mr. Miller and his prodigal children joined Mr. Stuart with the determination to follow him to St. Louis. These wanderers had been twice robbed by the Indians, had exhausted their strength, wasted their means, and saved nothing; and seemed on the present occasion quite overjoyed and happy at the prospect of once more returning to their native homes. Yet what will the reader think when he is told that only eight days after all these fine resolutions, they again expressed a wish to remain where they were, and try their fortune once more in the wilderness! Strange infatuation! Change of climate seldom makes a change of character. Mr. Stuart reasoned with them, but in vain; and at last, seeing them resolved, he supplied them with a new and full equipment of everything they wanted. So the parties separated; Mr. Miller following

Mr. Stuart and his [229] party, while the other three trappers bade them farewell, and stayed behind.

On the 7th of September they left the Great Snake River, and entered the defiles of the mountains. Here they met some saucily-disposed Crow Indians; but they got clear of them without harm, and Mr. Stuart continued his toilsome journey, winding his way among the rugged and rapid streams near the source of the Great Snake River to which they drew near again, in the hopes of avoiding the Crows; but it mattered little what course they steered, or what direction they took, the Crows were everywhere at their heels; and in front provisions were also scarce, and the party were now much reduced by hunger and fatigue.

On the 19th, early in the morning, the Crows, like a Scythian horde, dashed on their little camp, giving the Indian war-whoop, and swept all their horses off in a moment. This misfortune left them in an awful plight. They stood motionless and hopeless. They had now to turn over a new leaf, and from mounted cavalry, to become foot soldiers. They now set about making up each man's load, and what they could not carry they destroyed on the spot rather than let any of it fall into the hands of their implacable enemies, for their every movement was now watched with an eagle's eye by the Indians on the heights. To avoid, therefore, the hostile Crows, they had to shun the buffalo, and run the risk of starving or of going right into the jaws of the Blackfeet; but there was no [230] alternative, and to lessen the evil as much as possible they bent their course northward, through a country, in Mr. Stuart's own words, "more fit for goats than men;" and so closely were they watched by the savages, that they could not venture to separate for the purpose of hunting. They had likewise to keep watch by night, and were every moment in danger of being surrounded or waylaid in the narrow and intricate defiles through which they had to pass.

Yet these trying circumstances, when danger stared them in the face, failed to unite them together in heart and hand. Mr. M'Lellan, with a fool-hardiness and wayward disposition peculiar to himself, left the party in a pet, nor was it till the tenth day afterwards that he was picked up, lying in his cheerless and forlorn encampment, without fire or food, and reduced through hunger, fatigue, and cold to a mere skeleton. Always perverse and stubborn, he had now become peevish and sullen, yet in this torpid and reduced state he revived on seeing his friends, became cheerful, and joyfully joined the party again; but being unable to carry anything, or even to walk, the party halted for two days that he might recruit a little, and then his rifle, pistols, and other things being carried by the others, the party set forward on their journey. They wandered about for five days and nights without a mouthful to eat, and were now reduced to the last extremity; nor had they strength to make use of their rifles, although now and then some deer were seen.

[231] On the 15th of October, the sixth day of their fasting, just as the party had halted for the night, Le Clerc, one of the Canadians, proposed to cast lots, saying, "It is better one should die than that all should perish." Mr. Stuart reproved him severely; and as the fellow stood haggard and wild before him, with his rifle in his hand, he ordered the others to wrest it from his grasp. A watch was kept all night, nor did Mr. Stuart himself close an eye. During this scene, M'Lellan, scarcely able to

move, kept eyeing Le Clerc all the time, and looking round
for his rifle; but Mr. Stuart had put it out of the way.
Next day, however, Providence directed their forlorn
steps to an old and solitary buffalo-bull, which they
managed to kill, and this fortunate rencontre saved their
lives.

On the 18th, the wanderers fell in with a straggling
camp of Snakes, from whom they purchased a sorry old
horse, the only one the ruffian Crows had left with them.
This horse appeared in their eyes a prize of no small
value. With him they set out, not a little cheered and
comforted by the two lucky acquisitions — the old bull
and the old horse. Our party were then wandering
between the lofty Pilot-knobs and the head-waters of the
Missouri; but far from the latter. They now kept
veering more to the east, and advancing irregularly, as
the valleys and ravines opened a road for them to pass,
till the snow and cold weather precluded all hopes of
getting much farther for this season, so that they began
to look [232] out for a place of security, and rest from
their fatigues.

On the 2nd of November they pitched their camp for
winter; built a log-hut, and the buffalo being plenty,
and the party tolerably recovered in strength, they soon
laid in an ample stock of provisions; but in the wilderness
all plans are precarious, hopes delusive. Our friends
had not been long in their comfortable quarters before
they were pestered with unwelcome visitors, for a war
party of Arapahays discovered their retreat, and annoyed
them so much that they thought it best to look out for
some other quarters, more secluded and secure.

On the 13th of December they abandoned their
dwelling with infinite regret, and setting out through

deep snows, over a rugged and inhospitable country, they travelled for fifteen days, when a bleak and boundless plain presented itself before them. Here they held a consultation. The plain before them, destitute both of animals and firewood, appeared like an ocean of despair. The more they reflected, the more awful did their situation appear. At last they retraced their wearied steps for about eighty miles, and took up a second position.

On the 30th of December they again pitched their winter camp, built a house, laid in a stock of food, and found themselves once more in comfortable quarters. In this last retreat the Indians did not find them out, and there they awaited the return of spring.

[233] On the 20th of March they broke up their winter-quarters, and in two canoes, made during the winter, they essayed to push their way down a broad but shoal river. In this, however, they failed, and leaving their canoes they took to land again with their old but faithful Snake-horse. All this time they were wandering in hopes of reaching some known branch of the Missouri: for they had lost their way, and did not know where they were for the last three months.

On the 1st of April the party fell in with an Indian of the Otto tribe. This stranger gave them to understand that they were then treading on the banks of the River Platte, and not far from white men. The same Indian then conducted them to Messrs. Dornin and Roi, two Indian traders, established in that quarter. From these gentlemen Mr. Stuart got the first news of the war between Great Britain and the States; and they also undertook to furnish him with a canoe for the voyage down the Missouri, in exchange for the old and faithful Snake-horse.

On the 16th they all embarked, and after descending
about fifty miles on the River Platte they found themselves on the broad and majestic Missouri, down which
with buoyant spirits they now pushed their way, without
accident or interruption, till they reached St. Louis on
the 30th of April.   Mr. Stuart lost no time in acquainting
Mr. Astor with his safe arrival at that place with
despatches from Columbia, [234] and that the success
and prospect of affairs there were such as to warrant the
most flattering results.

The information conveyed by Mr. Stuart was hailed
by Mr. Astor as a sure presage of future prosperity:
and, in his exultation, he said, "That will do; I have hit
the nail on the head."   Mr. Stuart's journey with so
small a party, across a region so distant, wild, and hostile,
was fraught with many perils and privations.   During
the period of ten long months, he was never free from
danger and anxiety.   The eventual success of that
expedition, so often reduced to extremities, reflects great
credit on him who conducted it.   Leaving now Mr.
Stuart to enjoy himself among his friends at St. Louis,
we shall go back to Columbia again to see what has been
doing in the Wallamitte quarter.

The Wallamitte quarter has always been considered
by the whites as the garden of the Columbia, particularly
in an agricultural point of view, and certain animals
of the chace; but in the article of beaver, the great staple
commodity of the Indian trader, several other places,
such as the Cowlitz, Blue Mountains, and She Whaps,
equal, if not surpass it.   In the spring of 1812, Mr.
M'Kenzie had penetrated some hundred miles up the
Wallamitte River, but more with the view of exploring

the southern quarter, seeing the Indians, and studying the topography of the country, than for the purpose of procuring beaver. This year another party, fitted out by M'Dougall on a beaver-trading excursion, spent some months [235] in that quarter, among the Col-lap-poh-yea-ass. These parties penetrated nearly to the source of the Wallamitte, a distance of five hundred miles. It enters the Columbia by two channels, not far distant from each other; the most westerly is the main branch, and is distant from Cape Disappointment from eighty to ninety miles, following the course of the river. The Wallamitte lies in the direction of south and north, and runs parallel with the seacoast; that is, its source lies south and its course north. In ascending the river the surrounding country is most delightful, and the first barrier to be met with is about forty miles up from its mouth.

Here the navigation is interrupted by a ledge of rocks running across the river from side to side, in the form of an irregular horse-shoe, over which the whole body of water falls at one leap down a precipice of about forty feet, called the Falls. To this place, and no farther, the salmon ascend, and during the summer months they are caught in great quantities. At this place, therefore, all the Indians throughout the surrounding country assemble, gamble, and gormandize for months together. From the mouth of the Wallamitte up to the falls it is navigable for boats only, and from the falls to its source for canoes, and it is sufficiently deep for the ordinary purposes of the Indian trader. The banks of the river throughout are low, and skirted in the distance by a chain of moderately high lands on each side, interspersed here and there with clumps of [236] wide-spreading oaks, groves of pine, and a variety of other kinds of wood. Between these high lands, lie what is called the Valley of the Wallamitte, the frequented haunts of innumerable herds of elk and deer.

The natives are very numerous and well disposed; yet they are an indolent and sluggish race, and live exceedingly poor in a very rich country. When our people were travelling there, the moment the report of a gun was heard forth came the natives; men, women, and children would follow the sound like a swarm of bees, and feast and gormandize on the offal of the game, like so many vultures round a dead carcass; yet every Indian has his quiver full of arrows, and few natives are more expert with the bow. The names of the different tribes, beginning at the mouth of the river and taking them in succession as we ascend, may be ranged in the following order:— Wa-come-app, Naw-moo-it, Chilly-Chandize, Shook-any, Coupé, She-hees, Long-tongue-buff, La-malle, and Pee-you tribes; but as a great nation they are known under the general name of Col-lap-poh-yea-ass, and are governed by four principal chiefs. [80] The most eminent and powerful goes by the name of Key-ass-no. [81] The productiveness of their country is, probably, the chief cause of their extreme apathy and indolence; for it requires so little exertion to provide for their wants,

---

[80] The Kalapuya, an isolated family, were once a numerous people dwelling at the falls of the Willamette. In 1841 they numbered less than five hundred, and by the middle of the century were practically extinct. In civilization they occupied a middle position between the wandering tribes of the interior and the debased Indians of the coast. It is impossible to reconcile the names of the Kalapuya tribes given by Ross with other lists of lower Willamette Indians. He alone extends the Kalapuya to its mouth, while Lewis and Clark, Morse (*Report to the Secretary of War*, Washington, 1822), and Hale (*United States Exploring Expedition*, Philadelphia, 1846, vol. vi) confine them to the falls, and place Chinook tribes below that point.— ED.

[81] For an account of this chief, see Franchère, note 51.— ED.

that even that little is not attended to; they are honest
and harmless, yet there is a singular mixture of simplicity
and cunning [237] about them. The river, towards its
head-waters, branches out into numerous little streams,
which rise in the mountains. There is also another fine
river near the source of the Wallamitte; but lying rather
in the direction of east and west, called the Imp-qua;
this river empties itself into the ocean. [82] The finest
hunting-ground on the Wallamitte is towards the Imp-qua.
There beaver is abundant, and the party that went there
to trade this year made handsome returns; but the
Indians throughout are so notoriously lazy that they can
hardly be prevailed upon to hunt or do anything else that
requires exertion.

Yet, with all their apathy and inertness, we find that they
can be roused into action; for while M'Kenzie was visiting
their country, a slight quarrel took place between some
of them and a white man, named Jervais, at the Wa-
come-app village. Jervais had beaten one of the Indians,
which gave great offence to the tribe; and they had been
muttering threats in consequence. [83] M'Dougall, hearing
of the circumstance, sent off a letter to apprize M'Kenzie,

[82] This is the Umpqua, the largest river between the Sacramento and the
Columbia. It rises in the Cascade Range and empties into the Pacific Ocean
about two hundred and twenty-five miles south of the Columbia. The fur-
trading post Fort Umpqua, was on the southern bank about forty miles from the
ocean.— ED.

[83] Joseph Gervais, a French Canadian, came to Astoria with Captain Hunt
in 1811. After the abandonment of that post, he became a "free trapper," and
married the daughter of a Clatsop chief. Desiring a more settled life, in 1828
he selected a place on the Willamette, a short distance below the present Salem,
and raised wheat. A few years later other French Canadians, retired Hudson's
Bay clerks, became farmers along the Willamette and the district became known
as French Prairie. Gervais took an active part in establishing the provisional
government of Oregon in 1843. He became prosperous, and lived on French
Prairie until his death (1861) at the age of eighty-four years.— ED.

that he might keep a good look-out on his way back, as the Indians intended to intercept or waylay him. M'Kenzie arrived at the hostile camp, situate at the mouth of the Wallamitte, crossed to the opposite or north side of the Columbia, and then went on shore, without in the least suspecting what was going on, although he had remarked once or twice to his people, the unusual multitude of Indians collected together, and their bold and daring appearance; and [238] also that Key-ass-no, the chief, had not come to see them. On his way up, M'Kenzie had left his boat at the falls till his return, and now took it down with him. While he was revolving in his mind those suspicious appearances, one of a neighbouring tribe slipped into his hand, privately, M'Dougall's letter. The moment he read the letter he was convinced of his critical situation, and whispered to his men to be ready to embark at a moment's warning. But, behold, the tide had left his boat high and dry on the beach. What was now to be done? Always fertile, however, in expedients, he feigned the greatest confidence in the Indians, and at the same time adopted a stratagem to deceive them. He told them he had some thoughts of building among them, and would now look for a suitable site; for which reason, he said, he would stay with them for the night, and requested them to prepare a good encampment for him, which they immediately set about doing. This threw the Indians off their guard, as they could then accomplish their purpose more effectually, and with less risk. This manœuvre had the desired effect. Some of the Indians were busied in clearing the encampment; others he amused in looking out for a place to build, till the following tide set his boat afloat again; then taking advantage of it, he and his men instantly embarked and pushed before the current, leaving the Indians in painful disappointment, gazing at one another. Next morning they arrived safe among their friends at Astoria.

[239] Before we close the account of this year's campaign, we must take up the subject of the ship *Beaver*, Capt. Sowle, from New York, with the annual supplies, who arrived at Astoria, as we have before noticed, on the 9th of May, after a voyage of 212 days. The *Beaver* remained at the infant establishment of Astoria till the 4th of August. On the 6th, she crossed the bar with some difficulty, having grounded twice, which so frightened old Sowle, the captain, that he was heard to say "I'll never cross you again." Having cleared the bar, she left the Columbia on a three months' cruise along the coast, towards the Russian settlements at Kamtschatka, intending to be back again about the latter end of October, and as had been settled upon in the council of partners. Mr. Hunt was on board. It may, however, be easily inferred that this was a part of Astor's general plan, that the man at the head of affairs should accompany the ship on her coasting trip. It was so with the *Tonquin*, as well as with the *Beaver*; and this again goes far to prove how little Astor cared about the Columbia, or those carrying on the business there, when the man at the head of the establishment was liable to be removed from his important charge, and sent as a peddling supercargo on board the ship, merely for the purpose of receiving a few seal-skins from old Count Baranhoff, at Kamtschatka. [84] This, as I have already said, was done by Astor's orders; for he, in his arm-chair at New York, regulated all the

[84] For further information regarding Baranoff and the Russian settlements, see Franchère, note 93.— ED.

springs of action at [240] Astoria, just as if he had been on
the spot.   Work well, work ill, his commands remained
like the laws of the Medes and Persians: there was no
discretionary power left to alter them.

The ship, therefore, with Mr. Hunt on board, reached
her destination without any accident or delay;   visited
New Archangel, Sitka, and St. Paul's, taking in at these
places a valuable cargo of furs, chiefly seal-skins;   but was
detained in these boisterous seas much longer than had
been calculated upon, for she had not left the most northern
of these parts, which is St. Paul's, before the beginning of
November.[85]

And here we have another instance of that fatal policy
pursued by Astor in giving to his captains powers which
made them independent of the consignees.   This was
the case with Captain Thorn, who left what he pleased,
and carried off what he pleased;   and when M'Dougall
and the other parties remonstrated with him for leaving
the infant colony so bare, he put his hand in his pocket
and produced his instructions from Astor, which at once
shut their mouths.   The same game was now played by
Captain Sowle.   Mr. Hunt could not prevail upon him,
on his way back from the Russian settlements, to touch
at Columbia;   and when Mr. Hunt threatened to remove
him and give the command to another, he then, as
Captain Thorn had done before him, produced his
private instructions from Mr. Astor, justifying his proceedings;   for after Mr. Hunt's arrival [241] at Columbia,
he often repeated, in the anguish of his soul, that "the

---

[85] A brief account of Sitka will be found in Franchère, note 68.   Sitka and
New Archangel were identical.   Sitka was destroyed by the Indians in 1802 and
in 1804 a post called New Archangel, was built at the same place.   It is
situated on Sitka Sound, Baranoff Island, in latitude 57° north.   St. Paul is on
the northeast shore of Kadiak Island, off the coast of Alaska, in latitude 58°.—ED.

underhand policy of Astor and the conduct of his captains had ruined the undertaking." In this perplexing situation, Mr. Hunt had to submit, and Captain Sowle, spreading his canvass, steered for the Sandwich Islands direct, carrying Mr. Hunt, like a prisoner, along with him. From the Sandwich Islands, the *Beaver* sailed for Canton, in the first week of January, 1813; a serious loss to Astor, and the ruin of Astoria.

It was a part of Mr. Astor's general plan to supply the Russian factories along the coast with goods; and it would appear, from the conduct of his captains, that to this branch of the undertaking he devoted his chief attention; reserving for them the choicest part of all his cargoes, and for Columbia the mere refuse. This alone gave great umbrage to the partners at Astoria; it soured their dispositions to see many articles which they stood in need of pass by their door.

While at Woahoo, Mr. Hunt heard some faint rumours of the war, but nothing certain. The Boston merchants had, at a great expense, fitted out, it was said, a despatch ship for the Pacific, in order to apprise the coasting vessels there of the declaration of war. But Mr. Hunt could gain no certain information on that head; because Astor had not contributed his mite towards the expense of fitting out the vessel, they were determined not to let the least hint of it reach Hunt, who was therefore left in the dark. [242] Can anything point out in a clearer light Astor's indifference about the fate of his little devoted colony at Columbia, than his not joining the Boston merchants, or taking any steps whatever to apprise the Astorians of the war?

In the mean time, Mr. Hunt waited at the Sandwich Islands, in the hope that another annual ship from New

York might cast up for the relief of Astoria; but waited in vain. At last, by the arrival of the ship *Albatross*, Captain Smith, from Canton, he was no longer in doubt as to the declaration of war; and this increased his anxiety to get back to Astoria. Chartering, therefore, the ship *Albatross*, he sailed in her, after a ruinous delay, and arrived safe at Astoria on the 20th of August. And this brings the parties once more to Astoria, and closes the transactions of the year.

[243] CHAPTER XV

Meeting of the partners — Warm discussion — M'Kenzie — Eloquence of the times — Reasons for dissolving the company — Dissenting partners converted — Final resolve — The deputy's powers — Departure of the brigade — A canoe lost — A man's leg in jeopardy — Rumours at the narrows — Snake party — Rumours renewed — Tummeatapam's counsel — Hostile appearance at the forks — Number of Indians — Nez Percés' fleet — Fears of the whites — Indian visit — Strong guard — Mr. Clarke — Relic of the silver goblet — Mr. Hunt at Astoria — Face of affairs changed — Mr. Hunt departs from Astoria — North-West squadron — A great Eri duped — Bill of sale — Petty manœuvring — Rumours of ships — The Astorians at their post — Bills signed — Astoria delivered up — North-West Company.

ASTORIA now became the scene of business and bustle. A council was convened, and a second meeting of the partners took place. Last year their expectations were raised to the highest pitch, and everything promised an abundant harvest of wealth and glory: the present state of affairs was somewhat clouded with reverses and cross-purposes. The resolutions of M'Dougall and M'Kenzie last winter, to abandon the undertaking, were now discussed anew: on the one hand, M'Dougall found great [244] fault with Clarke and Stuart for not taking such steps for leaving the country as were pointed out in the resolutions alluded to; on the other hand, these gentlemen were equally displeased with M'Dougall for having acted, as they considered, prematurely and without their consent. Two days were spent in mutual recrimination: at last M'Kenzie, who had hitherto left both parties to settle the dispute the best way they could, now sided with M'Dougall, and poured forth such a torrent of persuasive eloquence, backed by facts, that the opposite party were reduced to silence.

"Gentlemen," said he, "why do you hesitate so long between two opinions? your eyes ought to have been opened before now to your own interests. In the present critical conjuncture, there is no time to be lost: let us then, by a timely measure, save what we can, lest a British ship of war enter the river and seize all. We have been long enough the dupes of a vacillating policy — a policy which showed itself at Montreal on our first outset, in refusing to engage at once a sufficient number of able hands.

"At Nodowa that policy was equally conspicuous. Did not Astor's private missive to Mr. Hunt at that place give umbrage to all? Did not his private orders to Mr. Hunt to put his nephew, with one scratch of his pen, over the heads of all the clerks in the concern add to that umbrage? Could there be anything more impolitic and unjust? Could there be any measure more at variance with the letter and [245] the spirit of the articles of agreement? Did not his private instructions to his captains annihilate the power and authority of the partners? When the unfortunate *Tonquin* left this, what did she leave behind? did she not, by virtue of Astor's private instructions to her captain, carry everything off that was worth carrying off? Has not the same line of policy been pursued in the case of the *Beaver*? And this year there is no ship at all! Has it not been obvious from the beginning, that under Astor's policy we can never prosper? and, besides, there are other untoward matters over which Mr. Astor had no control, such as the delay of the *Beaver*, the absence of Mr. Hunt, our formidable rivals the North-West Company, and, to crown all, the declaration of war.

"Now, gentlemen, all these inauspicious circumstances taken together point out, in my opinion, the absolute necessity of abandoning the enterprize as soon as possible. We owe it to Astor — we owe it to ourselves; and our authority for adopting such a course is based on the 15th and 16th articles of the copartnership, which authorize us at any time within the period of five years to abandon the undertaking, should it prove impracticable or unprofitable. Not, gentlemen, that there is any fault in the country — no country, as to valuable furs, can hold out better prospects; but Astor's policy, and a chain of misfortunes, have ruined all. Astor, with all his sagacity, either does not or will not understand the business. The system we were bound to follow was [246] bad, and that system we cannot alter; so that we are bound in honour to deliver the whole back into the hands from which we received it — and the sooner the better." These representations, stamped with the authority of experience, had the desired effect; the resolution to abandon the country was adopted, and Messrs. Stuart and Clarke gave it their cordial consent: as it was now too late to carry it into execution this year, it was postponed till the next;

and the 1st of June was the time fixed upon for our departure.

These preliminary arrangements being now completed, a resolution was signed on the 1st of July, by all the partners present, to dissolve the concern and abandon the enterprize the next year. It was then resolved that Mr. Stuart should betake himself to his post at the She Whaps, and that Mr. Clarke should proceed to Spokane, while Mr. M'Kenzie was to winter on the Wallamitte, with the express understanding that we were all to meet again at Astoria next May, and to take our final departure from that establishment on the 1st of June, unless a new supply should arrive, and peace be concluded before that time. That Mr. Reed, with some hunters and trappers, should pass the winter in the Snake country, collect the stragglers still wandering through that quarter, and at a certain point await the arrival of the main body, and join it on its way across.

Meanwhile, Mr. M'Dougall was still to continue in the command of Astoria until Mr. Hunt's return. [247] M'Dougall was also empowered, in the event of Mr. Hunt's non-arrival, to treat with Mr. M'Tavish for the transfer of all the goods and furs belonging to the Pacific Fur Company in the country, at certain fixed prices, should that gentleman be disposed to purchase on behalf of the North-West Company, considering a sale of this nature, under all circumstances, to be a safer speculation than the conveyance of so much property across the long and dangerous route to St. Louis. Such were the resolutions passed on the present occasion, and copies of them all were delivered over to M'Tavish, to be forwarded to Mr. Astor by the North-West Company's winter express. The parties then left Astoria for the interior on the 5th of July.

We have now so often related the voyage up and down
the Columbia, that on the present occasion it will not be
necessary to dwell on minute details; suffice it to say,
therefore, that we reached the cascades or first barrier
without any remarkable occurrence, till we got opposite
to Strawberry Island, where one of the canoes in ascending
the rapid, sheered out in the stream, whirled round and
round, and upset. With great difficulty and danger the
men were saved, but a good deal of property was irre-
coverably lost, and, among other things, a box of mine,
containing books and mathematical instruments, quadrant,
sextant, and a valuable pair of pistols — all went to
the bottom. It is a singular fact, that we have never yet
once been able to pass [248] this Charybdis without
paying tribute either to the natives or the whirlpools:
but misfortunes seldom come alone, and to add to the
confusion, as we were all running to and fro saving the
men's lives and the property, Mr. Cox's gun, being held
in some awkward and careless position, went off, and
both balls passed through the calf of Mr. Pillet's right
leg, but fortunately without breaking the bone.

Proceeding onwards, we passed the long narrows and
the Wyampam banditti, for the first time, without any
trouble. It was, however, rumoured here that we were
to be attacked in passing the forks; that the Indians had
assembled there in hostile array. And here Mr. Clarke
would fain have avoided the encounter; he made several
attempts, but in vain, to engage a guide to lead him
through the interior by a back path. At the Umatallow,
the small party bound for the Snake country left us, and
departed in the direction of the Blue Mountains.

On reaching the Walla Walla, about six miles from
the forks, Tummeatapam made signs for us to go on

shore. Here the good old Sachem appeared much agitated, and sat for some time without uttering a single word. At last he broke silence, and exclaimed —"White men! white men!" then pointing to a dark cloud of dust rising near the forks, said, "There they are — there they are!" Then taking up a handful of sand and throwing it in the air, exclaimed again — "They are as numerous as the grains of sand; the Indians have bad hearts: I am hoarse with speaking [249] to them; but they will not listen to me." He advised us earnestly to turn back; but seeing us determined to ascend the river, he asked leave to embark and accompany us: but this we refused. We took him, however, to one of our boats, and showed him a brass four-pounder, some hand-grenades, and sky-rockets; then giving him some tobacco to smoke, we embarked, and crossing over to the right-hand side, pushed on along shore; the Indians being all on the left bank. As we advanced, the Indians, mounted in numerous squadrons, kept flying backwards and forwards, seemingly bent on some great design. We paddled on, however, without a moment's delay, anxious to get to a certain point a little beyond the forks, but on the opposite side of the river, which is here nearly a mile broad. When we came just opposite to the Indians, they all formed into one mass, and could not have been less than two thousand, with a fleet of one hundred and seventy-four canoes along the beach. Their appearance was certainly very imposing and formidable; and the noise of the war-dance and war-song, mingled with whooping and yelling, was terrific. We in the mean time reached the wished-for point, landed, took our stand, fortified our camp, and awaited the threatened attack. This took place in the afternoon, about two hours before sunset. All at once the canoes were launched, and we beheld fifty-seven of them filled with people making for our camp. All was suspense. Every man squatted down with his gun in his hand, and his finger on the trigger. As [250] the fleet approached our anxiety increased, till Mr. Stuart, who kept eyeing them all the time with a spy-glass, called out — "There is nothing to fear; there are women and children in the canoes." This was glad news to some of our party, who were more intent on saying their prayers than on fighting. By this time they had got almost close to us, when they all disembarked at the distance of about two hundred yards. Mr. Stuart, advancing to meet them, drew a line on the sand, as much as to say, "Do not pass this:" they obeyed — the pipe of peace was smoked, and laid aside. After a short pause, a few harangues were made. They smoked again; a trifling present followed; the business was ended, and at dusk the Indians returned quietly to their camp. We supposed that Tummeatapam's account of our big gun influenced their conduct not a little. Their peaceable behavior, however, did not altogether quiet our apprehensions; a strong watch was set for the night, and before the morning dawn every man had his gun in his hand; but the Indians had disappeared. This demonstration of the Indians prevented Mr. Clarke from proceeding to his destination by the usual route. He had therefore to continue with us, and pass by Oakinacken for Spokane, making a circuitous route of more than three hundred miles.

From the forks, we proceeded without interruption till we reached Oakinacken on the 15th of August, where I was to winter; and here we shall leave the different parties to proceed to their respective [251] quarters, while we, in the mean time, return back a little to see what is going on at Astoria.

It has already been stated that Mr. Hunt arrived at Astoria, in the ship *Albatross*, on the 20th of August. He was mortified to find, from the resolutions of the 1st of July, that the partners had made up their minds to abandon the country. M'Dougall and M'Kenzie now exerted their reasoning powers to convince Mr. Hunt of their desperate and hopeless situation. Nor could that gentleman, with all his zeal for the interest of Mr. Astor, and the success of his enterprize, shut his eyes or close his ears against facts so self-evident. After weighing, therefore, all the circumstances of our situation, Mr. Hunt acquiesced in the measures that had been taken, and likewise confirmed the powers given to Mr. M'Dougall to transfer the goods and furs to the North-West Company. These points being settled, Mr. Hunt, after remaining a week at Astoria, left the Columbia again in the *Albatross*. This vessel was bound for the Marquesas, and Mr. Hunt took a passage in her with the view of purchasing a ship to carry the furs at Astoria to market, in the event of no transfer being made to the North-West Company, as well as to convey thirty-two Sandwich Islanders, now in the service of the Company, back to their own country; and here I shall take my leave of Mr. Hunt for the present, and return to my post at Oakinacken.

Everything now assumed a calm and tranquil [252] aspect; the dye was cast; we were now but sojourners for a day; the spring would remove us to other scenes, and till then we had to make the best we could of the passing hour. Under this impression, I soothed myself with the hope of passing a quiet winter, thinking at times on our

disappointments. After all our labours, all our golden
dreams, here is the result! Well might we say, with
Solomon, that ''all is vanity!'' While musing one day
on passing events, I was surprised all at once by the arrival
of a strong party of North-Westers, seventy-five in number,
in a squadron of ten canoes, and headed by Messrs.
M'Tavish and Stuart, two North-West bourgeois, on
their way to the mouth of the Columbia, in high glee,
to meet their ship, the *Isaac Todd*, which was expected
daily. Mr. Clarke also accompanied the North-West
brigade, on his way to Astoria. With the craft peculiar
to Indian traders, they had crammed down Mr. Clarke's
throat that nothing could be done at Astoria without
him, although his accompanying them was like the
third wheel to a cart; but it answered their purpose:
for his leaving Spokane threw at once all the trade of
the district into their hands, and Mr. Clarke found out,
when it was too late, that he had been duped. At
Astoria, the party arrived safe on the 7th of October.

Here it was that the negotiation between the two great
functionaries, M'Dougall and M'Tavish, commenced.
The terms were soon adjusted, and the prices fixed.
The whole of the goods on hand, both at Astoria [253]
and throughout the interior, were delivered over to the
North-West Company, at 10 per cent. on cost and charges.
The furs were valued at so much per skin. The whole
sales amounted to 80,500 dollars: M'Tavish giving bills
of exchange on the agents for the amount, payable in
Canada. This transaction took place on the 16th of
October, and was considered fair and equitable on both
sides.[86]

[86] Astor felt that he had been cheated in the transfer of Astoria, and charged
McDougal with betraying his interests. See his letter to John Quincy Adams,
January, 1823, in Lyman, *History of Oregon*, ii, pp. 298–301; also Irving,

But, after all, a good deal of petty manœuvring took place, not very creditable to the representative of a great body. M'Tavish expected the armed ship *Isaac Todd*, fitted out as a letter of marque, into the river daily, and in that case Astoria would have been captured as a prize, and become the property of the North-West Company without purchase; and besides, he had learned that the British Government had despatched a ship of war to cruise on the coast of the Pacific, and that she might be looked for hourly; and the moment she entered the river all the American property, as a matter of course, would have been seized as a prize. In either case, M'Tavish would have saved his bills of exchange. Under this impression he put off from time to time, under various pretences, the signing of the documents. M'Dougall and M'Kenzie, however, saw through this piece of artifice, and insisted that the business should be ratified at once. M'Tavish, however, full of commercial wiles, tried to evade and retard every step taken. M'Dougall, in the mean time, had a squadron of boats in readiness, should any suspicious vessel come in [254] sight, to transport the furs and goods up to the Wallamitte out of her reach. While matters were in this unsettled state, Mr. M'Kenzie suggested a decisive measure, which brought the negotiation to a speedy close.

M'Tavish and his party were encamped at the time within a few yards of the fort, and sheltered, as it were,

Astoria, chap. 29. Astor stated that McDougal sold the entire property for about $58,000, less the wages due the men; that beaver was sold for two dollars and otter for fifty cents a skin, both of which were at the time worth five or six dollars each in Canton, China. Altogether he considered the property worth nearly $200,000 above the sum received. Bancroft defends McDougal at length — *History of Northwest Coast*, ii, pp. 221-230. Admitting that the property was sold at a loss, he contends McDougal was justified in thinking Astoria could not be maintained, and that it was better to get what he could for Astor, before fort and furs were captured by a British ship-of-war.— ED.

under the protection of our guns. They were also
indebted to the generosity of the Astorians for their
daily supplies; being themselves without goods, ammunition, or provisions.

One morning before daylight Messrs. M'Dougall and
M'Kenzie summoned all hands together, seventy-two
in number, and after a brief statement of the views of the
North-West in reference to the negotiation, ordered the
bastions to be manned, the guns to be loaded and pointed,
and the matches lighted.   In an instant every man was
at his post, and the gates shut.   At eight o'clock a message
was sent to M'Tavish, giving him two hours, and no
more, either to sign the bills or break off the negotiation
altogether and remove to some other quarters.   By
eleven o'clock the bills were finally and formally signed,
and Astoria was delivered up to the North-West Company
on the 12th of November, after nearly a month of suspense
between the drawing and the signing of the bills.

[255] CHAPTER XVI

Mr. Franchere — Comecomly's anxiety — His report of a
sail — His attachment to the Americans — Lafram-
boise, the interpreter — Mr. M'Dougall's visit — The
Racoon sloop-of-war — Comecomly grows partial to the
British flag — North-West partners — British officers
— Astoria changed to Fort George — Captain Black's
character — Mr. Hunt's voyage — Commodore Porter
— Mr. Hunt leaves the Marquesas — Arrival at the
Sandwich Islands — Rumours — The ship *Lark* —
Eight persons perish — Columbian affairs — The
property delivered — No ice — The people assembled
— Voyage — The Cascade banditti — Two North-
West canoes — North-West affray at the cascades
— Mr. Stuart wounded — Mr. Keith's conduct —

Preparations for war — The great expedition — Conduct of the Cath-le-yach-é-yach Indians — Expedition
fails — The effect — Remarks.

THE fate of unfortunate Astoria being now sealed, and
the place in the possession of the North-West Company,
the Astorians looked on merely as indifferent spectators.
Mr. Franchere was the only clerk in the American service
who showed a wish to join the new comers. He was a
Canadian from Montreal; and in those days the North-
West stood high in Canada, and particularly in Montreal.[87]
There they were everything, and the Canadian voyageurs
[256] had a liberal share of their bounty. It was therefore
natural for him to join that body which was the admiration
of his countrymen.

On the 29th of November, Comecomly arrived in
great haste at Astoria, with a report that a sail had been
seen off the Cape, and expressed great alarm lest it might
be a King George ship. He did not wish, he said, to see
any more Britons among them. He and his people were
fond of the Americans, and would make war against any
other people entering the river. The old chief uttered
this threat in an angry determined tone. Then turning
to M'Dougall, he said, ''See those few King George
people who come down the river: they were poor; they
had no goods, and were almost starving; yet you were
afraid of them, and delivered your fort and all your goods
to them; and now King George's ships are coming to
carry you all off as slaves. We are not afraid of King
George's people. I have got eight hundred warriors,
and we will not allow them to enslave you. The Americans are our friends and allies.'' M'Dougall tried to

---

[87] For a brief discussion of Franchère's attitude toward the North West
Company, see the preface to volume vi of our series.— ED.

console him, and told him that the British would not hurt the Americans. He also rewarded the chief's devotedness to the American cause with a new suit of clothing; then told him to keep a sharp look-out to discover whether the ship was British or American; forbidding, at the same time, either himself or his people to go on board. This he promised faithfully to do, and went off highly pleased.

[257] The moment Comecomly left Astoria, Laframboise, the interpreter, was called in, decked and painted in the full Chinook costume, and despatched to Cape Disappointment to report whether a vessel was to be seen, and if so, whether British or American.[88] In the mean time, M'Dougall prepared to start the instant a ship was seen. Laframboise had scarcely reached the Cape when the ship hove in sight, and soon afterwards came dashing over the bar in fine style, and anchored in Baker's Bay, within the Cape. Laframboise immediately returned, and on his way back met Mr. M'Dougall, in a boat well manned, going to the ship, and told him that the new arrival was a British ship of war. M'Dougall proceeded, and after remaining for about an hour on board returned to Astoria and reported the vessel to be the *Racoon* British sloop of war, of twenty-six guns, Captain Black, commander.

As soon as M'Dougall had left the *Racoon*, his royal father-in-law, with a squad of followers, repaired to the

---

[88] Michel Laframboise came to Oregon on the "Tonquin." When Astoria was transferred to the British, he entered the service of the North West Company, and throughout the remainder of his life was with them and the Hudson's Bay Company. He obtained a small piece of property on French Prairie, but his restless disposition was unsuited to farming. In his later years he conducted exploring parties through the country between the Columbia and California, serving as Captain Wilkes's guide in 1841.—ED.

ship to pay their homage to the British captain. Then
the crafty old chief traduced the Americans and extolled
the British; expressing his joy that he had lived long
enough to see once more a great ship of his brother King
George enter the river. Then, with a grin of contempt,
he remarked, "The Americans have no ships to be
compared to King George's ships." Saying this, he
laid a fine sea-otter skin at Captain Black's feet, and
prepared to leave the ship. The captain called [258]
him back, gave him a good bumper of wine, and in
return for so much loyalty presented him with an old
flag, a laced coat, cocked hat, and sword. His Chinook
majesty then left the *Racoon*, and returned to shore as
staunch a Briton as ever he had previously been an American partisan. But the best part of the farce was to see
Comecomly sailing across, the very next day, to Astoria
in full British uniform, with the Union Jack flying at the
masthead.

On board of the *Racoon* was Mr. M'Donald, one of
the senior partners of the North-West Company, generally
known by the name of Brascroche. [89] He assumed
forthwith the direction of affairs at Astoria. Comecomly
soon got into his sleeve; and before the former was
twenty-four hours in office, the latter had a new chief's
suit on.

On the second day after the *Racoon* came to anchor,
Captain Black and his officers landed at Astoria, and
found they had been baulked in their expectations; the
place being already in the possession of the North-West
Company by an amicable arrangement. They laughed
heartily at their own disappointment, for they had made
up their minds that the capture of Astoria would yield

[89] A brief sketch of John McDonald is given in Franchère, note 104.— ED.

them a rich prize; but in place of a golden egg they found
only an empty shell. After visiting the place, Captain
Black, turning round to one of his officers, said, ''The
Yankees are always beforehand with us.''

On the 12th day of December, the death-warrant [259]
of short-lived Astoria was signed. On that day, Captain
Black went through the customary ceremony of taking
possession, not only of Astoria, but of the whole country.
What the vague term of ''whole country'' in the present
case meant, I know not. Does it mean the Columbia?
Does it mean all the country lying west of the Rocky
Mountains? Or does it merely mean the coast of the
Pacific? That part of the ceremony which referred to
the ''whole country'' might have been dispensed with;
for the country had already been taken possession of in
the name of his Britannic Majesty, and that many years
ago, by Drake, by Cooke, by Vancouver, and lastly by
Black. The name of Astoria was now changed to that
of Fort George; and this done, the *Racoon* prepared to
leave the Columbia. Captain Black was a gentleman
of courteous and affable manners. He was never once
heard to utter an oath or indecorous expression all the
time he was in the river; and there was a general and
sincere regret felt when he left Fort George.

Having now detailed the principal occurrences at
Astoria, we return to take up the subject of Mr. Hunt's
voyage. The reader will bear in mind that Mr. Hunt
sailed in the *Albatross* in August last, for the Marquesas,
where he arrived safe. Nor had he been long there till
he met with Commodore Porter,[90] of the United States'
frigate *Essex*, from whom he learned that a British frigate
called the *Phœbe*, with two sloops of war, the *Cherub* and

[90] For an account of David Porter, see Franchère, note 105.— ED.

Racoon, were on [260] their way to Columbia. Hearing this, Mr. Hunt tried his uttermost to get some assistance from Captain Porter in order to secure the American property now in jeopardy at Astoria, but to no purpose. The commodore would not budge, having no instructions from his government to that effect; and having besides learned, no doubt, that Mr. Astor refused to join the Boston merchants in their praiseworthy designs. Mr. Hunt, now finding all his efforts at the Marquesas fruitless, sailed for the Sandwich Islands, and landed at Woahoo on the 18th of December. While at that island, he received the disastrous intelligence that a vessel bound for Columbia had been wrecked some time previous, at the island of Tahvorowa. [91] Thinking it possible that it might be a vessel from Astor bound for Astoria, he repaired thither with all possible despatch, and found, to his mortification, that his conjectures were but too true.

The vessel in question proved to be the *Lark*, Captain Northcop, bound for Astoria. The *Lark*, which ought to have sailed in September, 1812, did not leave New York till the 6th of March, 1813, the very time when she was expected to arrive at the place of her destination. And this unaccountable delay of six months accelerated the downfall of unfortunate Astoria; for had the *Lark* left New York at the usual time, and reached the Columbia, her seasonable arrival would have beyond a doubt changed the face of affairs.

[261] But there was a fatality attending the ships bound for Columbia, and the loss of the *Lark* added another link to the chain of misfortune. This ill-fated vessel upset in a squall, about 250 miles from the

[91] This is the island of Maui, northwest of Hawaii. There are two high volcanic islands, east Maui and west Maui, connected by a low isthmus.— ED.

Sandwich Islands, and so sudden and unexpected was the violent wind, that not a hatch was shut at the time, so she filled with the second wave and became completely water-logged. The sufferings of the crew were extreme: they remained lashed to the bowsprit for four days and four nights without drink, food, or sleep! the rest of the vessel being completely under water. On the eighth day after the accident, a jury-mast was rigged, and a small scaffolding erected, on which the men could sleep. Still their sufferings from thirst and hunger were intolerable, their only drink a little wine, and a very scanty supply of raw pork their food. On the twelfth day they came in sight of land, and six days after that they abandoned the ship and got to shore. Up to the time of their leaving the ship, six men, a boy, and one of the officers perished, and the rest of the crew were so reduced from various causes, that they were utterly incapable of helping themselves, much less the sinking ship. Soon after the vessel was abandoned, it neared the beach, stranded, and went to pieces. Nor could all the efforts of the captain prevent the savage horde from seizing and destroying everything that came in their way; and not only that, but they effectually prevented him or any of the crew from approaching the wreck, or touching anything the [262] waves threw on shore. Nor did the tumultous spirit of the rabble subside till they stripped the shipwrecked men of their clothes, as well as the vessel of her cargo; so that the condition of the sufferers was very little improved by their getting to land.

During these proceedings, Mr. Ogden, the supercargo, set off for Woahoo, the residence of king Tammeatameah, to claim protection and restitution of the property; but behold! his majesty told him in few words that the

wreck belonged to the state. "Who," said Tammeatameah, "brought the ship to shore?" "The waves,"
replied Mr. Ogden. "Then the waves are mine,"
rejoined the king. "Had you brought the vessel to
land," said his majesty to Mr. Ogden, "the ship and
cargo both would have belonged to you, and I should
have granted you protection and restitution; but as you
abandoned the wreck at sea, and fortune drove it on my
territories, the wreck is no longer yours but mine. The
clothing you and your people brought to shore, shall be
restored; but whatever was in the ship, at the time of her
stranding or grounding, belongs to me:" and here the
conversation ended.

Such, then, was the fate of the unfortunate *Lark*, and
such the statement of her commander to Mr. Hunt on
his arrival at the Sandwich Islands; and here again we
must leave Mr. Hunt in the happy isles, while we go back
to see what is passing in the Columbia interior, and after
that we shall return [263] again to the subject of Mr.
Hunt's voyage: by so doing, we shall conform better to
the natural connection of the different subjects, without
perplexing the reader's attention. In the mean time,
it may be stated that Messrs. M'Kenzie and John Stuart
proceeded to the interior, to see the property delivered over
to the North-West Company, agreeably to the late
contract. After these gentlemen had settled the business
at Spokane, and assembled all the people of the late
concern belonging to that district, they came to me at
Oakinacken on the 15th of December: here also Mr.
Stuart, from the She Whaps, had arrived with the men
of that quarter. Finishing, then, the business at Oakinacken, we all prepared to embark, and left that place for
Fort George on the 20th of December.

On our way down the Columbia, such was the mildness
of the winter that not a speck of ice was to be seen.   At
the head of the cascades, a place always notorious for
its bad population, we encamped, and were disturbed
all night by the whooping and yelling of savages, who
kept prowling in the woods round us.   Notwithstanding
the strictest watch, several arrows were shot into our camp,
and a man named Plessis was wounded in the ear.   We
fired several shots into the woods, from a three-pounder,
which kept the Indians at a distance.   In the morning
we passed the cascades peaceably, and arrived safe at
Fort George on the 7th of January, 1814.   The people
from the Wallamitte had just reached that place before us.

[264] Below the cascades, there is no impediment
whatever to the navigation of the river, by night or by day.
The brigade, therefore, went sweeping down the current
in the dark.   In passing the last of the bad places,
however, my boat happening to get broken, we had to
put ashore to repair, and, by the time we got under weigh
again, the brigade had left us far behind.   Next morning
at daybreak, I met, opposite to the Wallamitte, two
North-West canoes and twenty men, under the direction
of Messrs. Keith and Alex. Stuart, two partners of the
North-West Company, on their way to the interior. [92]
We breakfasted together, and I strongly advised them
to turn back, since so small a party, and strangers too,
could never hope to pass through the hostile tribes in
safety.   They, however, made light of the matter, giving
me to understand that they were North-Westers! so we
parted, and they proceeded.   While talking on the subject
of danger, one of those swelling fellows, such as may

---

[92] Concerning James Keith and Alexander Stuart, see Franchère, notes 108,
102.—ED.

be ordinarily seen stuck up in the end of a north-west canoe, with a bonnet of feathers surpassing in size the head of a buffalo bull, turned round to my men and said,— "Do you think we are Americans? we will teach the Indians to respect us." In the darkness of the night, they had not seen our people on their way down. The moment Mr. M'Kenzie reached Fort George, he represented to M'Donald and M'Tavish the folly and danger of the attempt; consequently, a canoe with twelve men, under the direction of Mr. Franchere, was immediately [265] despatched to bring them back; but it was unfortunately too late.

On Messrs. Keith and Stuart's arrival at the portage of the cascades, the Indians collected, as usual, in great numbers; but did not attempt anything till the people had got involved and dispersed in the portage; they then seized the opportunity, and began to help themselves; they drew their bows, brandished their lances, and pounced upon the gun-cases, powder-kegs, and bales of goods, at the place where Mr. Stuart was stationed. He tried to defend his post, but owing to the wet weather his gun missed fire several times, and before any assistance could reach him he had received three arrows, and his gun had just fallen from his hand as a half-breed, named Finlay, came up and shot his assailant dead. By this time the people had concentrated, and the Indians fled to their strongholds behind the rocks and trees. To save the property in this moment of alarm and confusion was impossible; to save themselves, and carry off Mr. Stuart, was the first consideration. They, therefore, made for their canoes with all haste, and embarked. Here it was found that one man was missing, and Mr. Keith, who was still on shore, urged the party strongly to wait a little; but the people in the canoes called on Mr. Keith, in the tone of despair, to jump into the canoe or else they would push off and leave him also; but he, being a resolute man and not easily intimidated, immediately cocked his gun and threatened to shoot the first man that [266] moved. Mr. Stuart, who was faint from loss of blood, seeing Mr. Keith determined, and the men frightened out of their wits, beckoned to Mr. Keith to embark. The moment he jumped into the canoe they pushed off and shot down the current; nor had they proceeded far before they met Mr. Franchere, who had been sent after them. Both canoes then hastening day and night, reached the fort the second day. During this time Mr. Stuart suffered much, and was very low, nor had his wounds been yet examined. The barbs of the arrows were of iron, and one of them had struck on a stone pipe which he carried in his waistcoat pocket, and to that fortunate circumstance he perhaps owed his life: one of these barbs it was found impossible to extract, and he suffered great pain, and was confined to bed for upwards of two months. He then began gradually to recover. On the ninth day the man who had been abandoned in the affray with the Indians reached the fort in a state of nudity, having torn his clothes wandering through the woods, suffering at the same time the miseries of cold and hunger; and thus terminated the first adventure of the North-West on the Columbia.

The object of this expedition was threefold — to forward despatches for the east side of the mountains, to convey supplies of ammunition to the interior, and thence to proceed to the Snake country for Mr. Reed and his party; but the unlucky affair at the cascades knocked the whole on the head, and taught the [267] strutting and plumed bullies of the north that, although they were North-Westers, the lads of the cascades did not respect their feathers.

This disaster set the whole North-West machinery at Fort George in motion. Revenge for the insult, and a heavy retribution on the heads of the whole Cath-le-yach-é-yach nation, was decreed in a full council; and for a whole week nothing was to be heard about the place but the clang of arms and the sound of war. Every man worth naming was armed *cap-à-pie,* and besides the ordinary arms and accoutrements, two big guns, six swivels, cutlasses, hand-grenades, and handcuffs, with ten days' provisions, were embarked; in short, all the weapons and missiles that could be brought into action were collected and put in train for destroying the vile banditti of the cascades, root and branch.

Eighty-five picked men and two Chinook interpreters, under six chosen leaders, were enrolled in the expedition, and the command of it tendered to Mr. M'Kenzie, who, however, very prudently declined the honour, merely observing that as he was on the eve of leaving the country, he did not wish to mix himself up with North-West affairs; but that he would cheerfully go as a volunteer. The command then devolved on Mr. M'Tavish; and on the 20th of January, with buoyant hearts and flags flying, a fleet of ten sail conveyed the invincibles to the field of action, where they all arrived safe on the third day, and cast anchor at Strawberry Island, near the foot [268] of the rapids. On their way up, the name of this formid-able armament struck such terror into the marauders along the river, that they fled to the fastnesses and hiding-places of the wilderness;   even the two Chinook interpreters could neither sleep nor eat, so grieved were they at the thoughts of the bloody scenes that were soon to follow.

On the next morning after the squadron came to anchor, the Indians were summoned to appear and give an account of their late conduct, and they were desired if they wished mercy to be extended towards them, to deliver up at once all the property plundered from the expedition of Messrs. Keith and Stuart.   The Cath-le-yach-é-yach chiefs, not the least intimidated by the hostile array before them, sent back this answer, ''The whites have killed two of our people, let them deliver up the murderers to us, and we will deliver to them all the property in our possession.''   After returning this answer, the Indians sent off all their wives and children into the thick woods;   then arming themselves, they took their stand behind the trees and rocks.   M'Tavish then sent the interpreters to invite them to a parley, and to smoke the pipe of peace.   The Indians returned for answer, that ''When the whites had paid according to Indian law for the two men they had killed, they would smoke the pipe of peace, but not till then.   Their wives and children were safe, and as for themselves they were pre-pared for the worst.''   And this was all the progress that was made during the first day.

[269] The next day the interpreters were sent to sound them again.   Towards noon a few stragglers and slaves approached the camp and delivered up a small parcel of cloth and cotton, torn up into pieces, and scarcely worth picking up, with this message from the chiefs:—''We have sent you some of the property;   deliver us up the murderers, and we will send you the rest.''   Some were for hanging the Indians up at once;   others for detaining

them: at last, however, it was resolved to let them go, and they departed. In the evening two of the principal Indians surrendered themselves to M'Tavish, bringing also a small parcel of odds-and-ends, little better than the last. Being interrogated on the subject of the stolen property, they denied being present at the time, and had cunning enough to make their innocence appear, and also to convince M'Tavish that they were using their utmost influence to bring the Indians to terms, and deliver up the property. A council was then held to decide on the fate of the prisoners. Some were, as in the former case, for hanging them up without judge or jury; some for taking them down to Fort George in irons. The council was divided, and at last it was resolved to treat the prisoners liberally and let them go; and, to the disgrace of the expedition, they were set at liberty — nor did they ever return again; and thus ended the negotiations of the second day.

The third day the interpreters were at work again; but in place of making any favourable impression on [270] the Indians, they were told that if they returned again without delivering up the murderers, they would be fired upon. During this day, the Indians came once or twice out to the verge of the woods. Some were for firing the big guns where they were seen thickest; others, more ardent, but less calculating, were for storming their haunts, and bringing the matter to a speedy issue. Every movement of the whites was seen by the Indians, but not a movement of the Indians could be discerned by the whites; and the day passed away without any result. Next morning it was discovered that some of the Indians lurking about had entered the camp and carried off two guns, a kettle, and one of the men's bonnets, and the

Indians were seen occasionally flying from place to place, and now and then whooping and yelling, as if some plan of attack were in contemplation. This was a new symptom, and convinced the whites that they were getting more bold and daring in proportion as their opponents were passive and undecided. These circumstances made the whites reflect on their own situation. The savages, sheltered behind the trees and rocks, might cut them all off without being seen; besides, it was intimated by the interpreters that the Indians might all this time be increasing their numbers by foreign auxiliaries; and whether true or false, the suggestion had its effect in determining the whites that they stood upon dangerous ground, and that the sooner they left it the better. They therefore, without recovering the property, firing a gun, or securing [271] a single prisoner, sounded the retreat, and returned home on the ninth day — making the matter ten times worse than it was before. This warlike expedition was turned into ridicule by the Cath-le-yach-é-yachs, and had a very bad effect on the Indians generally; but the best of it was, on their way back, some turned off towards the Wallamitte to hide their disgrace, others remained for some days at the Cowlitz, and M'Tavish himself reached Fort George in the night; and so ended this inglorious expedition, which promised so much and did so little.

Here it may be observed that the nature of the ground along the cascades, on both sides of the river, is such as to afford no position secure from attack or surprise; and it showed a manifest want of judgment, not only in a military commander, but in an Indian trader, to expose his people in such a dangerous situation, where the Indians might have waylaid and cut them off to a man, and that without quitting their fastnesses; whereas the whole difficulty might have been easily obviated — for a very simple stratagem on the part of the whites might have quietly secured, as hostages, three or four of the principal men, and that would have soon settled effectually the whole affair, without noise or any warlike demonstration.

[272] CHAPTER XVII

Party to the Wallamitte — Hunt's voyage concluded — The brig *Pedlar* — M'Dougall suspected — His character vindicated — Mr. Hunt's remarks on the late concern — His liberality — His farewell address to the clerks — Final departure from Columbia — The party for Canada — Efforts and disappointments — Snake expedition — The melancholy story of Pierre Dorion's wife — Massacre of the Snake party — Remarks — A winter in the Blue Mountains — List of casualties — Astor's hopes disappointed — Comment on the late concern.

AFTER the late expedition to the cascades, in which our people had mixed themselves up with the North-West Company, and of course came in for a share of the general odium, they retired to pass the remainder of the winter in the Wallamitte — a place notorious for gormandizing; and here we shall leave them to enjoy, in peace and quietness, the fruits of the chace, while we turn again to take up and finish the wanderings of Mr. Hunt, who, it will be remembered, was left at the Sandwich Islands in quest of a vessel.

After Mr. Hunt had learned the fate of the unfortunate *Lark*, as already related, he had but one course [273] left, namely, to purchase a ship and return to Columbia with all possible despatch. On meeting with Captain Northcop, he bargained for and purchased a snug little

brig for ten thousand five hundred and fifty dollars, called
the *Pedlar*, from Boston, and giving the command of
her to the captain of the *Lark*, they embarked, bade a
farewell to the Sandwich Islands on the 22nd of January,
and sailed direct for the Columbia River, where they
arrived, after a rather tedious voyage, on the 28th of
February.

When Mr. Hunt arrived, he expressed himself dissatisfied with some points of the negotiation that had
taken place; but chiefly with that part of it which related
to the sale of the furs.   But it was now too late: the
whole business was irrevocably settled.   To repine or
find fault was therefore useless; and, under all circumstances, Mr. M'Dougall had perhaps made the best
bargain he could.   Nor was it likely that two men placed
in different positions, such as Mr. Hunt at the Sandwich
Islands and M'Dougall at Columbia, could view the same
object in the same light.   The circumstance, however, of
M'Dougall having joined the North-West Company, and
having already become a partner in that concern, threw
suspicion on his conduct, and this perhaps, weighed
more heavily on Mr. Hunt's mind than anything else; and
certainly, to say the least of it, M'Dougall's conduct, in
this particular, was indiscreet, and might in some degree
justify imputation — at least, his enemies made a handle
of it; yet there is not the least proof that he [274] had
betrayed his trust.   M'Dougall always bore the character
of integrity; he was a man of principle, faithful to his
word, and punctual to his engagements; but at times he
was overbearing, peevish, haughty, and obstinate; and
this unfortunate temper had well nigh proved fatal to the
undertaking in the commencement of his career at Astoria.
With these slight exceptions, however, M'Dougall's con-

duct was fair and unimpeachable. He was not a man of fortune; he had already sacrificed four years of his time on the Columbia; and, besides, it was not M'Dougall that proffered his services, nor was he more than half inclined to accede to the offers made to him — this we know; but it was the North-Westers themselves who wished to secure him, being aware that he was a man of ambition, and fond of enterprize. His experience also gave him a strong ascendant. M'Dougall had been with the nabobs of the North-West before, and did not leave them without tasting of the bitter cup of disappointment; he could, therefore, have had no predilection in their favour. Add to this, that previous to any arrangement with the North-West Company, he had finally closed Mr. Astor's affairs, and delivered up all the papers and documents of that concern into the hands of Mr. M'Kenzie. This delivery was confirmed by Mr. Hunt.

On the 27th of March, as soon as the people from all quarters were assembled together, and the papers and drafts belonging to Mr. Astor delivered over to Mr. M'Kenzie, Mr. Hunt called all the clerks before [275] him, and, entering into a full detail of the unfortunate circumstances which brought about the failure of the enterprize, he expressed his deep and sincere regret that so much talent and zeal had been employed to no purpose, and thrown to the winds; that we had been the pioneers of a more successful and fortunate rival; that the North-Westers would now reap the fruits of our industry; and the only consolation left us was that every man had done his duty, and to circumstances over which we had no control might chiefly be attributed the failure of our undertaking. He then went on:—

"My friends, I am now about to leave you, and it

may be that we part to meet no more. I am exceedingly
sorry that it is not in my power to reward you according
to your zeal and merit. There are two of you, however,
to whom I am in honour bound to make some acknowledg-
ment before leaving this place; they having come here
not for salary, but for promotion. As a small testimony
of my regard, I have placed at their disposal five hundred
dollars each, and wish it were even more for their sakes.
I am to leave this place by sea, and those of you who
prefer that course may embark with me; while for those
who feel disposed to remain in the country, I have made
such arrangements with the North-West gentlemen as
may turn to their advantage. For those that will accompany me I shall do my utmost to provide; the same I'll
do for those that remain, or go home by land, if in my
power." These words were [276] not the hollow efforts
of cunning or deceit; they were the genuine expressions
of the heart. For Mr. Hunt was a conscientious and
upright man — a friend to all, and beloved as well as
respected by all. I found five hundred dollars placed
to my account, and Mr. Seaton the same; we being
the pair alluded to by Mr. Hunt.

On the 3rd of April Mr. Hunt, accompanied by
Mr. Halsey, Mr. Seaton, Mr. Clapp, and Mr. Farnham,
embarked on board the *Pedlar* at three o'clock in the
afternoon, and took their final departure from Fort
George. Mr. M'Lennan, Ross Cox, and myself, entered
the North-West service; and I proceeded to resume
my former charge at Oakinacken.

On the 4th of April the North-West brigade left Fort
George for the interior, and along with it Messrs.
M'Kenzie, Stuart, and Clarke, with all those of the late
concern intending to leave the country, set out on their

journey across land for Montreal, Mr. Franchere among
the number. It will be recollected that he had entered
the North-West service; but by mutual consent he
became free, and preferred accompanying the party for
Canada. We shall now leave the Montreal party on their
journey, and turn to another subject.

It will be remembered, that one of the objects of the
unfortunate expedition of Messrs. Keith and Stuart was
to proceed to the Snake country in search of Mr. Reed
and his party, who were sent [277] thither last summer;
but that expedition having failed, it was now proposed
that Mr. Keith with a small party should undertake the
business, and proceed to Spokane Fort. From the mouth
of the Umatallow, Mr. Keith was to have taken his
departure, and a guide was there engaged for the purpose;
but when everything was arranged, and the party ready
to start, the guide expressed a wish to continue with the
brigade as far as the Walla Walla, and from thence set
out for the Snake country. Mr. Keith and his party
accordingly reembarked, and we reached the Walla Walla
early the next day; here, again, we were on the eve of
starting, when a few Indians arrived, and with them
the wife of Pierre Dorion the interpreter. [93] The timely
arrival of this poor unfortunate woman put an end to the
Snake expedition; and we shall relate her melancholy
story in her own words:—

"About the middle of August we reached the Great
Snake River, and soon afterwards, following up a branch
to the right hand, where there were plenty of beaver, we
encamped; and there Mr. Reed built a house to winter
in. After the house was built, the people spent their
time in trapping beaver. About the latter end of Septem-

---

[93] For a sketch of Pierre Dorion, see Bradbury's *Travels*, note 7.— ED.

ber, Hoback, Robinson, and Rezner came to us; but
they were very poor, the Indians having robbed them
of everything they had about fifteen days before. Mr.
Reed gave them some clothing and traps, and they went
to [278] hunt with my husband. Landrie got a fall from
his horse, lingered a while, and died of it. Delaunay
was killed, when trapping: my husband told me that he
saw his scalp with the Indians, and knew it from the
colour of the hair. The Indians about the place were
very friendly to us; but when strange tribes visited us,
they were troublesome, and always asked Mr. Reed for
guns and ammunition: on one occasion, they drove an
arrow into one of our horses, and took a capot from
La Chapelle. Mr. Reed not liking the place where we
first built, we left it, and built farther up the river, on the
other side. After the second house was built, the people
went to trap as usual, sometimes coming home every
night, sometimes sleeping out for several nights together
at a time. Mr. Reed and one man generally stayed at the
house.

"Late one evening, about the 10th of January, a
friendly Indian came running to our house, in a great
fright, and told Mr. Reed that a band of the bad Snakes,
called the Dog-rib tribe, had burnt the first house that
we had built, and that they were coming on whooping and
singing the war-song. After communicating this intelligence, the Indian went off immediately, and I took
up my two children, got upon a horse, and set off to
where my husband was trapping; but the night was dark,
the road bad, and I lost my way. The next day being
cold and stormy, I did not stir. On the second day,
however, [279] I set out again; but seeing a large smoke
in the direction I had to go, and thinking it might proceed

from Indians, I got into the bushes again and hid myself.
On the third day, late in the evening, I got in sight of the
hut, where my husband and the other men were hunting;
but just as I was approaching the place, I observed a
man coming from the opposite side, and staggering as if
unwell: I stopped where I was till he came to me. Le
Clerc, wounded and faint from loss of blood, was the
man. He told me that La Chapelle, Rezner, and my
husband had been robbed and murdered that morning.
I did not go into the hut; but putting Le Clerc and one
of my children on the horse I had with me, I turned
round immediately, took to the woods, and I retraced
my steps back again to Mr. Reed's: Le Clerc, however,
could not bear the jolting of the horse, and he fell once
or twice, so that we had to remain for nearly a day in
one place; but in the night he died, and I covered him
over with brushwood and snow, put my children on the
horse, I myself walking and leading the animal by the
halter. The second day I got back again to the house.
But sad was the sight! Mr. Reed and the men were all
murdered, scalped, and cut to pieces. Desolation and
horror stared me in the face. I turned from the shock-
ing sight in agony and despair; took to the woods with
my children and horse, and passed the cold and lonely
night without food or fire. I was now at a [280] loss
what to do: the snow was deep, the weather cold, and
we had nothing to eat. To undertake a long journey
under such circumstances was inevitable death. Had
I been alone I would have run all risks and proceeded;
but the thought of my children perishing with hunger
distracted me. At this moment a sad alternative crossed
my mind: should I venture to the house among the dead
to seek food for the living? I knew there was a good

stock of fish there; but it might have been destroyed or carried off by the murderers; and besides, they might be still lurking about and see me: yet I thought of my children. Next morning, after a sleepless night, I wrapped my children in my robe, tied my horse in a thicket, and then went to a rising ground, that overlooked the house, to see if I could observe anything stirring about the place. I saw nothing; and, hard as the task was, I resolved to venture after dark: so I returned back to my children, and found them nearly frozen, and I was afraid to make a fire in the day time lest the smoke might be seen; yet I had no other alternative, I must make a fire, or let my children perish. I made a fire and warmed them. I then rolled them up again in the robe, extinguished the fire, and set off after dark to the house: went into the store and ransacked every hole and corner, and at last found plenty of fish scattered about. I gathered, hid, and slung upon my back as much as I could carry, and returned [281] again before dawn of day to my children. They were nearly frozen, and weak with hunger. I made a fire and warmed them, and then we shared the first food we had tasted for the last three days. Next night I went back again, and carried off another load; but when these efforts were over, I sank under the sense of my afflictions, and was for three days unable to move, and without hope. On recovering a little, however, I packed all up, loaded my horse, and putting my children on the top of the load, set out again on foot, leading the horse by the halter as before. In this sad and hopeless condition I travelled through deep snow among the woods, rocks, and rugged paths for nine days, till I and the horse could travel no more. Here I selected a lonely spot at the foot of a rocky precipice in the Blue Mountains, intending there to pass the remainder of the winter. I killed my horse, and hung up the flesh on a tree for my winter food. I built a small hut with pine branches, long grass, and moss, and packed it all round with snow to keep us warm, and this was a difficult task, for I had no axe, but only a knife to cut wood. In this solitary dwelling, I passed fifty-three lonely days! I then left my hut and set out with my children to cross the mountains; but I became snow blind the second day, and had to remain for three days without advancing a step; and this was unfortunate, as our provisions were almost exhausted. Having recovered my sight a little, I set out again, and got clear off the mountains, and down [282] to the plains on the fifteenth day after leaving my winter encampments; but for six days we had scarcely anything to eat, and for the last two days not a mouthful. Soon after we had reached the plains I perceived a smoke at a distance; but being unable to carry my children farther, I wrapped them up in my robe, left them concealed, and set out alone in hopes of reaching the Indian camp, where I had seen the smoke; but I was so weak that I could hardly crawl, and had to sleep on the way. Next day, at noon, I got to the camp. It proved to belong to the Walla Wallas, and I was kindly treated by them. Immediately on my arrival the Indians set off in search of my children, and brought them to the camp the same night. Here we staid for two days, and then moved on to the river, expecting to hear something of the white people on their way either up or down."

This ended the woman's story of hardships and woe. That it was the Snakes who killed the party there is not the least doubt. The Dog-ribbed tribe have always passed for bad Indians; and besides, in the dead of winter, neither the Blackfeet on the east, nor the Nez Percés on the north, can wage war with the Snakes at that season of the year.

In recapitulating the number of casualties or disasters which befell the Pacific Fur Company during its short existence, we cannot help lamenting so great a sacrifice of human life in so limited a period. The tragical list stands thus:—

[283] Lost on the bar	8
Land expedition	5
Tonquin	27
Astoria	3
Lark	8
Snake country	9
Final departure	1
Total	61

Well might we, with Virgil, say, "Who can relate such woes without a tear!"

We have now brought together, and within a small compass, the accounts of all the different and widely extended branches of the concern. That concern which proposed to extend its grasping influence from ocean to ocean, and which, to use the projector's own words, "was to have annihilated the South Company; rivalled the North-West Company; extinguished the Hudson's Bay Company; driven the Russians into the Frozen Ocean; and with the resources of China to have enriched America." But how vain are the designs of man! That undertaking which but yesterday promised such mighty things, is to-day no more.

Various in those days were the opinions entertained

as to the merits of the undertaking in a speculative light; but few there were who saw clearly through the mist inseparable from a novel and remote design. The means were ample, the field [284] unbounded, and the River Columbia was the contemplated centre of a trade conducted by talent, and in the hands of a nation which, in the natural course of events, must soon encircle the remotest parts of the earth, and draw within its sphere of action the fairest portion of the fur trade.

It is therefore not surprising that the jealousy of the Canada traders should have eagerly seized on the first opportunity to check the encroachments, or extinguish the rising fame of this infant but gigantic rival. The course of events was favourable to their ambition, and the end justified the means conducive to their future aggrandizement.

The multifarious avocations of Mr. Astor must inevitably have prevented his bestowing the requisite degree of attention on each particular subject which came under his consideration. Hence, matters within his immediate reach, or which appealed to his own experience, engrossed his special care as objects of primary importance; while, on the other hand, those referring to a distance, or which he had not habitually at heart, were neglected by him as comparatively trivial.

During the slow progress of a distant and struggling establishment, exposed to the cruelty and rapacity of savages, or the perils of uncertain navigation, it may be naturally expected that the owner should lean to such other parts of the undertaking as may hold out a fair promise of recompensing for the hazard of the adventure. Hence it was that [285] his ships were the chief objects of his solicitude; that the captains retained his special trust; that the settlement was ill supplied; and hence the ungenerous dispensation of his confidence among its venturesome though too credulous leaders.

Had he, however, acquired such insight into the practice of the Indian as he so eminently attained in all other branches of trade; had his mind been as liberal as it was acute, or as ready to reward merit as to find fault; or were he as conversant with human nature as he was expert in a bargain; and had he also begun his undertaking not at the commencement of a war, but at its close, then competency and ease might have been the lot of his servants, instead of misery and want — success might have crowned his ambition, glory finished his career, and the name of Astor might have been handed down with admiration, as having borne away the palm of enterprize.

[286] CHAPTER XVIII

Origin of the Oakinackens — Religion — Good Spirit — Evil Spirit — Ideas of a future state — Ceremonies — End of this world — Extent of country — Names and number of tribes — Warriors — Population — Royal family — The great chief, or Red Fox — Wild hemp — Long journeys — Barter — Emblem of royalty — Government — Indian ideas — Council of chiefs — Manners — Employments — Plurality of wives — Brawls — Dress and clothing — Stratagems — A savage in wolf's clothing — Painted faces and sleek hair.

AFTER closing the drama of the Pacific Fur Company we shall now raise the curtain a little, and take a cursory peep at the Indians of the interior; but more particularly of the Oakinackens.

The origin of savage nations is mixed up with so

much fable that it is scarcely possible, through the mist of tradition, to trace their descent clearly to any source: nor can this surprise us when we consider how unsatisfactory the most learned inquiries often prove, with respect to the origin of many civilized nations. Indeed, all that can be aimed at is to state distinctly and fairly the opinions handed down from one generation to another, and currently believed by the people themselves.

[287] The origin of the Oakinackens is thus related:— Long ago, when the sun was young, to use their own expression, and not bigger than a star, there was an island far off in the middle of the ocean, called Samahtuma-whoolah, or White Man's Island. The island was full of inhabitants of gigantic stature, and very white, and it was governed by a tall white woman, called Scomalt. The good woman Scomalt, possessing the attributes of a deity, could create whatever she pleased. The white people on this island quarrelled among themselves, and many were killed in the affray, which conduct so enraged Scomalt that she drove all the wicked to one end of the island, then broke off the part on which they stood, and pushed it adrift to the mercy of the winds and waves. There they floated about for a length of time, not knowing whither they went. They were tossed about on the face of the deep till all died but one man and woman, and this couple finding the island beginning to sink with them made a canoe, and paddling for many days and nights, going in a westerly direction, they came to a group of islands, and kept steering through them till they made the main land — the land which they now inhabit — but they say that it has grown much larger since that time. This couple, when first expelled from the island of their forefathers, were very white, like the other inhabitants

of the island; but they suffered so much while floating on the ocean that they became dark and dingy from the exposure, and their skins [288] have retained that colour ever since. From this man and woman all the Indians of the continent have their origin; and as a punishment for their original wickedness, they were condemned by the great Scomalt to poverty, degradation, and nakedness, and to be called Skyloo, or Indians.

The religion of the Oakinackens, like that of all Indian tribes, is difficult to understand, and still more difficult to explain. They, however, believe in a good and an evil spirit, who preside over the destinies of man, and that all good actions will be rewarded, and all evil deeds punished in a future state. The good spirit, or master of life, they call Elemehum-kill-an-waist, or Sky-appe; and the bad spirit, Kisht-samah, or Chacha; both are invincible, and keep constantly moving to and fro through the air, so that nothing can be done unknown to them. They believe that all good Indians after death go to the Elemehum-kill-an-waist, and that the wicked who kill and steal, go to the Kisht-samah. On all solemn occasions they offer up a short prayer to the good spirit for his assistance and help. They have no places of worship, public or private. The god whom they adore is invincible. In all their religious ceremonies the great pipe of peace is smoked as a peace-offering to the Eleme-hum-kill-an-waist, and also on all occasions of peace or war, or other matters of state; and this is done by holding the pipe (when filled and lighted) first to the east, or rising sun, and drawing three whiffs; then to the west or setting sun; next to the heavens above; and, [289] lastly, to the earth beneath — in each case taking care to draw three whiffs. This religious part of the ceremony is gone through only by the chief when the first pipe is filled, before entering upon business. Then the chief hands the pipe to his next neighbour, who smokes without any ceremony, and he to the next, and so on. At the conclusion of the business there is no ceremony observed.

They believe that this world will have an end, as it had a beginning; and their reason is this, that the rivers and lakes must eventually undermine the earth, and set the land afloat again, like the island of their forefathers, and then all must perish. Frequently they have asked us when it would take place — the its-owl-eigh, or end of the world.

The Oakinackens inhabit a very large tract of country, the boundary of which may be said to commence at the Priest's Rapids on the south; from thence, embracing a space of upwards of one hundred miles in breadth, it runs almost due north until it reaches the She Whaps, making a distance of more than five hundred miles in length; within this line the nation branches out into twelve tribes, under different names. These form, as it were, so many states belonging to the same union, and are governed by petty chiefs, who are, in a manner, independent; nevertheless, all are ready to unite against a common enemy. These tribes, beginning at the southern boundary and taking each according to its locality, may be classed as follows:— Ska-moy-num-achs, Ke-waught-chen-unaughs, [290] Piss-cows, Income-can-étook, Tsill-ane, Inti-étook, Battle-le-mule-emauch, or Meat-who, In-spellum, Sin-poh-ell-ech-ach, Sin-who-yelp-pe-took, Sa-milk-a-nuigh, and Oakinacken, which is nearly in the centre. [94]   All these tribes, or the great Oakinacken nation, speak the same language; but often differ a good deal from one another as to accent.   The whole nation, or twelve tribes taken together, could never muster above six hundred warriors.   The number of souls I was never able to ascertain correctly; but, considering the extent of country they possess, they are far from being numerous.   I should say there are not more than fifteen persons to every square mile.   The Oakinackens are not a warlike people; fishing and hunting, and not war, are their usual occupations.

The principal family of the Oakinacken nation bears the title or name of Conconulps, being the name of the place where the members of it generally reside, which is situate about nine miles up the beautiful stream of the same name. [95]   The head, or principal chief of this family, died last year, leaving the inheritance or chieftainship to Quills-chin-eigh-an, his eldest son, about twenty-five years of age.   The old man himself was called Who-why-laugh, or Red Fox.

The old chief was a venerable and worthy savage: his influence was great over a wide circle, not only at home, but abroad among the neighbouring tribes.   The Red Fox had been many times with his young [291] men at the Great Salt Lake, as they call it, meaning the Pacific, the direct road to which, across the mountains, is almost

---

[94] Ross is here enumerating all the Salishan tribes living on the Columbia between the Yakima and Spokane rivers, and on the lower Okanagan.   For the first seven, see notes 42, 44, 45, 48, *ante*.   The Inspellum were east of Okanagan.   The Sinpohellechach were the San Poils at the mouth of San Poil River. forty-five miles west of Spokane River.   They were closely related to the Spokane Indians.   Samilkamigh is, of course, Similkameen, a tribe on the river of the same name.— ED.

[95] The Conconully River is an affluent of the Okanagan, entering a short distance above its mouth.— ED.

due west to where they fall on the sea-coast, in about the 49th degree of north latitude. They take generally fifteen days to make the journey, sometimes more, sometimes less, according to circumstances. Traffic is their object: they carry along with them the wild hemp of the interior, prepared and neatly put up into small parcels, which they give in exchange for the higua and trinkets. The hemp is used for making fishing-nets, and is always in great demand on the coast. The higua, which has already been noticed, is the most valuable commodity among the Indians to be found west of the Rocky Mountains, being the circulating medium throughout the country.

The royal insignia of an Indian king or chief is simple, and is always known in the camp. The Oakinacken emblem is a white wolf-skin, fantastically painted with rude figures of different colours — the head and tail decorated with the higua, bears' claws, and the teeth of different animals — suspended from a pole, in a conspicuous place near the chief's lodge.

On our first arrival among this people, the wolf-skin was always to be seen waving conspicuously from the pole; but as they began to associate and got accustomed to us, they became less particular in exhibiting the ensigns of royalty. But although they occasionally threw off the savage ferocity and wild aspect peculiar to savages in general, yet they could [292] not be brought, even after years of friendly intercourse, to change their habits of life. The morose, sullen, and unsociable disposition still remained the same; whereas, on the contrary, the white man almost immediately falls into the customs and ways of the savages. An Indian accustomed to squat on the ground, and double himself up in the lodge, is

long, long indeed before he can reconcile himself to sit
in a chair; but the white man is at once at home in the
Indian lodge, and becomes as easy and contented sitting,
squatting, or lying amongst dirt and filth, dogs and fleas,
as if in his arm-chair at home — showing how much
more easy and natural it is for civilized men to degenerate,
than for the savage to elevate himself to the habits of
civilized men; but here I should observe, that the Oakinackens are by no means ferocious or cruel, either in
looks, habits, or dispositions; but are, on the contrary,
rather an easy, mild, and agreeable people.

The government, or ruling power among the Oakinackens, is simple yet effective, and is little more than
an ideal system of control. The chieftainship descends
from father to son: it is, however, merely a nominal
superiority in most cases. Their general maxim is,
that Indians were born to be free, and that no man has a
natural right to the obedience of another, except he be
rich in horses and has many wives; yet it is wonderful
how well the government works for the general good,
and without any coercive power to back the will of the
chief, he is seldom [293] disobeyed: the people submit
without a murmur. On all state occasions, of peace or
war, the chief has the assistance of a council; that is,
he calls all the great men together, they form a ring, sometimes in the chief's lodge, sometimes in the open air.
No one is admitted into the council, except he can show
some marks or trophy of war, or has performed some
praiseworthy deed, according to their ideas, or else he
must be rich in horses or have many wives; or, lastly,
he may be called by the chief, and that entitles him to a
seat without any other qualification. The council being
seated, and the ceremonial pipe smoked, the chief, in

his usual sitting posture, holds down his head, as if looking to the ground, then opens the business of the meeting by a speech, closing every sentence with great emphasis, the other councillors vociferating approbation. As soon as the chief is done speechifying, others harangue also; but only one at a time. The decision of the council is sure to be zealously carried into effect; but, in all ordinary matters, the chief is not more conspicuous than any other individual, and he seldom interferes in family affairs, or the ordinary routine of daily occurrences: and this, I think, adds greatly to the dignity of his character.

Each nation or principal tribe has generally two chiefs; one for the village, and another called the war-chief. The former is the head of the tribe; and, as already observed, holds his office by lineal descent: the latter is elective, and chosen by the voice or [294] whim of the majority of the people. Every morning at the dawn of day, the head chief rides or walks round the camp or village, and harangues as he goes: the business of the day is then and there settled; but he never interferes with the affairs of families or individuals. All the movements of the camp, as a whole, as well as hunting and other matters of consequence, are settled by the chief's authority alone; and all weightier matters, of peace or war, are settled by the chief and council.

The manners of the Oakinackens are agreeable, easy, and unassuming, and their dispositions mild. They are at times subject to gusts of passion, but it soon blows over; and, on the whole, they are a steady, sincere, shrewd, and brave people. They are generally of the middle size, light, and well made, and better featured and hand-somer in their persons, though darker, than the Chinooks or other Indians along the sea-coast. The circumstances of climate will perhaps account for this difference of complexion. Their hair is generally jet black, long, and rather coarse; they have dark black eyes, with teeth white as ivory, well set and regular.

The women wear their hair neatly clubbed on each side of the head behind the ears, and ornamented with double rows of the snowy higua, which are, among the Oakinackens, called Shet-la-cane; but they keep it shed or divided in front. The men's hair is queued or rolled up into a knot behind the head, and ornamented like that of the women; but [295] in front it falls or hangs down loosely before the face, covering the forehead and the eyes, which causes them every now and then to shake the head, or use the hands to uncover their eyes. The young persons of both sexes always paint their faces with red and black bars, extremely well designed.

The men live an active life; between hunting, fishing, war, and making canoes and domestic implements, they are always employed and industrious. Nor are the women less busy — curing fish, drying meat, dressing leather, collecting roots and fire-wood; with their domestic and family affairs, their whole time is occupied; and, indeed, they may be said to serve in the double capacity of wife and slave. They have in general an engaging sweetness, are good housewives, modest in their demeanour, affectionate and chaste, and strongly attached to their husbands and children. Each family is ruled by the joint will or authority of the husband and wife, but more particularly by the latter. At their meals, they generally eat separately and in succession — man, woman, and child.

The greatest source of evil existing among this otherwise happy people is polygamy. All the chiefs and other great men have invariably a plurality of wives: for he that has not one is neither chief nor great man, according to their ideas of greatness, and is looked upon with contempt. Many have two, three, four, or five, according to their means and influence; but those wives do not at all times remain [296] together,— indeed, that would be utterly impossible,— but at different camps where their relations are; so that the husband goes from camp to camp occasionally to visit them, keeping seldom more than one or two at a time with himself. The greatest favourite is of course his constant companion. Indeed, brawls, and squabbles constantly ensue when several wives meet; and what is still more revolting, the husband of the eldest daughter of the family is entitled by their laws to take to wife all her sisters as they grow up, if able to maintain them.

The dress or costume is nearly the same for men and women. It is simple, neat, and convenient, and serves unchanged for both winter and summer, hot and cold, wet and dry, day and night. That of the young females consists of a robe or garment of deer-skin, down to their ankles, well dressed, and soft as chamois, with long, wide sleeves, fringed and ornamented with beads, and the more valuable higuas with a belt around the waist, adorned with the teeth of animals, beads, and trinkets, and is far from being unbecoming. Leggings, or Indian stockings, trimmed with all the showy ornaments of Indian fancy; shoes, and a loose robe of deer-skin, thrown carelessly round the body, constitute the whole of their dress at all seasons of the year. While new, white, and clean, it has a pleasing appearance; nor does clothing of our manufacture ever become an Indian woman so well as her own [297] native dress; but as they have no change of clothing, nor any bedclothes excepting an additional skin thrown over them, their garments soon become shabby and unsightly. A new garment once put on remains until it is either worn to rags, or rotten with grease and filth on their backs. Those, however, worn by young people of a certain age, both male and female, are frequently bestowed on their elders when half worn, and replaced by another new suit; so that the younger folks of good circumstances are always well dressed and clean.

The men's garments seldom descend below the knee; and in lieu of being ornamented like those of the women, with gaudy trinkets, they are wrought and garnished in a very fanciful manner with porcupine-quills. During winter the men wear long detached sleeves or mittens up to their shoulders, made of the wolf or fox skins, which are united or fastened together by a string across the shoulders. While on their hunting excursions, they also wear caps made of the skins of the wolf or bear, with the ears erect; their heads being thus metamorphosed into wolves' or bears' heads, they are enabled to approach the game with greater facility. But it is not the head alone that is masked or disguised: I have seen a fellow get into a deer-skin, stripped for the purpose, with the skin of the head and horns complete, walk off on all fours, and get actually among a herd of deer without their taking notice of the deception. But the wolf is the animal they [298] seem to imitate the best. An Indian concealed in a wolf's hide, pulls the skin of the wolf's head, with the face, eyes, and nose entire, over his own head, the ears erect, and tail in its proper place, will walk, run, and frisk about on his hands and feet, so that he can scarcely be distinguished from the real animal itself. There is no bird nor beast of which they cannot imitate the voice so as to decoy it within their reach. Hunting is a favourite exercise with all Indians; and the Oakinackens are very fond of displaying their dexterity in riding, and decoying the animals of the chase. All classes of them paint the face, particularly the young. Painting, and dressing, and decking the hair, is their chief glory; but they are nowise particular about other parts of their persons.

[299] CHAPTER XIX

Marriage contracts — National custom — Exchange of presents — Nocturnal visits — The object — Purchasing the bride — Customs on the occasion — Feuds and quarrels — Tla-quill-augh, or Indian doctor — His office — Precarious life — Mode of paying him — Manner of treating the sick — Customs and ceremonies on the occasion — Hard duty — Superstitions — Knowledge of roots and herbs — Curing wounds — Diseases, or general complaints — Gambling — Tsill-all-a-come, or the national game — Manner of playing it — Bets — Gambling propensities — Hot baths — Manner of using them — On what occasions — Indian qualifications — Gymnastic exercise — Comparison — General remarks.

WE now come to the mode of courtship and the rites of marriage observed among these people. The law of the land, or rather the established custom of the country is, that parents betroth or promise their children in marriage while they are still very young; and these contracts are in most cases held valid when the minors come of age.

When a marriage alliance is thus entered into between parties on behalf of their infant children, reciprocal presents exchanged immediately between them serve as a seal to the marriage contract. These [300] presents are occasionally repeated afterwards; but not by both parties, as in the first instance. The friends of the young woman cease to give, but are always ready to receive what the friends of the young man may from time to time choose to bestow, until the parties come of age. What these presents consist of is immaterial, and depends on the means of the parties. Sometimes horses, or a horse, or a dressed skin, or a few trinkets of but little value; but as soon as the young man attains the age of fourteen or fifteen years, and the young woman that of eleven or twelve, he then goes and pays his addresses to her in person; which is done in this way:— After the people are all in bed, the young man goes to the lodge or wigwam of his intended bride, enters it in the dark, makes a small fire, and sits by it till he is observed by some of the inmates. The whisper then goes round If he be welcome, the girl's mother gets up, and without speaking to the young man herself, she awakens her daughter, who sits up with him by the fire; but the matron immediately retires to rest, leaving the young couple by themselves. During the *tête-à-tête*, no person in the lodge ever interrupts them. The interview is not long: the young man then departs, and the girl retires to rest again. These visits are repeated some three or four times, or more; and if the suitor be welcomed on every occasion, all goes on well. He then goes in the day-time, pretty sure of success, to his intended father-in-law, accompanied by some [301] near relative, and bringing with him the purchase-money; that is, horses, robes, skins, and trinkets, more or less, according to the rank of the parties. On arrival they sit down opposite to the door of the lodge. If invited in, all is well; then the pipe of peace is smoked; one side of the lodge is put in order; a new mat is spread out, and the young man seated thereon. The young woman is then brought by her father and mother, each taking her by an arm, and placed near her intended husband. They are thenceforth considered lawfully married. This done, the pipe of peace is again produced; and during the ceremony of smoking, the father-in-law and young man's relative expatiate on the worth of their respective families; after which the parties regale, the bridegroom's companion returns home, and the whole business is ended.

Now in all cases of first marriage the wife must be purchased by her husband; for there is no greater disgrace to a family than for a parent to give his daughter away in marriage for nothing, as they call it. In this, as in many other instances, the custom here is exactly the reverse of that which prevails in civilized life; for in place of giving a portion with the daughter, the parents require a portion for her; and the nobler the family the greater must be the donation, for the quality of the bride is on all occasions measured by the price paid for her by the husband. I have seen, however, the property tendered more than once refused; nor is [302] it uncommon to increase the offer once or twice till it is accepted. We have now shown the fair and natural side of the question, and shall next turn to take a view of the reverse side.

It sometimes happens that the plighted virgin rejects the parents' choice. The parents themselves also change their sentiments in this case; and the young woman marries, not the person she was betrothed to, but another. This never fails to produce feuds and quarrels between

the families concerned; the tide of animosity runs high —
so high, sometimes, that the tribe splits into two portions,
which separate from each other, perhaps permanently.

We need not touch on second or subsequent marriages;
they are made and unmade according to circumstances,
whim, or fancy, without being subject to any other law
than the will of the parties themselves.

We now come to a rather mysterious part of our subject,
which I could never rightly understand, and therefore we
do not expect to guide the reader satisfactorily through
this labyrinth of superstition and jugglery. It refers
to a class of functionaries called medicine-men, or priests,
or perhaps, what would be nearer the true meaning,
conjurors; for I know not exactly which of these terms
would be the most applicable to them, as the class of
men to which we allude act occasionally in all these
capacities. They are called Tla-quill-aughs, which
signifies, in their language, men of supernatural gifts,
who pretend to [303] know all things, and can kill and
cure by magic whom they please. Among the whites they
go by the name of doctors or jugglers.

There are no acquirements, so far as I know, deemed
essential to qualify a person for the office of a tla-quill-
augh. In all Indian tribes there are three or four
characters of this description. The tla-quill-aughs are
men generally past the meridian of life; in their habits
grave and sedate, with a certain shyness and cunning
about them. Like most Indians, they possess a good
knowledge of herbs and roots, and their virtues. All
classes stand in awe of the tla-quill-aughs' power or ill
will, and their opinions have much influence in most
matters. They are consulted in all cases of sickness.
All classes avoid, as much as possible, giving them offence,

from a belief that they have the power of throwing, as they express it, their bad medicine at them, whether far or near, present or absent. The people believe they can converse with the good and the bad spirits; and the tla-quill-aughs, on their part, make it their chiefest study to impose on popular credulity, leading others to credit what they do not believe themselves.

During our stay among these people, it sometimes happened that the tla-quill-aughs were offended with us for our want of faith. On such occasions, the other Indians, seeing us act with so much unconcern in matters which they considered so hazardous to ourselves, would stare at our ignorance, and look on us as the barbarians of old did on St. Paul when the [304] viper fastened on his hand, expecting every moment to see us fall down dead!

From what has now been said on the subject, the reader will no doubt at once conclude that the tla-quill-aughs are of all men the most happy. Let him not, however, be deceived, but look upon them as of all men the most miserable. Every misfortune, sudden death, mishap, or unexpected disaster that happens to any of the people, is immediately attributed to some tla-quill-augh, and he, however innocent, pays with his life for the calamity. On whomsoever the imagination fixes, be he far or near, he is secretly hunted out, waylaid, and put to death; and this is generally the fate of all of them!

When any person is dangerously ill, a tla-quill-augh is consulted, and the price of his services fixed, without his ever seeing the patient. As soon, therefore, as this preliminary part of the business is arranged, the price agreed upon is forthwith sent to his abode, and he repairs to the sick person and begins his operations. He is always paid beforehand — that payment being according to the quality of the sick person; and it is believed that the more is given the sooner and the better will be the case. It is no wonder, therefore, that they should be liberal on such occasions; but if the patient dies the fee is all returned again.

When the tla-quill-augh enters the wigwam or lodge, he views the patient with an air of affected gravity, such as we see some of our own doctors assume on entering the dwelling of a sick person, and [305] tells the by-standers, with a shake of the head and a groan, that the case is a very bad one, and that without him the patient would have surely died. The first thing he then does is to paint himself; and while this is going on he keeps constantly eyeing the patient, ties up his head with a leather strap and his waist with a thong, then lays the patient on his back, takes a piece of strong line, and girds him round the waist as tight as possible; in which position he is not allowed to stir, or to receive any kind of nourishment, until the whole ceremony is ended, which lasts for upwards of three hours every morning and evening until there is a change; and I have known them for weeks together to continue the business without intermission, when it would be hard to tell whether the doctor or the patient was most exhausted.

After the patient is thus placed, the tla-quill-augh, standing over him in a stooping position, bends down, and with his whole force presses him with his two fists in the pit of the stomach, as if intending to push through his body; then, suddenly standing up again, he opens his fists, and keeps blowing through his fingers, every now and then ejaculating a short prayer in a loud and frantic manner, stamping with his feet, blowing with his mouth, and making various gesticulations with his body and arms, always ending the last sentence, in a tremulous voice and quaver of the lips, in these words — "Ho! ho! ho! ho! oh! oh!" All this, the doctor says, is necessary to drive away the evil spirit, for he must be expelled before a cure [306] can be effected! The moment the bad spirit is gone out of the sick person, the tla-quill-augh sucks the part affected with his mouth to extract the bad blood through the pores of the skin, which, to all appearance, he does effectually. How he manages to do it I know not; but I have often watched him, and seen him throw out whole mouthfuls of blood, and yet not the least mark would appear on the skin. I have also examined the tla-quill-augh's mouth, supposing he might have cut it, but I could never discover anything of the kind. By the colour and quantity of the blood he announces the character of the disease. He goes through the same ceremony with various parts of the body till he expels the evil spirit altogether; or if he fails to do so, and the patient dies, he fixes the death on some rival in the profession.

Having now detailed the course pursued by the honest and zealous tla-quill-augh himself, we next come to describe the accompaniment performed by his assistants. The moment the tla-quill-augh commences his operations, four other persons, men and women indiscriminately, are placed in the same wigwam with the doctor and the sick person, two and two, face to face — that is, opposite to each other, and sitting tailor fashion, with a small stick in each hand. Between these four persons is then laid, flat on the ground, a piece of wood about eight feet long, and on this they keep beating time with their sticks in a loud and noisy manner, singing all the while; but the moment the tla-quill-augh comes to the words

[307] ''Ho, ho, ho!'' the assistants who keep drumming
on the piece of wood stop singing, and with their sticks
beat one, two, three, for three successive times, by way
of an *amen* to the doctor's invocations. Then silence
ensues for about two minutes, when the whole commences
anew, and so on to the end of the ceremony, which, as I
have already said, continues every morning and evening
about three hours.

The noise made by drumming on the stick, in conjunction with the tla-quill-augh's hallooing, is intended
to frighten away the evil spirit, and prepare the patient
for medicine; so that, between the doctor's bawling and
stamping, and the drummer's beating and singing,
the noise may be heard a quarter of a mile round. With
all this absurdity, many extraordinary cures are performed by these people. They have a profound knowledge of all simples, and if the complaint be manifest, as
in cases of cuts and wounds, or the like, their skill is
really astonishing. I once saw an Indian who had been
nearly devoured by a grizzly bear, and had his skull split
open in several places, and several pieces of the bone
taken out just above the brain, and measuring three-
fourths of an inch in length, cured so effectually by one
of these jugglers, that in less than two months after he
was riding on his horse again at the chase. I have also
seen them cut open the belly with a knife, extract a large
quantity of fat from the inside, sew up the part again,
and the patient soon after perfectly recovered. The
bite of the rattlesnake [308] they cure effectually; and
as to vomits, purges, decoctions, and the knowledge of
phlebotomy, none can be more expert and successful than
the tla-quill-aughs; and I have witnessed two or three

cases, which baffled the skill of a regular surgeon, cured by them.

The diseases most frequent among these people, are indigestion, fluxes, asthmas, and consumptions. Instances of longevity are here and there to be found among them, but not very often.

From the doctor we now turn to the gambler. Play or gambling is a favourite pastime among all classes of the Oakinackens. The principal game is called tsill-all-a-come, differing but little from the chall-chall played by the Chinooks or Indians along the sea-coast. This game is played with two small, oblong, polished bones, each two inches long, and half an inch in diameter, with twenty small sticks of the same diameter as the bones, but about nine inches long.

The game does not set any limits to the number of players at a time, provided both sides be equal. Two, four, or six, as may be agreed upon, play this game; but, in all large bets, the last number is generally adopted. When all is ready, and the property at stake laid down on the spot, the players place themselves in the following manner: the parties kneel down, three on one side, and three on the other, face to face, and about three feet apart; and in this position they remain during the game. A [309] piece of wood is then placed on the ground between them: this done, each player is furnished with a small drum-stick, about the size of a rule, in his right hand, which stick is used for beating time on the wood, in order to rivet attention on the game. The drumming is always accompanied with a song. The players, one and all, muffle their wrists, fists, and fingers with bits of fur or trapping, in order the better to elude and deceive their opponents. Each party then takes one of the two small polished bones, and ten of the small sticks, the use of which will hereafter be more fully explained. In all cases the arms and body are perfectly naked, the face painted, the hair clubbed up, and the head girt round with a strap of leather. The party is now ready to begin the game, all anxious and on the alert: three of the players on one side strike up a song, to which all keep chorus, and this announces the commencement. The moment the singing and drumming begin on one side, the greatest adept on the other side instantly takes the little polished bone, conceals it in one of his fists, then throws it into the other, and back again, and so on from one fist to the other, nimbly crossing and recrossing his arms, and every instant changing the position of his fists. The quickness of the motions and the muffling of the fists make it almost impossible for his opponents to guess which hand holds the bone, and this is the main point. While the player is manœuvring in this manner, his three opponents eagerly watch his [310] motions with an eagle's eye, to try and discover the fist that contains the bone; and, the moment one of them thinks he has discovered where the bone is, he points to it with the quickness of lightning: the player at the same time, with equal rapidity, extends his arm and opens his fist in the presence of all; if it be empty, the player draws back his arm and continues, while the guesser throws the player one of the little sticks, which counts one. But if the guesser hits upon the fist that contains the bone, the player throws a stick to him and ceases playing, his opponent now going through the same operation: every miss costs a stick on either side. It is not the best of three, but three times running:

all the sticks must be on one side to finish the game. I have seen them for a whole week at one game, and then not conclude, and I have known the game decided in six hours.

It sometimes happens, however, that after some days and nights are spent in the same game, neither party gains: in that case, the rules of the game provide that the number of players be either increased or diminished; or, if all the parties be agreed, the game is relinquished, each party taking up what it put down: but so intent are they on this favourite mode of passing their time, that it seldom happens that they separate before the game is finished; and while it is in progress every other considera-tion is sacrificed to it; and some there are who devote all their time and means solely to gambling; and when [311] all is lost, which is often the case, the loser seldom gives way to grief. They are a happy people, never repining at what cannot be remedied. Various other games and amusements occupy their time: among which, the females have several that are innocent and amusing; but singing and dancing are their delight, and in these they often indulge to excess.

Next we come to the description of their hot baths, or rather fiery trial. To construct one of these baths a good deal of trouble and labour is required. A hole, fifteen feet in diameter, and about four feet deep, is dug in some convenient place for wood and water. The hole is then covered over with a thick coat of earth, as close as possible, leaving only a small aperture or opening in one side, barely sufficient to admit a single person to creep in and out on all fours. This done, a pile of wood, with a considerable number of stones laid thereon, is set on fire in the centre; and when the wood is consumed, and the stones red hot, water is thrown over them, causing a dense vapour and intense heat; yet in the midst of this suffocating cloud, where one would suppose a salamander itself could hardly live, the Indians enter stark naked, and no sooner in than the aperture or hole is closed upon them. Here they keep singing and recounting their war adventures, and invoking the good spirit to aid them again, rolling and groaning all the time in this infernal cell for nearly an hour; when all at once they bound out one by one, like so many [312] subterranean spectres issuing from the infernal regions. Besmeared with mud, and pouring down with sweat, they dash into the cold water, and there plunge and swim about for at least a quarter of an hour, when they return again to their cell, going through this fiery trial twice — morning and evening — on all great occasions. On all occasions of peace or war; of success in their enterprises, and good luck in hunting, the bath is resorted to. In short, great virtues are supposed to arise from the regular observance of this general custom of purification.

In the wide field of gymnastic exercise, few Indians — I might say none — have been found to cope with civilized man. In all trials of walking, of running, of fatigue, feats of agility, and famine, even in the Indian's own country, he has to yield the palm of victory to the white man. In the trials of the hot bath alone the savage excels.

The ceremony of the bath is not peculiar to the Oak-inackens: it is practised by all the aboriginal tribes on the American continent.

[313] CHAPTER XX

Social habits — Winter habitations — Economy of the winter — Summer employments — Collecting of food — Fish barriers — Salmon — Division of labour — Roots and berries — Scenes at the fish camp — Mode of catching the deer — Preparation of food — Furnaces or ovens — Implements of warfare — Spampt, how made — Pine moss — Bread, how prepared — Great war-dance — Manner of fighting — Treaties of peace — Scalps — Slaves — Funeral ceremonies — Mode of interment — Graves — Superstitions — Emblems — Customs — Mourning — Punishments — Sedate habits and docile dispositions.

THEIR winter habitations are constructed chiefly of mats and poles, covered over with grass and earth; and are made very commodious, comfortable, and roomy. The inside being dug about a foot or two below the surface of the ground, a precaution which adds much to their warmth. They are invariably open at the ridge pole all along, and the reason is obvious; for without any chimney, the smoke by this means has a free vent upwards. These lodgings resemble in appearance the roof of a common dwelling-house removed from the walls and placed on the ground; the fires are made in the centre, directly under the ridge pole, and about six or eight feet apart, and are in proportion to the number of [314] families who live under the same roof; each family having generally one fire. The doors are but few, and situate to suit convenience; in the front, in the back, or the gable ends, and are merely oblong holes, over which mats are suspended by means of a wooden hinge, which mat or door must be lifted up and down every time a person goes in or out.

Although these dwellings have neither partition nor division in any of them, yet the property of each individual, the privacy of each family, and the place each occupies, are so well secured and ascertained as to afford to a rude people all the advantages, and even conveniences of a more complicated building. These dwellings are generally long and narrow, and contain each from one to five or six families, whose winter supplies of provisions are considered as one common stock, and as such are served out in winter by each family in turn, until the whole is consumed.

We must now relate the manner in which these people pass the summer season, and provide food for the winter. As soon as the snow begins to disappear in the spring, the winter camps break up, and the whole tribe disperse here and there into small parties or families; and in this unsettled manner they wander about till the middle of June, when they all assemble again in large bands on the banks of the different rivers, for the purpose of fishing during the summer season. Here, then, their fish barriers are constructed, by the united labour of the whole village or camp assembled in one place. The salmon being then in the utmost abundance, no sooner are the barriers finished than one [315] or more of the principal men are appointed, by general consent, to superintend each. The person or persons thus chosen divide the fish every morning, and settle all matters respecting the barrier and fish for the current year. Their authority is law in all those matters till the end of the fishing season, which is generally about the beginning of October. During the season the camp is divided into four parties, for the various purposes of daily life, and of laying in a stock of food for the approaching winter. The men are divided into two parties; one for hunting, and the other for fishing: and of the women also, one party cure the fish, another collect roots and berries. All these different productions are dried and seasoned in the sun, and require much attention and labour. The fish when properly cured is packed up into large bundles or bales; the roots and berries into bags made of rushes. The stock for the winter, thus daily and weekly produced, is then, during the nights, conveyed in secret, and put in *caches*; that is, hidden under ground among the rocks; each family having its share apart, secure from wild beasts and the eye of thieves. During the continuance of the fish season, the Indian camp is all life. Gambling, dancing, horse-racing, and frolicking, in all its varied forms, are continued without intermission; and few there are, even the most dull and phlegmatic, who do not feel, after enjoying so much hilarity, a deep regret on leaving the piscatory camp on these occasions.

As soon as the fish season is over, the Indians again all withdraw into the interior or mountains, as in the [316] spring, and divide into little bands for the purpose of hunting the various animals of the chace. In their mode of ensnaring the deer and other animals, they are generally very successful. Exclusive of hunting these animals with their guns, bows, and arrows, and running them down with their horses, which latter practice is a favourite amusement, they frequently select a valley or favourable spot of ground between two mountains, having a narrow outlet or pass at one end; and the better to decoy the unwary game into it, bushes are planted on each side of the pass, contracting, as it were, the passage as it advances into the form of a funnel, until, at the outlet, it becomes quite narrow. Here the animals, being pressed forward by their pursuers, fall an easy prey to those who in ambush await their arrival, and by whom they are generally all killed while struggling to extricate themselves from the snare.

The Indians, after passing a month or six weeks in this roving state, congregate again into large bands for the purpose of passing the winter on the banks of small rivers, where wood is convenient and plentiful. During this season they remain in their habitations, constructed as already described; nor do they break up their winter camps till about the 1st of February. During this cold and tedious period, they chiefly subsist on the stock laid in during the summer season, and in severe winters, when little can be obtained from the chace, they are reduced to great extremes before the snow disappears, or the spring invites them to rove about again.

Their food is boiled in watape kettles, a mode [317] common to all the aborigines throughout the continent. The process is simple, and similar to that practised by the Chinooks and other tribes along the Pacific. The dish or kettle being placed on the ground, and nearly filled with water, the meat, fish, or other viand, is cut or torn into small pieces, and after being put into the kettle, some heated stones, by the help of wooden tongs, are immediately thrown in also, which is no sooner done than the water in the dish is in a state of ebullition. After a few minutes' boiling the stones are taken out and instantly replaced by others, also red hot, which second set generally suffices to complete the process. The contents are then served up, and each individual receives his portion on a piece of bark or mat. The broth, in which the food is boiled, is likewise carefully dealt round with a wooden ladle into bark or wooden dishes, and is, with all the ashes and dirt incident to the process, considered as the most delicious part of the repast. Their culinary vessels are seldom washed or cleaned. The dog's tongue is the only dish-cloth known.

Roots and vegetables of every description are cooked during the summer by means of furnaces in the open air; they are then baked on stones, formed into small cakes, and dried in the sun, after which the whole is carefully laid by for winter use. And while speaking of a furnace and baking, we ought not to omit stating how they bake their bread, and what kind of bread they generally make use of.

On the pines of this country there is a dark brown moss which collects or grows about the branches. [318] This moss is carefully gathered every autumn, when it has the appearance of dirty coarse wool. It is soaked in water, pressed hard together, and then cooked in an oven or furnace, from which it comes forth in large sheets like slate, but supple and pliable, resembling pieces of tarpauling, black as ink, and tasteless; and when cut with a knife it has a spotted or marbled appearance, owing to the number of small sprigs of wood, bark, or other extraneous substances, unavoidably collected with the moss in taking it from the trees. This cake when dried in the sun becomes as hard as flint, and must always be soaked in water before use. It is generally eaten with the raw fat of animals, as we use bread and butter. It is viscous and clammy in the mouth, with but little taste. Thus prepared it will keep for years; is much liked by the natives, and sometimes eaten by the whites. It is called squill-ape.

We now come to their warlike weapons and manner

of fighting. Generally speaking, they are rather a trafficking commercial people than a nation of warriors; yet, when called to war, they are resolute and brave.

Their implements of warfare are guns, bows, and arrows (in the use of which they are very expert), shields, knives, and lances, and a bludgeon, for close combat, called spampt. This deadly weapon is made in the following manner: — A piece of hard wood, about nine inches long, and half an inch in diameter, of a cylindrical form, resembling a short rule, is tightly covered over with a piece of raw hide, which being large at one end forms a bag, in which is [319] enclosed a round stone of the size of a goose-egg. This has the appearance of a ball at the end of the staff: the space between them about an inch, serving as a joint; the other end is tied round the wrist of the right hand with a thong. An Oakinacken thus accoutred, and mounted on his fleetest steed, is ready for action.

The hot bath, council, and ceremony of smoking the great pipe before war, is always religiously observed. Their laws, however, admit of no compulsion, nor is the chief's authority implicitly obeyed on these occasions; consequently, every one judges for himself, and either goes or stays as he thinks proper. With a view, however, to obviate this defect in their system, they have instituted the dance, which answers every purpose of a recruiting service. As soon, therefore, as war is resolved upon, a large ring or circle is marked out, into which the war chief enters; the belligerent declaration is published in a loud voice, and the great war-dance commenced, which is carried on with much spirit and shouting; every man, therefore, who enters within this ring, and joins in the dance, thereby pledges himself, and is, according to the laws of the tribe, in honour bound to assist in carrying on the war, or in other words, is a soldier, and bound to obey the great war chief.

Stratagem and ambuscade, so peculiar to all savages, is always resorted to by these people, who dislike an open attack; and for the want of proper discipline and subordination, never stand face to face in the fight if they can avoid it. If they fail to surprise their enemy in the darkness of night, or [320] the dawn of morning, which is their favourite mode of attack, they skirmish at a distance, occasionally dashing at full speed near enough to have a flying shot at each other, without any kind of order, shouting and yelling all the time in the most wild and frantic manner, capering and cowering on their horses to evade their adversaries fire. If one on either side happens to fall, a rush is made for the scalp, which brings the foes into close contact. The firing with guns then ceases, and the quick shooting of arrows commences; but the arrows soon cease also, and the spear comes into play; but this in turn is soon laid aside, and gives place to the bloody knife and deadly spampt. These are the last weapons used, except, perhaps, a few random shots at retiring. This last stage of the encounter or conflict is often severely contested, but does not last long. The moment a chief or principal man falls, fighting gives place to mourning; they get discouraged, and instantly fly without disgrace, and the battle is ended.

The number slain on these occasions is comparatively few; and when the conquerors bear off in barbarous triumph a dozen scalps or so, it is thought a great victory. Their treaties of peace, though made with the utmost solemnity, are but the words of children, no sooner uttered than forgotten. With all this barbarity, however, they are kind and indulgent to their slaves. War not being their trade, there are but few slaves among them, and these few are adopted as children, and treated in all respects as members of the family.

Next in order are their funeral ceremonies, mourning, [321] and manner of interment. When a chief, or other principal personage, is on his deathbed, he is surrounded by his relatives, who observe a strict silence and calm indifference while the zealous tla-quill-laugh goes through the solemnities of his office; but the moment the patient dies, the house or lodge is abandoned, and loud clamorous mourning commences: the whole camp, during the first burst of lamentation, join in the tumultous uproar. This lasts for some hours without intermission, and then gives way to a dead silence; during which the body, wrapped in a new garment, is removed to the open air, and the house or lodge is razed to the ground. Every now and then the mourning bursts forth anew. The moment one begins, the whole instantly join; the cry being reinforced by the howling of dogs and screaming of children. A few hours after death the body is interred. For this purpose, a round hole is dug in some convenient spot, and the body is placed in a sitting posture, but inclining a little backwards, with the knees raised up nearly to the breast. All the most valuable trinkets and trophies of war possessed by the deceased are laid on his breast, supported by his knees, and interred along with the body. If any of these articles be withheld from the grave, the spirit of the deceased, according to the popular belief, can never be at rest; consequently the custom is religiously observed. After the grave is filled up with earth and stones, a small pile of wood is placed over it, and several articles are suspended from the pile, indicating the quality of the deceased. If he be a warrior, the bow and scalp mark his grave; if a [322] hunter, an animal is portrayed thereon; the spear and salmon in like manner point out the fisherman's place of rest. Immediately after the interment, all the valuable property, such as horses, guns, bows, and other things not put into the grave, are destroyed and scattered around it as a sacrifice. The near relations then cut their hair short, scarify their flesh, besmear their faces and bodies, clothe themselves in old tattered garments, and abandon themselves to excessive mourning for many months together; strictly taking care not to mention the name of the deceased.

If a husband dies, the widow, according to custom, must remain two years single; during which time she never paints, combs her hair, nor puts on new clothing. After some months, their loud lamentation is confined to the morning and evening; but in their grief, during the first months, they howl incessantly and desperately, as if excess of grief were to be measured by excess of noise. Yet no sooner are these wild fits over than they seem all of a sudden to forget their anguish, and at once resume a tranquil, placid, and cheerful countenance.

They have no place appropriated for the reception of the dead; but their graves are generally on some eminence, rocky ground, or stony place, and the spot is always held sacred.

Among these people there are no regular punishments instituted for crimes or offences of any kind; yet all transgressions are cognizable and punished by their laws, so as to ensure security to life and property. Theft, in particular, is held in the utmost abhorrence, so that it rarely occurs among them. [323] The property of each individual, even of the slave, is held sacred.

They perfectly understand the nature of barter and traffic, and may be called, in their way, a commercial and trading people; but, like all Indians, they cannot resist the temptation of European articles, and will give everything they possess for the toys and trifles of the whites. They are a sedate and docile people, and very susceptible of improvement, and could, with comparatively little trouble, I am confident, be brought round to a state of civilization. Their superstitions seem to be the only barrier between them and the attainment of a more refined state.

[324] CHAPTER XXI

Calculation of time — Singular manner of naming children — Peculiar modes of address — Anecdote of an Indian chief — Indian forbearance — Conduct of the whites in Indian countries — Comparison of crime between Indians and whites — Manner of swaddling infants — Hardships during infancy — Savage customs — Indian constitution — Chief cause of scanty population — A day's journey — Calculation of distance — Rough roads — Indian ideas — Social habits — Some remarks on the system adopted for converting Indians to the Christian faith.

IN calculating time the Oakinackens invariably use their fingers, and go by tens. A common mode of counting with them is by snows or winters. Ask an Indian his age, he immediately casts his eyes on his hands, calculates his age by his fingers, and answers by holding so many of them up to view, each finger standing for ten years. Some of the most intelligent among them will reckon to a thousand tolerably correct; but by far the greater part can scarcely count twenty.

Contrary to the customs in civilized life, the children are never weaned until they give up the breast of their own accord, or another child is born to supplant the former; nor is the child ever hand-fed [325] while at the breast, but lives solely on its mother's milk till old enough to feed itself. Yet the infant is generally robust and healthy; but the mother soon becomes an old woman. Here a singularity in their manners presents itself; for the child never receives a name till it has done sucking its mother's breast, and then it is named according to the disposition it evinced up till that time. If a male child, fractious and ill-humoured, it is named to please the ear, after some carnivorous bird or beast, such as the bear, the wolf or the vulture; if, on the contrary, it be mild and quiet, it will be named after the deer, the rabbit, or the pheasant, so that the name generally indicates the temper; and while we are speaking of names, it may be proper to follow that subject a little farther, because it is one that generally forms a striking characteristic of Indian manners.

Indians of all classes change their names periodically, taking new ones according to fancy or caprice; and it is a peculiar habit, even a national custom, for the male and female children to address their parents in a manner peculiar to their sex, if I may so express myself, and to name their brothers and sisters according to their respective ages, as shall presently appear. To explain this rather knotty point, we shall suppose a family to consist of six children, three boys and three girls, besides the parents; and in order to make the thing as intelligible as possible, we shall again suppose that one of the boys —

not the eldest, nor yet the youngest, but the middle one —
is to address each of the [326] other members of the
family. The boy then says, En-leo, my father; Es-koy
my mother; En-ketch-eck, my elder brother; E-shentsa
my younger brother; El-kick-cha, my elder sister;
El-shets-spo, my younger sister; E-she-she, my uncle;
and Es-wa-wis-saw, my aunt. We shall now take the
female in the same degree; that is, the middle one, who
must say, En-mistem, my father; En-toume, my mother;
El-keck-cha, my elder sister; El-shets-ops, my younger
sister; El-kack-itsa, my elder brother; El-she-shentsa,
my younger brother; Es-melt, my uncle; and Es-ta-ta-qua,
my aunt.

Age and change of circumstance have great influence
in causing change of names at different periods of life;
but no change ever takes place in the above family
mode of expression. During my first years among them,
the chief went by the name of Its-kay-kay-etsa, or painted
garment. After the death of the fox his father, he changed
his name to Quill-quill-is-tshen-ach-can, or public speaker;
and of late he has changed it again to that of Whist-as-ma-
whey-kin, or the white bear, a name only assumed by
chiefs or other great men; but in general these changes
may be classed under three heads; one for youth, one for
middle age, and one for old age.

On our travels one day, we overtook a party of Indians,
when one of my men accosted the chief, calling him by
name. The chief looked steadfastly at him, but made
no reply. Being called again by name, he turned half
round, and with a significant air, said, ''You white people
say you know all things; do you not then know that I
have changed [327] my name?'' ''No,'' said the man;
''how could I know? for you change your names as

often as the moon changes; but the whites, like the sun, never change." "And who made the moon?" said the Indian. "God, to be sure," rejoined the man. "And who made the sun?" continued the chief. "The same who made the moon," was the reply. "Then if God made us after the moon subject to change, and you after the sun unchangeable, why do you reproach us? In reproaching us, you reproach the master of life."

If you offend or even assault an Indian, he seldom resents at the moment, or shows any signs of violence or passion; but, on the contrary, he remains sullen, mute, and thoughtful. This forbearance, however, forebodes no good; for he broods over the insult or injury, and meditates revenge. Years may elapse, but the injury is still fresh in the savage breast; and there is but one way left for you to ward off the meditated blow, and regain his friendship, and that is, by a peace-offering or present; for here property pays for all offences.

If one Indian kills another, the murderer saves his own life by making a suitable present to the nearest relative of the deceased; and they draw no line of distinction between accidental or justifiable homicide and wilful murder: death caused in any way by another is looked upon in the same criminal light.

If a native flies into a passion with a white man, which is seldom the case, his passion or anger ought to be allowed to evaporate; and if you can muster [328] patience enough to keep your temper till his rage is past, you can then do with him just what you please; for nothing subdues and reforms a savage more than patience and silence on your part while he is giving way to anger. Forbearance and even-handed justice are far more successful instruments in governing Indians than powder

and ball. The confirmation of this statement will be
found in the spectacle of the millions of aborigines that
inhabit this quarter of the globe alone, and the comparatively few white men, not perhaps one to a thousand,
who live among them. Yet the white man does not
always observe the golden rule of forbearance and even-
handed justice, but often arbitrarily arrogates the right
of domineering over the natives; and yet these, in almost
all cases, yield without a murmur. And to our shame
be it said, that reason and right, humanity and forbearance, are as often to be found among the savages
themselves as among the whites, who live by sufferance
among them. The Indian in his natural state is happy,
with his trader he is happy; but the moment he begins
to walk in the path of the white man his happiness is at
an end. Like a wild animal in a cage, his lustre is gone.

However strongly we may abhor heathenism, and
deprecate the savage character in its natural state, as
compared to civilized humanity, yet we ought not, in
our zeal for the one or abhorrence of the other, to suppress
the truth; and the truth, therefore, compels us to admit
that there are many traits of virtue to be met with in the
Indian character. They are brave, generous, and often
charitable; and to their [329] credit be it said, that there
is less crime in an Indian camp of five hundred souls than
there is in a civilized village of but half that number.
Let the lawyer or moralist point out the cause.

Custom here constitutes law, not only in reference to
the great affairs of the nation or tribe, but in trivial things
also. A mother is not allowed to prepare swaddling-
clothes for an unborn infant; and, indeed, but little
preparation is required, for the whole paraphernalia
consists of but four articles — a rude piece of board,

which serves for a cradle; a bit of skin, which serves to
wrap the new-born babe in; some moss to lie on; and
a string to lash the whole together. Thus secured, the
bantling is carried about on its mother's back, or allowed
to sprawl on the ground, in all weathers and all seasons.

Tacitus found fault with the Roman ladies of his
day for giving their children to Grecian women to nurse,
and thus depriving the infant of maternal tenderness.
What would the historian have thought had he seen an
infant of the savage race, as practised in these parts,
tied naked on a hard board, and allowed to tumble and
roll about as it best could? and yet this very race, or
portion of the human family, is as perfect in form, as
healthy and vigorous, as any people on the face of the
earth.

In traveling, the distance of places is always calculated
according to time. If on horseback, a day's ride is
estimated at about seventy of our miles; if on foot, at
half that distance. This mode of calculating distances is,
however, very erroneous, and not to be depended upon
by the whites, as the natives seldom [330] take into
consideration either the good or bad state of the roads.
But interruptions which are grievous obstacles to us are
nothing in their way; for where a rabbit can pass, an
Indian horse will pass, and where a horse can pass, the
savage, who sticks on his back like a crab, passes over
hill and dale, rock and ravine, at full speed; so that
good roads or bad roads, rugged or smooth, all is alike
to him.

Nor is the fair sex less dexterous in managing the horse;
a woman with one child on her back and another in her
arms will course the fleetest steed over the most rugged
and perilous country. In conversation they seem to

possess but few ideas, and their answer is often a gesture expressive of approbation or dislike; at other times, simply yes or no; and yet, in their national harangues, they often display great energy of mind, inspire confidence, and frequently give a strong impulse to public opinion.

While on their journeys, and indeed at all times, the men willingly aid in alleviating the hardships of the women, and are indulgent husbands. On all occasions they evince a steady and temperate disposition, and every action of their lives is more or less marked by intelligence and moderation.

Having now performed, however imperfectly, the task we had undertaken, and brought to a close our description of the Oakinacken nation, we shall proceed to make a few remarks on the moral and spiritual condition of these people, as a portion of the great family of mankind, as well as on the system generally pursued by missionaries in converting Indians to Christianity.

[331] The Oakinackens are a people that might soon, and with but very little trouble, be induced to throw off their savage habits altogether, as they are reforming fast, and exhibit on most occasions a strong desire and capacity for receiving moral and religious instruction. The last time I visited them was in 1825, and it was encouraging to witness their continued improvement. [96]

When we contemplate the wide field open before us for missionary labours, even between the Rocky Mountains and the Pacific, and the large sums yearly spent in various parts of the world for the purposes of instructing

[96] From his residence among the Okanagan and his marriage to the daughter of a chief of this tribe, Ross had ample opportunity to learn their customs; he seems to speak wholly from observation. Ross Cox, who in 1816 was stationed at Okanagan, also gives a description of these Indians, which in the main agrees with Ross's account, although differing in some important details.— ED.

and converting the heathen, shall we not then hope and expect that at some future day those blessings may be extended to the Far West? Even a tithe of what is laid out in our country in England would, if rightly applied, be an inestimable blessing to these people. But the result would entirely depend on the manner in which the work of conversion was undertaken; and, with this impression on our minds, it seems to us expedient to make a few observations on the system generally followed in instructing and evangelizing the heathen in other parts of the world.

Where the rays of evangelical light beam forth, that light alone, if practically improved, will not only discover the errors of the past, but point out a remedy for the future. But the great evil is, hesitation takes the place of determination, and no person wishes to begin the work of reforming any great system which has been long in operation, and more particularly so if it be considered by its promoters [332] as working well; but in a case such as the present, in which the whole world is more or less concerned, others as well as the actual promoters ought to have a voice, and every voice inculcating improvement ought to be respected: yet I am not vain enough to suppose that any opinion or representation of mine, however correct, will either reform the old or perfect the new system, because such things are not the work of a day nor of an individual; but if the suggestions now presented draw the attention of abler writers to the subject, I shall be satisfied.

The pious and charitable world contribute with a liberal hand; the missionary is sent out to the wilderness to instruct and convert the heathen: so far all is well. The missionary reaches his destination, announces the gospel tidings, and commences his official duties; the young and the old are catechised, baptism is administered, and the sacrament of the Lord's Supper follows — and all these different glimpses of evangelical light succeed each other in such rapid succession as to stamp the whole proceeding with the character of a miracle. The calm and reflecting observer is confounded, and the pious Christian is struck with astonishment at the hurried and precipitate manner in which the wild and untutored savage is thus washed from all his sins, and received into the bosom of the Christian church. In all this, however, there is nothing real; on the contrary, it is utterly impossible for the missionary, or any other man alive, to cultivate the soil, sow the seeds of gospel vegetation, and bring forth the matured fruits of regeneration in so short a time. [333] The missionary, in all this, no doubt follows his instructions.

But this is not all: the missionary's journal goes home, more labourers are required for the vineyard, periodicals circulate the marvellous success, and all the world, except those on the spot, believe the report. Yet the picture is delusive: the savage is still a savage, and gross idolatry and barbarism have not yielded inwardly a hair's-breadth to the influence of civilization, far less is he made sensible of the obligations imposed upon him by his new creed. It is but a treacherous calm before a storm: the tree is known by its fruit.

These reports are no sooner laid before the public, than a pious interest is again excited, and the liberal hand of charity is again cheerfully held out to aid in civilizing mankind. Other missionaries are sent forth, who, to prove their own zeal and success, heighten if possible the colouring of the former picture, by the addition of still more marvellous reports; and in this manner they go on, as it were, at full gallop, according to the present system, without taking time to dispel that thick and heavy cloud of ignorance and barbarism so necessary to be removed from the savage mind before it is prepared to receive spiritual instruction, or appreciate the benefits of Christianity. The result is scarcely a form of godliness, the time allowed being insufficient for perfecting the work, or doing it as it ought to be done; and this very want of time is chiefly the rock on which the missionary bark universally founders.

Before concluding this part of our subject, we [334] might advert to another evil connected with the present system, and perhaps the worst of all evils, inasmuch as no effectual remedy can well be applied to it — that is, the interference of sects with one another; for no sooner does a missionary plant the standard of the Gospel in any foreign land, but others of different persuasions follow: and it is no uncommon thing to see, in many parts of the heathen world, Papists and Protestants, with all the different branches of the two great sects, like rivals in trade, huddled together, working confusion; not only distracting and corrupting their converts, but destroying in their obstinacy the fruits of each other's labour — forgetting that they are all God's husbandmen, labouring in the same vineyard, and for the same master.

Next to the British empire, few countries on the globe have pursued the present system with more success than the Americans have done; yet the Americans themselves have found from long experience, as they now declare, that the system is defective, that the results produced nowise correspond to the means employed: and the same observation may be applied to every other quarter of the earth.

Let us now consider the possibility of reforming this defective system. Considering the moral degradation of the heathen world, it behoves those who take an interest in changing the condition of the natural man, to apply the means best adapted for that purpose, and to recognise and avail themselves of every light that may in a practical way hold out a prospect of success; and if they do so, they will neither slight nor condemn, without an impartial and [335] patient investigation, any suggestions that may be offered with the view of forwarding the great and benevolent work of salvation.

In the first place, then, all men generally know, and history bears testimony to the fact, that Indians, whether of the open plains or of the deserts, universally rove about from place to place, like beasts of prey, without any settled or permanent home.   To counteract this habit ought to be the first step taken in order to bring about a healthy state of civilization, without which the missionary labours in vain: but this is not the work of an hour, nor of a day, but of years — I should have said generations; and time proportionate to the work must be allowed, moral restraints must gradually be imposed, and the savage, in place of his former precarious mode of living, must be taught not only to feel the wants, but to appreciate the blessings resulting from settled habits and practical industry; he must be taught to cultivate the ground, and be convinced from experience that his living and comforts are more certain from the soil than from the chace, before he can be brought a step farther: but according to the present system, in place of locating the Indians, as a preliminary step, and accustoming them to habits of industry and social order, the zealous missionary at once commences his course of religious instruction, without any step of the kind; and, while the savages have anything to eat, all goes on well, but the moment a new supply of food is required, that moment they disperse in all directions, according to their usual habits, leaving the missionary alone, and perhaps [336] months may elapse before they again reassemble on praying ground, losing to-day what they had gained yesterday; and this is generally the course pursued — a course productive of social evil and moral deterioration.

What are the qualifications of the men generally sent out for the purpose of converting the heathen? These men have seldom any other recommendation than a knowledge of books; they are ignorant of the language, habits, and feelings of the people they have gone to convert, and have little experience in human nature: this alone is of itself sufficient to protract and retard, if not to frustrate altogether, the working of the system satisfactorily. In every quarter of the globe there are not wanting, if sought after, pious and philanthropic men, possessing the advantages of long and close personal intercourse with the natives of almost all countries. These are the men to be selected and sent out as pioneers among the heathen — men who might, from their local experience, at once infuse the elements of much good by their presence and example; and if such men cannot always be found, persons possessing at least a general knowledge of mankind, as well as of books, can. The work requires practical as well as pious men to set things a-going during the first probationary time; for I wish it to be distinctly understood that religious instruction should not be mixed up with the primary part of the plan at all; but may be introduced at any subsequent period, according to circumstances, as soon, but no sooner, than the degrading influence of the savage character begins to yield to the more genial and rational habits of civilized life. For one of the greatest evils in the [337] present system is, that men generally begin where they ought to end. They commence with religion before the heart is prepared to receive it. A thing easily got is thought but little of: religion must therefore be kept for some time, as it were, at a distance from them; they must be taught to feel the want of it; they must ask for it; and they must be prepared to receive it with all thanksgiving.

The preparatory part of the plan, as regards time, ought, as I have already stated, to be regulated according to circumstances; but when a new field is opened for missionary labours, I cannot convince myself that a shorter period than ten years' location of the tribe or nation, under civilized guidance, would be sufficient to remove the deep-rooted apathy of the savage, and prepare his mind for religious instruction; or perhaps it would be still nearer the mark to adopt the more general opinion on this point, and that is, that an age is not too long for assembling, locating, training, and instructing the savage in the habits of civilization, industry, and economy, before introducing even public schools among them; another age under scholastic discipline might be required to prepare them for the next and most important step; and in the third generation only might religion, as practised in civilized life, be thoroughly introduced with effect among them. This would be laying the basis of a solid and permanent plan.

In reference to the missionary himself, whose pious

work is the conversion of souls, the apostle reminds us, "How beautiful are the feet of them that preach the gospel of peace;" and while the [338] missionary follows, in all its purity, the work of faith and labour of love, all men are in charity bound to contribute to his assistance, and aid in bringing about, by the application of appointed means, the great work of salvation; but then, to encourage all men to do so, the missionary, like the apostles of old, who in simplicity and godly sincerity told their Lord and master "what they had done, and what they had taught," ought to tell his masters, with the same simplicity and uprightness, what he has done, and what he has taught, without exaggeration or any false colouring. This course would indeed inspire confidence, and give such a direction and impetus to popular opinion as would lead all to co-operate for the good of mankind.

But the missionary at home and the missionary abroad are two distinct characters; the latter, from his position and the influence he acquires over the general conduct, as well as consciences, of the simple and ignorant people with whom he lives, and who on every occasion look up to him for advice in temporal as well as for instruction in spiritual matters, of course becomes a great man, not only in their estimation, but in his own also, till at last the force of habit gains an ascendancy over him, and often leads him astray from the path of evangelical duty. He is no longer the humble and zealous disciple he was when he left home, but considers himself the chief man in civil as well as in religious matters.

But the paramount evil which frustrates all the labours of the missionary is that arising from sects [339] of different persuasions interfering with one another, an evil which tends rather to destroy than promote religious feelings

among savages, and which nothing less than the potent
arm of Government can prevent; for it is no uncommon
thing in the wilderness to see the pious and persevering
evangelist, after undergoing every hardship to open a
new field for his labours among the heathen, followed
after by some weak zealot of another sect, who had
not energy or courage of himself to lead, but who no
sooner reaches the cultivated vineyard of his precursor
than he begins the work of demoralization and injustice,
by denying the creed and labours of his predecessor,
clothes some disaffected chief, and infuses animosity and
discord among all parties, in order to get a footing and
establish himself; and where envy and strife are, according
to the apostle's doctrine, there are "confusion and every
evil work;" and every additional zealot of a different
creed in this field of strife increases the disorder, for all
Indians are peculiarly fond of novelty; consequently,
the last creed is with them the best. Now where there
are two, three, or more conflicting creeds at one station,
as is often the case, it may truly be said, there is neither
religion nor religious fellowship to be found in that
community; but, on the contrary, every moral and
religious sentiment is destroyed, and the people are sunk
deeper and deeper in the gulf of moral degradation;
and not only that, but the missionaries, one and all,
labour in vain. Yet, strange as it may appear, such
unhallowed and demoralizing scenes seldom reach either
the public eye or the public [340] ear; for the missionary
or zealot of each sect, in writing home to the parent
society, so far from noticing and reporting, with official
uprightness, the true state of things, cheats the public
by exhibiting a picture of marvellous success. Solomon
hath declared that "he that soweth iniquity shall reap

vanity." Surely there ought to be some law existing to protect and secure to the first missionary the fruits of his enterprize and pious labour against all such corrupt and impious interference.

To exemplify this part of our subject still further: I was once travelling along the frontiers of Canada, when I came to a neat little Indian village, on the bank of the St. Lawrence, containing about three hundred souls. They had a missionary, a little white chapel, and a thriving school, and I thought them at the time, as they also considered themselves, perfectly comfortable and happy. Three years afterwards, a friend of mine happened to pass through the same village; but in place of finding them happy as they had been, everything in and about the place was changed, The inhabitants were less numerous: instead of one missionary and one church, they had, during the short interval, got three missionaries, all of different persuasions, and three churches; but so high did the tide of religious animosity among all parties then run, that one of the churches had been recently burnt to the ground, by some of the fanatics themselves; another was despoiled of all its ornaments, and deserted; and the third remained, a sad memento of the times, with but few hearers: and in place of one thriving school, there had been no less [341] three, but with scarcely a scholar in any of them. Such are the fruits that generally result from the unhallowed practice of one sect interfering with another.